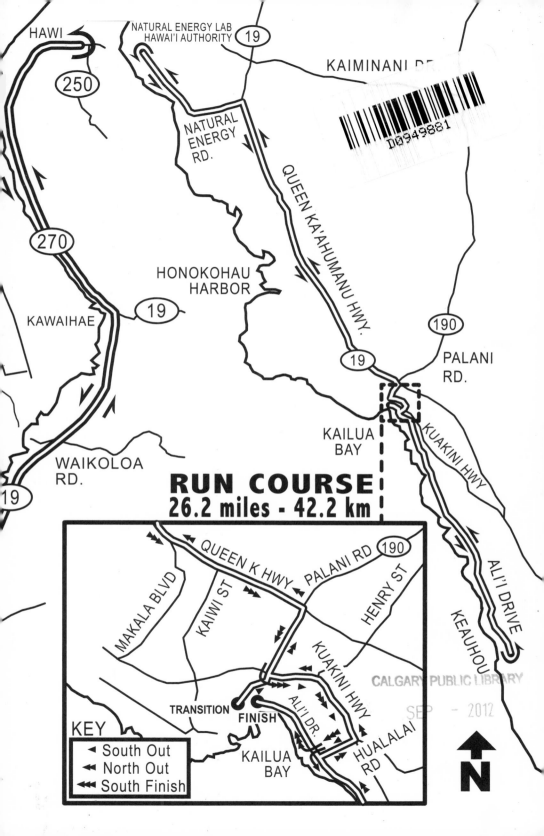

RUN COURSE
26.2 miles - 42.2 km

I'm Here to WIN

A WORLD CHAMPION'S ADVICE FOR PEAK PERFORMANCE

by **CHRIS McCORMACK**

with **Tim Vandehey**

CENTER STREET

New York • Boston • Nashville

Center Street
Hachette Book Group
237 Park Avenue
New York, NY 10017
www.centerstreet.com
Center Street is a division of Hachette Book Group, Inc.

The Center Street name and logo are trademarks
of Hachette Book Group, Inc.

The Ford Ironman World Championship map was created by Kirk Matkin
(www.matkindesign.com) and is reprinted with permission from
World Triathlon Corporation.

The publisher is not responsible for websites (or their content)
that are not owned by the publisher.

Printed in the United States of America

First Edition: May 2011

10   9   8   7   6   5   4

Library of Congress Cataloging-in-Publication Data

McCormack, Chris
    I'm here to win : a world champion's advice for peak performance / by
Chris McCormack with Tim Vandehey. — 1st ed.
        p. cm.
    ISBN 978-1-4555-0267-7
    1. McCormack, Chris, 1973-   2. Athletes—Australia—Biography.
3. Triathlon—Training.   4. Ironman triathlons.   I. Vandehey,
Tim.   II. Title.

    GV697.M37A3 2011
    796.092—dc22
        [B]

                                                            2011006729

*This book is for my mum and every woman
who has ever been touched by breast cancer.
Mum, I miss you so much.*

Contents

Foreword

by Mark Allen

Six-Time Ironman World Champion

Let me just start by saying: YOU HAVE TO READ THIS BOOK! Macca is a world champion, a person who turned down-and-out into golden victories and a human being who has had to overcome truly devastating personal hardships. But what most of you probably don't know about Chris McCormack is that he tells an exceptional story! What he penned in this book is a page-turner that I guarantee you will not be able to put down!

But before I get to some of the priceless pearls that Macca reveals, I must replay what I just saw a few months ago at the 2010 Ironman World Championship in Kona. It was a race that will have a very long shelf life because, frankly, it is very unlikely that there will ever be another race to top this one. Before the event the press was building up a hugely anticipated rematch between Craig Alexander and Andreas Raelert, both of whom had battled side by side with gazelle-running form for miles the previous year: 2009 was Raelert's first Kona and became Crowie's second crown. Then there was the usual mutterings about the whole slew of upstarts who might take the thunder out of this personal matchup.

Barely a blip on the radar was the obligatory mention of past champion Chris McCormack. He got the monkey off his back in

2007 by running a near perfect race and showing that all his claims that he would win the race were so much more than smoke. Unfortunately, he wasn't able to back it up with a successful defense in 2008. He dropped out within reach of the bike finish because a mechanical on the bike tore his legs to shreds. He followed up the next year with a second failed attempt to be the World Champion.

Was the third time going to be the charm? The press didn't think so. He was barely given better than a ten to one chance to walk away with victory number two.

Ironman 2010. Macca's swim was arguably his best ever. He made no secret about the fact that he had to get a cushion on Crowie if he was going to have any chance of victory, and victory was indeed his intent. Chris McCormack was not pitching up at Ironman to sign more posters of his 2007 championship.

I followed the leaders of the race from one of the infamous NBC vehicles. Nothing seemed out of the ordinary, as the bike unfolded hour after hour. Lieto did his flyer off the front. Norman Stadler seemed to be staging his own kind of comeback and became a factor on the bike. Macca seemed to be undecided when the moment was right to really build that critical gap he needed on Crowie, his main concern on the run. That moment came in the predictable winds of Hawi. He swiftly opened a gap that would stick and grow, giving him what seemed to be enough on the defending champ for victory.

Ironman is a race with a million questions. "It's not over until it's over" is the mantra we all mutter under our breaths when our favorites are behind, and it's the thought that haunts the leaders until it is undeniable that they will not be caught.

Off the bike anyone can look good. Not everyone can say that after 20 miles of running in 90-degree heat. Would Macca be able to suffer without consequence? Would the sub-6-minute pace he set through town put his body into total cramping spasms, as it had in the past? Even if his muscles cooperated, what was Raelert capable of with another year of Ironman experience under his belt? Within rea-

sonable striking distance of Macca, could Raelert put together a full
marathon at top speed?

I'll make you wait and read Chris's blow by blow of how the marathon unfolded. But I do need to tell you what I saw at mile 23. Raelert had caught Macca, but he didn't pass him. At that point of the
Ironman, if two competitors run side by side for even a moment it
seems like an eternity. They were running together for what seemed
like a thousand lifetimes. I was barely breathing, wondering what
was going to happen next. How was it going to play out? They both
looked incredible, and each appeared to be equally credible as the
one who would break the other. But then it happened: Raelert
extended his hand to give Macca a shake.

In that moment you could just feel something incredible happen.
It was like a caldron of energy was being poured into Macca's body
from above. It was the thousands of hours of experience Chris had
logged in training. It was every one of the intense lessons he had
learned about himself in the deepest darkest moments in his failed
assaults. It was the Big Island giving him the subtle nod that was saying something like, "You have earned the right to be here and to take
this race." In that moment he became invincible. When he would
make his move was still unknown, but it would happen.

I'm Here to Win shares the twists and turns that Chris took to
develop into one of the greatest competitors in our sport. A theme
that Macca threads throughout all his stories is that when you have a
feeling that something is calling you, that scratch that must be itched
even though your friends and family say it's not a good idea to do it,
that you have a choice. You can either live the safe route that many
others have done and will continue to do, or you can take that leap of
faith: Jump off the cliff that can send you into a world that is unpredictable, extremely challenging, and altogether unsupported by those
who see risk as a negative. Do that and you can truly live the life that
you were put here to live. And that is absolutely what Chris did.

If you think Macca is what the press has labeled him — brash, verbally combative, or just downright boastful—then you don't understand him and you're missing the gold of who he has become. At what was perhaps one of the most critical times in his racing career, when he was positioning himself to become part of the Australian Olympic team for the Games in Australia, when the triathlon would make its debut in the Games, Chris was broadsided by the death of his mother, Theresa. Feeling the guilt of not taking her cancer seriously enough, Macca had to bridge a huge chasm that had opened up before him. Why race? Is being so self-focused valid when it takes precious time away from those who mean so much to you and who, like all of us, will not be on this earth forever? 19455. That's the number of days Macca's mother was on this planet. And that number became a key to helping him refocus his efforts as a world-class competitor in the sport of triathlons.

You can read how that number and the passing of his mum changed Macca from the core of his being. But what is even more important to get from this turning point in his life are the insights he shares with us—insights that he gained from this devastating loss, insights that will help you to focus your efforts in the big dreams of your own life. As he says, "Believe me, when you've trained and suffered and traveled and missed your family for as long as I have, the prospect of winning just isn't enough to keep you hungry and working hard. You can't just race for yourself; you have to race for something or someone else."

One element of being a champion that very few athletes speak about is the necessity to truly understand what makes your opponent tick, and figuring out how you are going to sidestep their strengths and exploit their weaknesses to come up with the goods on race day. This poorly understood component to a champion's preparation is given a five-star treatment in this book. Forget someone telling you to just do your own race. Top-level performances are only made that way because of the competition. McCormack delves into his own fears and doubts and gives a template for how he crafted his mental game and verbal gamesmanship to turn the tables on his competitors. As he puts it: "In endurance racing, whether the race is two hours or eight hours, the biggest limiting factor is fear. The reason you get nervous before a race is that you doubt your ability to perform when it's all on the line...I handle it by creating folders in my brain."

Chris also expresses one of the most potent weapons an athlete—or any person, for that matter—has, and that is themselves. Greatness starts with what Macca depicts as a mantra for success, which is that you can't lie to the person in the mirror. Facing truth and admitting weakness is what will ultimately free you to find your strength, your power, and your dreams. Of course, that magnetic force called ego tries to keep each of us from opening our eyes to embracing our frailties, but like the weak link in the chain, unless we find it and fortify it, we will fail when tugged on by life's biggest missions.

Keeping Macca honest throughout his years was his support team of family, friends, and training partners who with love in their hearts would tell him exactly what he needed to see that would have been so tough to look at on his own. He was the CEO of his person, as he says, but he had advisors who helped him keep the ship in order and on course. And with those people, Macca turned two very rough and long years of Ironman disappointment that followed his first victory on the Big Island into a second championship in even more glorious fashion, in a race that stands alone as the single most competitive ever, with the battle being decided only in the closing mile of the race.

Chris also shares some of his personal secrets about training, hydration, and race nutrition that you would have a tough time finding anywhere else. Combining this knowledge with the vast array of stories where he reveals his mental strategies for success makes *I'm Here to Win* a superior book for anyone searching for keys to take their racing and life to the top level.

Introduction

They said there was no way I could win the 2010 Ford Ironman World Championship in Kona. It was simply out of the question.

Anyway, that was the conventional wisdom. I was too big, too old, too hot, and too comfortable with my accomplishments. I had won the race three years earlier, but most of the "experts" saw my 2007 win as nothing more than the big red ribbon that would wrap up a stellar career. In their eyes, I should have made it my graceful exit from a role as the leading figure in the sport. In other words, "Macca, here's your hat, what's your hurry?" The unspoken consensus was that I was no longer a force to be reckoned with in the world's most important one-day endurance race.

When I landed in Hawaii back in 2002 to do my first World Championships, people were saying, "This guy's going to win ten of these things." After all, I had won races on every continent and dominated World Cup short-course racing in Europe, Asia, and North America as far back as 1997. I had captured virtually every major title in the sport. I was Global Triathlete of the Year and Competitor of the Year in 2001, and the only triathlete ever to hold the USA Professional Championship Title and the USA Sprint Course Title in the same season.

Since moving to the Ironman distance in 2002, I had won Ironman Australia five years in a row. In 2003 I had lost my first European Ironman—the prestigious Challenge Roth in Roth, Germany—to five-time winner Lothar Leder in an incredible sprint to the finish, then come back to take that race every year from 2004 to 2007. I had crushed the field on the 70.3-mile half Ironman circuit. With that record, I think the entire world presumed that I would dominate in Kona in the same way. I blew into town in October of '02 cocky and confident. In my first television interview, I said simply, "Mate, I'm here to win!"

Well, that win took six years and was the toughest challenge of my career. Kona humbled me, as it does nearly everyone. In 2002, I failed to finish after I melted on the marathon in the infamous lava fields north of Kailua-Kona, where the baking heat can overwhelm a body that is already near the end of its endurance. In 2003 I walked to a humiliating 9:32:11 finish. In 2004 I quit on the run, unable to take the heat-induced cramping. In 2005 I came back from near failure on the bike to finish sixth with the fastest run split of the day. In 2006, I finished second to Normann Stadler, who had set the new bike course record that day, so I was moving in the right direction. Finally, in 2007, I mastered the heat and humidity and captured the title I had craved my entire career, the one that no one—including, from time to time, me—had believed I would ever win. It was the jewel in my triathlon crown, so to speak.

My return in 2008 was seen as a formality; of course I would defend my title, everyone said, but for me it was a big race—much more than a formality. Unfortunately, I had a mechanical failure on the bike that year and my fellow Australian Craig Alexander was crowned champion. When Craig won again in 2009, the sport was more than ready to pin the mantle on someone new. *Nice career, Macca, thanks for everything, time to make room for a new generation.*

It was a shock: I was the most accomplished triathlete on the planet at any distance, had already proven that I could win in Kona, and had come in fourth in 2009, yet I was being written off as irrelevant. It just goes to show you how quickly you can be dismissed in favor of the Next Big Thing.

Kona, 2008 and 2009

The thing is, I *knew* I could win in 2010. In 2008, my bike failure had torn me apart because I hadn't even had the chance to defend my title. I never said a word about it; Kona is a very small place, and I didn't want to take anything away from Craig or the other competitors by making excuses. I have too much respect for them and for the sport. After my gear breakdown forced me to quit in the bike stage, I went back to my room at the King Kamehameha Hotel, watched the top pros finish the bike stage and start the marathon, and saw Craig cross the line to win his first title. I've been left off Olympic teams and had a lot of things happen in my career, but that was the most difficult thing I have ever dealt with in the sport. I felt cheated. An equipment failure makes all the time, training, suffering, and pain meaningless. I hadn't lost; the race had been stolen from me by something beyond my control. It was galling.

I went away and studied the event, and I came back in 2009 ready to challenge Craig. Kona was a race that suited him; he's a smaller guy and he loves the heat and humidity, which are always a part of the challenge of Kona. I knew he was coming into his own in Hawaii. But in the prerace interviews I said, "Crowie (Craig Alexander's nickname) has borrowed my title, and he's never beaten me in Kona." Which he hadn't; since I had been forced to drop out because of an equipment failure, he hadn't really defeated me mano a mano. "I've raced him since 1994 in Australia, and in maybe a hundred races he's beaten me four times. I know he feels the pressure of that." Not everyone appreciated me saying that; speaking my mind hasn't always made me popular. But I was simply highlighting the fact that his bike is his weakness, telling everyone how I was going to win and creating some self-doubt in Craig—playing the mental game I've used so effectively over the years.

Well, you know what they say about best-laid plans. In 2009, I had a terrible swim. I put myself in a position to win on the bike but Craig ultimately caught me on the run—he's one of the best marathoners ever to compete at Kona—and won his second consecutive title. And that was it. *Macca's done.* But I knew that even after taking my awful swim into account, my 2009 performance had been spectacular, perhaps even better than my win in 2007.

I lost three and a half minutes in the swim for reasons we've still never figured out; I was behind blokes I've never been behind in my whole career. This is the problem with some people in our sport: they watch *results*, not *races*. If they knew anything about the trends of an athlete, they would have said, "Hold on, there's something wrong with Macca's swim there." I had never swum fifty-four minutes; I'd always swum fifty. I was on the back foot from the swim, fought to catch the front group on the bike and rode minutes into them (I cut into their lead). Then I fell apart in the marathon, dropped back to seventh, and pulled myself together to come in fourth in the event, four minutes down from the winner. If I have a more typical swim and don't lose that three and a half minutes early on, then boom—I'm only thirty seconds down from the leader and racing Craig for the title.

So I wasn't deluding myself. It wasn't that I couldn't compete with the guys who had finished ahead of me in the swim; I knew I could. Believe me, I never want to be that worn-out heavyweight boxer who keeps coming back looking for one more night of glory only to get his face punched in. Every athlete can feel when it's time to quit. When it's time for me to retire, I'll be happy to go home and spend more time with my wife and daughters. But in 2009, I didn't feel that way. Even as everybody in the sport was busy writing my obituary, I was ready to show that the reports of my demise were premature.

Hacking the Race

When I said I was coming back to Kona in 2010, everyone was stunned. I heard the word *dinosaur* a few times. People said things like, "Here goes McCormack, gobbing off again, he needs to convince himself so he goes out and tells anyone who will listen what he's going to do to win the event. He's a dreamer. He could never drop these guys on the bike, and Alexander's too good a runner. Macca's too old, he can't do it."

Well, I knew I could win. In the off-season I did what so many other triathletes don't do: I broke down the race and looked at it strategically. I think of myself as a computer hacker looking for a way to break into a system. When I watched film of the 2009 race, I saw that the runners were winning the event because of how the rest of us were handling the bike stage. I noticed that on the bike, from mile marker forty to mile marker eighty (where we turn off Queen Ka'ahumanu Highway and head up to the turnaround at the town of Hawi), the riders were tending to settle in instead of pushing to get position on the other athletes. The area is notorious for its treacherous crosswinds, and everybody was playing it safe in the winds. This meant that while on their bikes, the best runners got to rest their legs, their fitness brought them back to Kona, and then they ran away from the field in the marathon.

I knew that I had "hacked" the race. This was a distinct weakness in the way the nonelite runners were doing the race. Now I needed to convince the athletes I knew from the European racing circuit, who were intimidated by the dominance of the runners, that these guys were beatable with the right strategy. We needed to push the pace in that crosswind stretch of the bike. We would gain time on the top runners and force them to work on the section back into town, "burning up their matches" on those legs of theirs and preventing them from running their best times in the marathon. We were allowing these guys to kill us on the marathon because we were playing their game. No more. I intended to make the runners play my game!

In every interview I did with the triathlon press in the next year, I said the same thing: "Guys, this is the formula to break the runners. I'm going to do it. Come with me." Predictably, other competitors thought I was crazy. Everybody was so blinded by the new generation of Ironman athletes—Craig Alexander, Andreas Raelert, Terenzo Bozzone, Rasmus Henning—that they saw them as unbeatable. But then why show up at the race at all? I knew they were beatable, and I started calling it out in early 2010.

There was a method to my madness, of course. I was trying to build a pack, because Ironman biking is pack biking. Drafting (getting behind another cyclist so he blocks the wind for you) is illegal in Ironman, but riding in groups allows you to use other cyclists to help maintain your pace. That way, you avoid inadvertently slowing down and having to expend more energy getting back up to speed. Pack biking also lets me observe other athletes and watch for weaknesses I can exploit. So I started talking to athletes like the German Timo Bracht, a two-time Ironman Europe champion who also won the 2010 Ironman Arizona. I said, "Timo, you're a solid swimmer and an exceptional bike rider, but guys like Craig Alexander and Rasmus Henning are consistently better runners than you. Why would you want to get off the bike with them when you've got a weapon like the bike ride? Go home, speak with your coaches, and you'll see that we have to attack in the crosswinds. It will open up this race and we'll take their legs out from underneath them." I wanted to plant the seeds, because I assume everyone is there to win, and I was telling them a strategy that I knew would work.

Most athletes work themselves, not the race. But if all you have is a hammer, every problem becomes a nail, right? For many athletes and coaches, the only tool they have is training more. Slow in the swim? Train harder. Couldn't keep up with the pack on the bike? Ride more miles. They make the race all about the physical, and it's not. An

Ironman lasts eight hours for the pros, but races are won or lost in moments, when one athlete makes a move that either gives him an advantage or proves to be a mistake. Experience and strategy help you discover in which moments to spend your limited endurance in order to give yourself the best chance to win.

Each race is a puzzle, and if you know what to look for and are willing to get out of that training-only mind-set for a while, you can get an edge on the field. I think this mentality comes from when I was a runner as a kid. I would break down the race I had just done on the drive home with my father: "Dad, I was feeling good and then at four kilometers, they all took off up the hill!" My dad was very analytical, and he would say, "Why do you think that is?" And I'd say, "Well, it was hard."

My dad would say, "Exactly, son, that was a key point in the race. So what do you think you need to do when you race there next year?" And I'd say, "I need to be stronger on that hill, Dad." I would find the missing piece in my puzzle like this. Now I had found that missing piece for Kona, and I knew that if I could find other athletes to work it with me, I could win the race.

Unfortunately, my public campaign to find allies against the runners didn't make me popular. What I saw as honest dialogue about leveraging the limitations of other athletes, others called cocky and disrespectful. A lot of competitors, many of them amateurs, said I wasn't acting in the spirit of the race and all that. But I'm a professional athlete. I'm not looking for a finisher's T-shirt and for announcer Mike Reilly to say, "You are an Ironman!" as I cross the finish line. My job description is simple: *Win race.* That's how I make my living. So while I won't show poor sportsmanship, I will do everything I can within the rules to give myself an advantage, and if that ruffles the feathers of some age groupers, I'm sorry about that.

Still, I think I'm pretty misunderstood. So I'm here to set the record straight about who I am, what I do, and how I do it. My career has been about a lot more than physical talent or dedicated training. Other factors have set me apart: engaging in subtle psychological warfare with other athletes, looking honestly at my weaknesses and systematically finding ways to overcome them, looking outside the sport for solutions from other disciplines, and more. Put it all together and you get the most successful career in the history of the sport. This is the story behind the success.

I'm Here to Win

1

"I'm Here to Win!"

My journey to the Ford Ironman World Championship began years before I treaded the waters of Kailua Bay, Hawaii, on race morning, ready to turn the world's most prestigious endurance race into my latest conquest. Coming to Kona had been the only thing that my best mate, Sean Maroney, and I had talked about for more than a decade. As idealistic young swim-bike-runners, our scheme was both simple and utterly outrageous: we would work our way through the world's top triathlons one by one, not caring if we won or lost, only caring that we had the experience, met the pretty girls, and had a great time. We would conclude this "bucket list" of races by doing Ironman Hawaii together, and then probably return to Australia to bask in the glory of our adventures.

We actually went to some of those races. While I became a professional, Sean decided to pursue a career as a lifeguard in Hawaii (and who can blame him?) with some occasional swim and triathlon coaching mixed in. But if he found out that I was doing a race that we had on our "list," he would drop everything. "You're doing Chicago?" he'd say. "I'm coming." I'd buy him a ticket, he'd fly to the race, and I'd race. After I won the Mrs. T's Chicago Triathlon in 2000, we met Spencer Smith (a terrific British world champion in short-course racing who's also won races of Ironman distance) and other guys we had worshipped. We'd play it cool, but when we got back to the hotel room, we were jumping on the bed and shouting, "Look at the trophy with all the names!" We were like little kids let loose to play with their idols...which we were.

I'd become world champion, and Sean had been on the whole journey with me. And as 2002 rolled around, it looked like the most important part of our boyhood fantasy might actually become a reality. That was the year I'd turned my back on the Australian triathlon program and my short-course racing background and started racing Ironmans. Ignorance was bliss, I suppose: I showed up in May 2001 at the Wildflower Half Ironman without a strategy, so I just took what I did in short-course racing and doubled it. A half Ironman is twice the distance of a short-course race, so that made sense to me. I broke the course record.

Then I went to Ironman Australia and beat three world champions to win my first full Ironman, joining Luc Van Lierde and Dave Scott as the only athletes to win the first Ironman races we entered. Best of all, winning Ironman Australia qualified me to race at Kona in October 2002. I was going to Hawaii!

Joy and Sorrow

That was in April, and things got even better. In June 2002, Sean rang me so excited that I barely needed the phone to hear him. I'd been out training, so my phone had been ringing off the hook; clearly, he'd gotten to about beer number ten by the time I picked up.

"I'm in, you bastard!" he shouted. He'd been celebrating in typical Sean fashion because he had finished high enough in the Keauhou Kona Half Ironman race that he qualified for Ironman Hawaii as an age grouper. "We're going to Kona! I'm coming over to watch you win Alcatraz for the fourth time."

I had already won the Escape from Alcatraz triathlon three times, and I would be going for a fourth later in 2002, trying to equal the record set by American Mike Pigg. Sean absolutely idolized Mike Pigg. Mike was a swim-biker at heart, which was how Sean saw himself. Sean's mother knew that we lived for triathlon, but we'd drive her insane watching videos of Mike Pigg and Mark Allen, my favorite triathlete, all day long. She'd finally have enough, say something like, "Would you boys go outside and play?" and chase us outdoors. I raced Alcatraz because of Mike, so I was thrilled to be in a position to match his record.

Sean said, "I'm going out tonight to party, and then I'm going to come over and watch you in Alcatraz, you bastard. Can I stay with you?" I was traveling with my wife, Emma-Jane, but of course I said yes. Sean was my mate. We'd manage.

We were over the moon. I was going to match one of our childhood heroes, and then we were going to fulfill the dream that we'd cooked up as teenagers watching the Kona race on television in Sydney. I could hardly believe it. I was happier for Sean than I was for myself. Between the two of us he was the one with more raw talent, but he could never put aside the partying to focus on training. He was just a force of nature: loud, positive, generous, and always out for fun. I loved him for it. That was what drew us together as kids; life was a big party.

I went to bed, planning to call Sean the next day in midhangover. The next morning, I got an e-mail from Mrs. Maroney, Sean's mother. I had never gotten an e-mail from her before, which set off alarm bells in my head. I opened it and the message absolutely left me speechless:

Darling Chris, Sean died last night.

What? No details, just those few chilling words. I thought, *Maybe I read it wrong or something.* Immediately, I rang Sean's mobile phone. No answer. Again. No answer. Again. No answer. Now I was getting very scared. So I rang Mrs. Maroney.

"Mrs. Maroney, it's Chris." She burst into tears, and I knew right away that Sean really was dead. It was the hardest phone call I have ever made. He had been celebrating his Kona qualifier at a hotel in

Honolulu and fallen to his death from a twenty-seventh-floor balcony. He died on June 6, 2002. He was twenty-seven years old.

I said, "Mrs. Maroney, I'm getting on a plane right now. I'm coming home."

As soon as I got off the phone, crying myself, I bought my ticket. The earliest flight I could get didn't leave for twenty-four hours. I had to get back to Los Angeles and pack everything. Then my phone rang. It was Mr. Maroney, Sean's father. I remember that he said, "Chris, we've talked about it, and we want you to go on and do Escape from Alcatraz."

I said, "No, no, no, Mr. Maroney. That's the last thing on my mind."

I remember him saying, "Chris, Sean's last moment of glee was the thought that you would equal Mike Pigg's record."

My mind reeled. I said, "Mr. Maroney, he was my best friend. My mind's not in the right place. I can't win Escape from Alcatraz. I'm coming home."

Mr. Maroney was the assistant commissioner of police in New South Wales, and a very assertive man, an absolute gentlemen. "No," I recall him saying in a tone that had no room for compromise. "You do that race and you come home. But you are going to win that race."

I didn't know what to say. Then I said the only thing I could. "Okay, Mr. Maroney. I'll give it my best shot." Emma and I flew to San Francisco so I could do Escape from Alcatraz.

A Miracle

Escape from Alcatraz is a cold, tough race that starts off in the icy waters of San Francisco Bay. The main threat to my fourth win there was Greg Bennett, a guy I've raced my whole career. He had just won the World Cup and was in incredible running form. But Escape from Alcatraz is really won on the bike. I figured I could get away from the pack on my bike and then post the third- or fourth-fastest run to win.

I was wearing a black armband in memory of Sean, and everybody knew that my mate had died. It was big news in Australia. The commentators knew how close Sean's and my relationship had been, and I think they probably wrote me off as a threat on that day. I would have written myself off; my heart was halfway across the world with Sean's family.

The race started, and after the swim Greg Bennett surprised me by escaping on the bike. We got off the bikes and started the run, and Greg had a substantial lead over me. *Damn.* I looked at the sky as I ran and told Sean, "Sorry, mate." I was past the halfway point in the race, thinking, *Okay, I'm not going to win, fine. I'm going to get on the plane, get back to Australia, and just deal with my mate.* I had never rationalized defeat in races; it was one of my strengths. I always kept my mind positive and found ways to keep going. But that day, the only chance I had was if Greg Bennett blew up.

Then I saw an ambulance coming toward me, and they gave me a split. "One minute, Macca," meaning that Bennett was one minute ahead of me. I figured that he was really probably two minutes ahead by then; he's a great runner, better than I am. But then I kept getting more splits. People said, "Forty-five seconds, Macca!" "Forty seconds, he's gone!" *Impossible,* I thought. Greg Bennett never blew up. He had never, ever blown up in his entire career. This was only an eight-mile run. Greg could run eight miles in his sleep.

As we dropped down off the hilly section of the course, I was starting to hear something. It sounded like a motorbike. The race is on winding trails and you can't see far ahead. But there was this motorbike rising up out of the trees and going around the corner. It was the lead chase bike, following the leader—Greg Bennett. He was falling apart.

I couldn't believe it. I had been worrying about coming in second and now...I dropped down the hill and there was Greg Bennett going sideways, absolutely falling to pieces. I floored it and heard the crowd cheering. Greg was in such disarray that as I ran past him I said, "Bennett, are you all right?" But he was in another zone. I took off and ended up getting the win. Greg ended up finishing seventeenth.

It was a bloody miracle. I won my fourth title and equaled Mike Pigg's record. Mike himself greeted me at the finish line and said something like, "So sorry to hear about your friend." I was there with Emma, sobbing, telling her what happened. I still couldn't believe it. My win couldn't have been more unlikely if lightning had vaporized Greg on the spot. I went into the medical tent to see if he was all right.

As I recall, he said, "I don't know what happened, man. One minute I was cruising along, the next thing it was like someone punched me in the head, a knockout punch. I didn't know where I was." But walking out with Emma, I thought, *I know exactly what happened. Maroney was out here saying, "You're going to win this, you bastard."*

While I was racing, back home they were burying Sean. The cream of the city's triathlon and swimming community attended his funeral. I couldn't make it, but I sent a statement that Pauline Maroney, Sean's mum, read. In it, I called Sean "the Halley's Comet of friends," because they only come around once in a lifetime.

Tempting the Island Gods

Against that backdrop of events and emotion, I went to Kona for my first Ford Ironman World Championship. Outwardly, I was trying to be Mister Cool; inwardly, I was excited beyond excited. I went out to the Energy Lab (the Natural Energy Laboratory of Hawaii, a big facility and the place where the marathon course turned back toward town) and took pictures like a tourist. I had no idea how to act around the world-class triathletes who I saw all over town. I didn't know what protocol was. I felt like a tennis player walking onto the court at his first Wimbledon. Did I swing my racket? Wave at the crowd?

Even though I had never been there before, I felt like I knew the race. I'd watched it on television since I was a kid. I could tell you the names of the winners and their splits. I knew the legendary spots where the race was won or lost: Palani hill, the crosswinds coming down from Hawi, the lava fields. I couldn't wait to get to the lava fields, which just shows you how completely ignorant I really was. I was coming off dominating wins in my first two races ever over two hours—Wildflower (considered the unofficial half-Ironman championship) and Ironman Australia. I expected to do well at Kona.

When I got to town, I discovered that there was already talk about me. Older athletes were speculating about the twenty-nine-year-old who had crushed Wildflower and run through legends like Peter Reid at Ironman Australia. Apparently, the talk was that I was capable of anything in Kona. They were worried about me because I was a wild card, and I liked that. I felt incredibly confident.

But I also felt strange. Walking around Kailua with Emma was weird, because I had always felt that Sean, my best mate, would be there with me. We would have coffee at Lava Java together. We would swim the course off the Kailua-Kona Pier. But none of those things would happen now. Still, I was here, and after the gods somehow intervened to give me a near-impossible win at Alcatraz, I was sure I would be able to make Sean proud by dominating in Hawaii. I was excited, nervous, and ready.

It was with that spirit that I sat down for my first prerace interview. It's a standard thing: the network (that year, NBC) brings athletes into a media room and asks a series of pretty basic questions. Going into the interview, I had a goal: to make the other athletes worry about me, even fear me. But that wasn't the template the interviewer was reading from. The media was expecting the same kinds of answers they got from all the other athletes who'd come to Kona in recent years: "I've trained really hard, I'm just grateful to be here," and so on. But that's not what I gave them.

The reporter asked me if I was worried about the race because of my lack of experience. *What kind of a question is that?* I said, "No. I think I can win this race."

You could see and feel the eyebrows go up in the media room. No athlete had ever said anything like this before. But follow-up questions were negative and defeatist: "Can you do it?" "What about paying your dues?" I didn't understand this. I was used to the kinds of questions they asked in the cutthroat world of World Cup racing, questions about my bike strength or whether I could drop a certain athlete on the run. There, we had a seek-and-destroy attitude. These were soft, almost gentlemanly questions, and I didn't care for them. Was I not supposed to want to win?

Then the reporter started talking about the island gods and how you were supposed to pay your dues at Kona for a few years to satisfy the gods. That was enough for me. "Look," I said, "I don't buy into island gods. Everyone talks about respecting the island gods. But I'm part Maori, so if anything, they're my gods! I don't care about gods. I didn't come here for a holiday or to get a finisher's medal. I came here to win this race. I'm here to win."

A Target on My Back

After the camera was off, I remember the interviewer said to me, "Kid, if you pull this off, you could be very good for this sport." That was my first clue that I had said things never before heard in Kona. My statements filtered around the town in hours, and soon everybody was talking about that Australian rookie who had said he was going to win Kona his first time out.

The press was happy, as they've been my entire career when I've opened my mouth and something outrageous has come out. They had both sides of the story covered. If I won, they had the quotes to make me look like a hero; if I failed, they would make me look like an idiot. But I'd said what I'd said, and I owned it. I didn't hide during race week. What I hadn't realized was that I had really been offending people. I didn't get the Kona way of thinking about the race, which was all about gratitude and humility. I had set myself up and painted a nice big target on my back. Everyone thought I was rude and over-confident, and by race day they were ready for me to lose.

I knew I could win. Or at least I thought I knew. The truth was that no matter how well I thought I knew the race, I hadn't bled in those lava fields. But I was about to.

The Easiest Win Ever

On race morning, I was practically jumping out of my skin with pre-race nerves and excitement. I remember tripping out over the gear bags we had to use for transition, because they were so big. In short-course racing, you just had a pair of shoes and some shorts, because everything was so quick. But for Ironman, I had sunglasses, a hat, my nutrition bottles—stuff everywhere.

I checked in and started chatting to guys like Lothar Leder, Jurgen Zack (a five-time European Ironman champion who ran the second-fastest Ironman in history) and Tim DeBoom, who won it all at Kona in 2001. I was nervous, so I just ran my mouth, not knowing that most of the guys were in some intense personal zone and didn't want to talk. They looked at me like I was some kind of freak. I dove off the pier and just treaded water, looking at all the fans up early for the start of the swim. *Wow. I'm really here.* I had always seen the start of Kona from above—the aerial camera shot from the TV helicopter. This was a whole new angle.

Then the cannon went off and the race was on. I was next to Jan Sibbersen, a phenomenal swimmer who set many course records in Ironman races, and when he took off, I stayed with him. *Man, this guy is quick,* I thought. But I kept up with him, and before I knew it I was second or third in the swim. There was a lot of swell that day, but I was totally comfortable. After the frantic pace of a 1,500-meter World Cup swim, the 2.4-mile Ironman swim seemed slow and easy. I sat in a group of the top eight or so swimmers and we distanced ourselves from the pack.

We approached the turnaround buoy, and I thought for the first time, *This is a long way.* But I turned clean and stayed with the lead group, and I got out of the water sixth. I got my bike kit and nutrition and was out of transition so fast that I think I jumped to second, behind Sibbersen. I rode the first six miles and then looked back to see Tim DeBoom, Peter Reid, Spencer Smith, and a few others with me. But after the first ten miles, I decided the pace was too slow. I was out of there. My race was on, catch me if you can.

By mile twenty, I had caught Sibbersen and blown by him. Now I was leading at Kona. I started getting splits from the group I'd been riding with: two minutes behind me, then three minutes back. I thought, *This is going to be the easiest win ever!*

Mark Allen and Dave Scott, my idols, were covering the race and they pulled up next to me in a car. I said (I cringe to think about this now), "When does this start getting hard?" Mark said something like, "Be patient, kid." But I wasn't about to listen at that point. I thought I had Kona beaten.

MACCA'S (W)INSIGHTS

Ironman Hawaii doesn't end until the pier!

A triathlon is not a sprint, especially at Ironman or half-Ironman distance. Don't try to finish the race on the bike when you still have a run in front of you. Know the conditions, know your fitness level, and be patient. Take advantage of easier or downhill areas of the course to rest and conserve your energy for the later stages.

Zack Attack

I got to the community of Kawaihae and got the splits on Jurgen Zack and Thomas Hellriegel (who would play a pivotal role in my future Ironman career), probably the best bike riders in the field. Hellriegel had been one of Sean's favorite triathletes, and Zack had just missed the world record. I was a big fan; I had posters of Jurgen on my wall only five years earlier. Now they were coming after me.

I anticipated them passing me, and they blew by me on the way to the turnaround at Hawi. But as they did, I started putting out more power and stayed with them. They kept looking back, thinking they had dropped me, but it was becoming clear that I could ride with them.

However, I wanted to show some etiquette; I didn't want them to think I was looking to them to set the pace and just hang around behind them. So I rode up on them and took the lead for a while. That's what you do in a bike group: one guy does five minutes at the front of the pack, setting the pace, then another guy takes his turn, then another. At one point, when I was out front, Zack tore around me to take the lead—his signature move on the bike, known as a Zack Attack. I had fantasized about being on the receiving end of a Zack Attack, and it had just happened. Trying to be cool, I rode up next to him and said, "Man, that was a Zack Attack. I've waited my whole life for a Zack Attack." I was such a geek. But he took offense and I vowed to shut up and just ride.

We got closer to the turn and I started thinking about Sean. *Mate, look at me. I'm here with the big boys. Can you believe this?* We made the turn and started pushing, putting serious time into the chase group. Now I really put in the work leading our group. If Thomas did five minutes in front, I made sure I did ten. I think they started to respect me because everything they did, I matched or surpassed. When fatigue starts to set in, you get really annoyed with riders who aren't doing their share of the work.

Hellriegel also gave me my first taste of the psychological game at Kona. About eighty-five or ninety miles into the ride, he rolled up beside me and told me that Normann Stadler (who I'll talk about quite a bit later in the book) was coming across—that is, trying to close the gap and catch us. We watched Normann get closer and as soon as he was close enough to see us, Hellriegel changed gears and surged ahead. I loved the gamesmanship: he had given Stadler the chance to see us and get his hopes up, and then dropped him by setting a faster pace. Stadler dropped more than two minutes behind and never recovered.

"Welcome to Kona, Punk!"

I matched Hellriegel's pace, but Zack was having a harder time. He struggled with the crosswinds over the last fifteen miles. I got off the bike with Hellriegel, put on my sunglasses, and came out of transition leading the race. That year, transition was at the old Kona airport and it was a half-mile run into town. By the time I dropped down onto Ali'i Drive, I had picked up two minutes on Hellriegel in a mile and a half. The group of strong runners that had started with me wasn't even in yet, and I'd beaten them in Ironman Australia. *You guys are dead,* I thought.

I saw Emma by the course and winked. I got a split and I had a thirteen-minute lead on the runners group of Reid, DeBoom, and the rest. I was setting the tempo and I felt great. I saw my dad and said, "Bank the check, Dad." I was beyond confident. I was sure I already had the race wrapped up.

Then I got to the turn at five miles and headed back toward town. I started to think, *Man, this is a long way.* Next, I started to think, *Geez, it's hot.* I felt a few cramps and grabbed some Gatorade at the next aid station.

Heat started to dominate my thinking. *It's hot, it's hot, it's hot* was all my brain could seem to say. At mile marker six, I got a cramp and walked. Hellriegel picked me up just after mile marker six, so I had lost two minutes to him in two and a half miles. He ran in the middle of the road, where there's no shade, but I ran on the side, where tree branches provided me with a little shade. I was starting to suffer in the heat.

At mile marker seven I thought, *Oh God, nineteen miles to go. How am I going to do nineteen more miles?* I was cramping badly now and coming back into town, and people shouted that I needed salt. Back then, they actually kept salted pretzels at the aid stations, so I had some. The cramps kept coming and I kept walking.

At mile marker eight, Francois Chabaud caught me. He was a hard-looking bloke, covered in tattoos, and about the time he caught me he vomited. I thought, *Cool, someone else is hurting.* But then he straightened up and just kept running. He would finish sixth.

The main runner group was coming now; I had lost some serious time, most of my thirteen-minute lead. I knew I had to start running again. I was running past my hotel, the King Kamehameha, which is right near the pier where the swim starts, and I knew Emma and all my people would see me walking. I didn't want to embarrass myself, so I tried to run. But my hands were shaking, and my groin and hip flexors were bunched in agonizing cramps.

I made the turn onto Palani hill. If you don't know Kona, Palani is a modest hill that looks like nothing if you walk or drive it. But when you try to run up it on a 100-degree day after racing more than 120 miles, it's like one of the Himalayas. People break on Palani. Peter Reid and Tim DeBoom caught me on the hill and passed me, and then Tim's brother Tony, who was also a triathlete but there as a spectator, shouted something like, "Welcome to Kona, punk!"

Rationalizations

I hadn't made any friends here, but I was in too much pain to care. I finally got over the top of Palani, but the minute I started downhill on the other side, I couldn't put one foot in front of the other anymore. I had hoped to make it to the Energy Lab and at least compete in the lava fields, but I was starting to melt. I saw mile marker eleven and thought, *How am I going to do fifteen more miles?* That's when I started rationalizing. *You led at Hawi, mate. You've had a great year. You had thirteen minutes on the runners. You'll cover this nutrition thing, come back next year, and solve it.*

See how insidious that kind of thinking is? Those easy excuses for ending the suffering gave me the escape hatch I needed. There was an aid station right at mile marker eleven and I went over to it and sat down in a sun chair under an umbrella. I was cramping horribly. *That's it. I'm out.* That was my first Ironman at Kona.

The press was all over me. Later on, the papers ran a photo of me in my chair with a bucket of ice on my head. For years, every time a publication or website ran an article on dealing with heat, they ran that picture. It was my claim to fame: Chris McCormack, poster boy for heat intolerance.

Back at my hotel, I tried to hide. I had promised a win, believed I would win, and been humbled by the island gods. NBC had called me a "cocky rookie," and I had to wear that now. I told myself, *Okay, you needed this. Let them laugh at you. You had thirteen minutes on the runners and you know you can beat them.*

But despite my positive talk, I was bitter. I'd led in Kona, but I hadn't won or even finished, and I knew Sean would have been disappointed. Over all the years we'd followed the gods of triathlon, my wins were Sean's wins. When I won a world championship, he told people about it with so much pride that you would have thought he had won. I had loved having a guy in my corner who was happier about my success than I was. I had wanted to win Kona for him.

Most of all, I had been exposed as a fraud. I should have fought on. Thomas Hellriegel ran a 3:03 marathon and finished third. If I'd kept it together to run a 3:10, I would have finished in the top ten. If I'd had more Ironman experience I would have told myself, *You've done fifteen miles a million times, so you can do it now.* Back then, I didn't have the psychological tools I do now, and I certainly didn't have the maturity.

Today, I do. I've developed strategies that have changed the sport, faced my weaknesses and overcome them, and mastered the mental game enough to win Kona not only in 2007, but in 2010, in what many people have called one of the greatest Hawaii performances ever. But I'm getting a little ahead of myself. If you really want to know how I became the oldest man ever to claim the top spot on the Kona podium, we have to start at the beginning.

MACCA'S 2002 SEASON

- Kurnell Triathlon, Sydney—FIRST
- Dubbo Triathlon Australia—FIRST
- Ironman Australia—FIRST
- Wildflower Half-Ironman, US—FIRST
- Carlsbad Triathlon, US—FIRST
- Escape from Alcatraz Triathlon—FIRST
- San Jose International Triathlon—FIRST
- Tempe Triathlon, US—FIRST
- Commonwealth Games Triathlon—FIFTH
- Bonn Triathlon, Germany—FIRST
- Ironman Hawaii, DNF

Season Statistics and Interesting Facts

- Flight miles accumulated: 76,450
- Days away from home: 241
- Countries visited: 7

Training miles for the year

- Swim: 720
- Bike: 18,275
- Run: 2,907

2

Too Proud to Go Home

I grew up in southern Sydney, Australia, in a town called Heathcote, right along the Royal National Park. It was a phenomenal place for a runner, full of trails through the forest and a great fraternity of runners. When I was five years old, my dad, Ken, took up running to quit smoking, and my two brothers and I just started running with him. Running became what we did together.

When I got to Kirrawee High School, I discovered that I had a natural talent for running and I started competing in cross-country, winning numerous awards including the NSW Sporting Blue, given to the best high school athlete in New South Wales. But surfing was my first love. When you grow up near the water in Australia, you surf every spare moment. My brothers and I surfed five days a week. I would watch anything on television that had to do with Hawaii in the hopes of seeing a big North Shore wave or some of the Hawaiian surfers, who were supposed to be the best in the world. In 1987, when I was fourteen, I saw my first Ironman World Championship on the old ABC *Wide World of Sports* program. It was only the tenth Ironman in Kona, which Dave Scott won in 8:34:13. Triathlon was years away from blowing up into the worldwide phenomenon it is today. But I was intrigued.

I thought, *They don't run that fast. I can swim and bike—man, I can do this one day.* And that was it—back to surfing and school and daily life. In my house, sport was always an important part of the family, but it was definitely something you did only on weekends—it was not a respectable, reliable way to earn a living. So the year would go by and the next October would come along and the Ironman would come on and I'd say, "Oh, there's that race again." I would sit for the whole day and watch it and think, *This is cool,* but that was it.

In my mind, I wasn't a triathlete. I didn't even really know that there was such a thing. I was a runner. Running landed me a scholarship at the University of New South Wales, where I ran for the track club while I majored in commerce and pursued a degree in economics, which my parents thought would allow me to get a steady job. Then in 1991 I met Sean Maroney.

Sean was an incredible swimmer who had been ranked the fastest in the world as a twelve-year-old. I knew of his family already because of his twin sister, Susie, who had swum the English Channel twice and set the world record. We don't have many champions in Australia, so Susie was quite famous. So I was impressed with Sean first because he was a Maroney, second because he was such a great swimmer, and third because he was also a triathlete who followed Ironman Hawaii the same way I did.

He and I would talk for hours about the race and greats like Dave Scott and Mark Allen. Mark and Dave are the legends of Kona, probably the two top athletes in the history of Ironman. They each won Kona six times, and their 1989 showdown in the marathon at Kona, on what has come to be known as "Mark and Dave Hill," is probably the most famous moment in the sport. I've known Mark and Dave for years, and have tremendous respect for them, but back when I was a kid, they were demigods. Over this common ground Sean and I became partners in crime.

Sean had started racing triathlons in 1990, but he wasn't in college like I was. Instead, his life had four components: bartending, swimming, doing triathlons, and partying. I may have spent part of my time as the dutiful student, but we had our share of fun together and became best mates. During this time Sean was also trying to push me into doing triathlons. "You should do them, Chris!" he would say. "You run so fast!" I was a good runner, but I was apprehensive about the swim. It's not easy when your mate is one of the best swimmers in the world. True, he'd lost his motivation for swimming. He'd hit the age where you either become an elite competitor or fall short, and he hadn't made it to Olympic caliber. But I was still intimidated to go to the pool with him because the guy would swim five laps to my one.

Finally in 1991 and 1992, I started doing some duathlons, races that are run-bike. I did pretty well and enjoyed them, but I was still a college scholarship athlete and my college was doubtful about this triathlon movement. My running coach, Helen McGuckin, was supportive, but she saw triathlon as a fad and believed that my natural affinity for running would bring me back into the fold. Still, she gave me a lot of athletic freedom, and I kept doing these multisport races for a noble, pure-hearted reason.

The girls.

Hey, I was eighteen or nineteen years old! When you're that age, girls are all that matter. Running was bland, and I knew all the running girls. I'd go with Sean to duathlons and triathlons and there would be gorgeous girls in bikinis. It was summer, the sun was shining, and I thought, *This is fantastic! This is the sport for me!*

My First Triathlon

Pumped up by adolescent hormones and a growing love of triathlon, I finally agreed to join Sean's swim squad in the fall of 1992 and learned proper swim technique from his coach, Dick Caine. On November 11 of that year I did my first triathlon. It was the Daihatsu Wollongong Triathlon in Wollongong, a city south of Sydney. Among other things, that was where I met Mick Gilliam, a trainer and physiologist who is one of my closest mates and advisors to this day, and also the vainest man I've ever known. Mick is quite a character; more on him later.

No one knew who I was at the triathlon, which was by design. I was still an Australian champion university runner, so I was trying to slip in under the radar. If my college had found out I was doing triathlons, they could have made life difficult for me. I was riding and swimming in secret, trying to squeeze training in between parties and girls. I turned up race morning with my dad and I saw all these guys in wet suits. I thought that it must be cold in the water, because that's why you wore a wet suit. That's how much of a novice I was: I didn't know that you wore wet suits to swim faster. All I had was this thick surfing wet suit, so I put it on and got in the water.

It was an Olympic distance race—1,500-meter swim, 40k ride, and 10k run (.9315 miles, 24 miles, and 6 miles, respectively)—and I was entered in the junior category. I think I was last out of the water. But I rode through a lot of the other juniors, and I ran a thirty-one-minute 10k—faster than all the juniors and the pros—to win the junior category. I got up on stage and found out that I had won a trip for two to New Caledonia and five hundred bucks. *Far out!* I was used to winning little medallions, so this was incredible. I called Sean and told him we were going to New Caledonia to race. Then I went surfing the rest of the day.

Coincidentally, as I walked in the door that night the phone rang. My father said, "There's someone from Triathlon Australia on the phone." It turned out that the Wollongong race had featured the best juniors in the country, sponsored by the candy company Cadbury. I'd beaten every one of them. This freaked out Triathlon Australia, the national federation, because they had no idea who I was. I told the guy on the phone my name and he said, "Did you do the whole course?"

Ah, so that was it. They were tripping over me beating all their best juniors, so they were basically saying I'd cheated. In my head, I was panicking, but not because I cared about winning the race—I didn't want to give the tickets to New Caledonia back! I'd already told Sean that we were going! I said, "Of course I did the whole course. You're not getting your tickets back. They're mine." And I hung up. It was the beginning of a long, tumultuous relationship with Triathlon Australia.

They rang me back and told me they were very suspicious of my run time. I started to get angry; these guys were wasting my time when a little homework would have saved all of us a lot of stress. "I'm the best junior runner in Australia," I said. "Check it out." They did their due diligence and found out I was a good runner, and that changed everything. Next time we talked, they invited me to Canberra, the Australian capitol, to do my next race. If I did well, they wanted me to fly all the way across the country to Perth for another race.

I didn't know what to say. When you run in Australia, even if you run for the national team, you pay for everything. We were by no means a wealthy family. It was $600 for the flight plus accommodations. I told my father and his reply was "Well, I'm not paying for that, mate. You're a big boy now." I was a college kid with no money, so I rang them back to say I couldn't do the Canberra race, and they said, "Oh, we'll pay for your travel." I was shocked. My father was only too happy to let me go if someone else was picking up the bill, so I went to Canberra and finished second. Even though the powers that be were still trying to figure out who I was, I was picked for the Cadbury Junior Elite Squad, which meant more racing. Suddenly I was on the fast track, even though I wasn't quite sure how I'd gotten there.

A Champion Abroad

I suppose this was the beginning of what's become a lifelong pattern for me: defying the conventional way of doing things. I hadn't come out of the heavily recruited junior circuit, but shown up at a race as an unknown and won it. That's the story of my entire career. I've bypassed the typical path of ascension for a triathlete by simply showing up for races and winning them. I've said things that other competitors won't say, trained my body and mind in ways that are completely foreign to our sport, and won races I wasn't supposed to win. I guess I'm the Frank Sinatra of my sport: I've done it my way. And it's worked.

Not that it's always been easy. After winning an Australian junior title, I was given the chance to compete in my first Junior Triathlon World Championship in Manchester, England, in August 1993. This would mean starting college two weeks late. My father was not happy about this. "You know you haven't finished college yet, mate," he said. To my parents, no matter how successful I was as a triathlete, it was strictly a hobby. Their goal was for me to get my degree, settle into a good, safe job at a company, and race on the weekends. I wanted—well, I wasn't sure what I wanted anymore.

I told my dad, "Don't worry, I'll be back," and went to Manchester. That race gave me my first taste of humiliation as well as giving me something of a party-boy reputation. I had second place wrapped up, but as I was coming down the final run before the finish line, I was high-fiving the spectators and being a goose, and two guys ran right past me just before the finish. So I finished fourth. *Welcome to the big leagues, kid.* Triathlon Australia was livid that I had done this. I'd had the silver medal wrapped up, which would have proved that their program worked and gotten them more funding. And there I was doing airplanes down the chute and getting phone numbers from girls!

Even so, I qualified for the World Juniors, which was phenomenal. A French club invited me to join them and start competing immediately. In my first negotiation ever, I somehow convinced them to pay for my mate Kevin Schwarze, who qualified as an amateur age grouper for the Worlds, to go to France with me, and we both started racing for this club.

Of course, I had to call my father and tell him that I was deferring college for a year so I could travel around with my mate and race triathlons in Europe. What else could I do? I was young and single, and I couldn't pass up this opportunity! I think that was the angriest I had ever heard my father. "You're going to lose your running schol-arship," he said over the phone. I could almost see his face turning red. "You've already put yourself in jeopardy if anyone finds out you're doing this. Now you're deferring college?"

I had never gotten into trouble and had always been the obedient son. I knew this might be my only chance to get out on my own with my mate and see some of the world. "Dad, it's done," I told him. "I'll be back. I promise I'll go back to college." End of conversation. Kevin was worried about what my father might do, but I laughed. "We're in Europe. He's not going to fly out here to drag us home." We rang Sean and told him we were going to France, and he said, "Get as many pictures of French chicks as you can." At least some-body had his priorities straight.

So just like that, we started racing in France. It was my first time in Europe. It was the first time I had ever seen the Alps. Everything was new and unbelievable. We were meeting athletes we had never heard of, learning how to deal with different types of terrain and elevations and discovering new tactics and race strategies. We ate all kinds of food, met lots of women, and didn't learn a single word of French. It was an incredible experience. Then in November, it was over.

Only it wasn't over. I had won a lot of events. My team saw poten-tial in me if I could improve my swim, which I knew I could do since I'd only started working with a bona fide swim coach a few months earlier. But first, I had to go back home.

Back in Sydney, my father was ready to put my brief career as a European triathlete in the past. Then my French club offered me a contract for the 1994 season. I still had two years of college left, and my dad said, "There will be no more talk about professional European triathlon racing. There's no future in professional triath-lon racing. You are not going on mucking around swimming, biking, and running. You need to get your degree. You need to become an accountant. You need to grow up." I was twenty.

It had been great fun, and my dad appreciated that. He knew that boys needed to be boys. But I'd done that, it was over and now it was back to the business of school, school, school.

Dying a Day at a Time

I turned down the French contract, dropped out of the triathlon scene, and did my last two years of college. But Sean and I became triathlon junkies. For two years, we lived, ate, slept, and breathed the sport. All I wanted to do was see the world and do these races, but I was trapped by my obligation to my parents. So Sean and I sat down and started The List: a list of all the triathlons around the globe that we would one day compete in together. The plan was that I would finish college and get a job. Then in the summers, we would go on holiday, travel the world, and participate in these races. At the top of the list—our Holy Grail—was the Ironman in Kona. I still have that list today.

THE LIST:
(Some races have changed names or no longer exist)
Ironman World Championships
Ironman Europe (now Quelle Challenge Roth)
International Triathlon Union (ITU) World Championships
ITU World Cup
Chicago Triathlon
San Diego Triathlon
Old Sacramento Triathlon
San Jose Triathlon
Escape from Alcatraz
Wildflower
Santos, Brazil
Mountain Man Triathlon Series
French Grand Prix

Australian Races:
   Ironman Australia
   Australian Triathlon Championships
   Noosa Triathlon
   Nepean Triathlon
   Lake Macquarie Triathlon
   Bundeena Triathlon
   Taree Triathlon
   Nowra Triathlon
   Devonport Triathlon
Races that were gone by the time we raced:
   Nice Triathlon (France)
   World Cup Triathlon (Surfers Paradise, Australia)
   National Park Triathlon (Australia)
   Desert Princess Duathlon (USA)
   Frankston Triathlon (Australia)
   Bud Light US Triathlon Series Pro Championships:
     • St. Joseph Island Triathlon
     • Wilkes-Barre, Pennsylvania
     • Orange County Performing Arts Triathlon
   Coke Grand Prix Series

In October 1995 I finished college with my accounting degree and took a job at Bankers Trust, to the sheer elation of my parents. They were ecstatic that I had aced the interview and now here I was, twenty-two, wearing a suit to work every day, making a good salary. I moved into my own apartment. I bought furniture and my first television. I was racing domestically and doing pretty well, chasing girls with Sean, partying on the weekends, and living what for most young men would be a pretty good life.

I hated every minute of it. I sat at work thinking, *What the hell happened?* I had only become an accountant because my high school advisor told me I was good at mathematics; I had wanted to be a sports physiologist. I was caught in a conflict that's been playing out since time immemorial: My parents didn't understand my passion and they feared that if I followed it I would wind up wasting my life. Their mantra was, "Be sensible, son. Be sensible."

Now, instead of being worried, they were proud. Dad would pick me up at my apartment and drive me to the train each morning for my commute to work. And I thought, *This must be what life is about, right? Do what you're told and it all works out.* Then Sean took a job working at summer camps in America, worked in Hawaii as a life-guard, and sent me "I'm in Hawaii, mate" postcards. He seemed to be living this cool life. Meanwhile, I was dying a little every day.

I wanted to see the world and I was stuck in Sydney. I wanted to see the world so badly I could barely stand to go to the office each morning. One morning, on the peak hour train into the city, I noticed that no one was smiling. *That's why they call it work,* I thought. *It's not called fun for a reason. It sucks.* My next thought was, *I'm twenty-two. Am I going to do this for the next forty years?*

There was a guy who sat next to me at the office named Brian. Other than my parents, he was the oldest person with whom I had ever had a relationship. He was forty-four and had pictures of his kids in his cubicle. I used to sit there and think, *Dude, that's me in twenty-two years. Is this what I have to look forward to?*

That day, I made my decision. After just five months, I was done. I couldn't allow myself to become one of those bitter guys who looks back on his glory days and wonders what could have been. I thought I could go to my French team and get a contract, but it didn't matter. I knew the sport was blowing up in Europe, and I needed to be there. I wasn't going to be discovered in Sydney. I was ready to sell everything I owned and go all in on my swim, bike, and run.

I went to my boss that day and handed in my resignation. He was in shock. He said, "Can I ask you what your reason is?" I said, "I'm going to be a professional triathlete and use that money to travel. I'm going to race around the world and make money so I can travel for one or two years and then I'm going to come back and fall back on my degree."

He laughed. "You're a dreamer, but good luck," I recall him saying. I told him I'd give him two weeks, but he told me to finish by Friday. It was Tuesday. That was quick. Friday came and went and I was out of work. I thought, *I've done it. I've done it.* Now came the panic. Now what did I do? I thought, *Should I go back in and say I made a mistake?* Even bigger, *What am I going to tell Dad?* There was panic, but there was also relief. I had sworn that one day I would do this. Finally, that day was today.

I caught the train home and started planning things. I had some money in the bank, but I needed to start selling off things to get my ticket to Europe. The weekend went by, and I realized that my father would be coming Monday morning to pick me up for the job I no longer had. I wasn't ready to deal with telling my parents yet, so Monday morning I put my suit on and met my father downstairs. He drove me to the train station as usual, and we talked but I just couldn't tell him. He dropped me off at the station and I waved as he drove away. Then I ran back home and spent the day training and getting organized.

A while before he would have been at the station to pick me up from the job I no longer had, I put my suit back on and ran back to the station. Dad picked me up, asked me how my day was, and I said, "Fine." I did the same thing for the next two weeks.

Finally, two Fridays later, I asked if I could come to dinner Saturday night. That evening, I went to Mom and Dad's and said, "I've quit work and I'm going to go to Europe in nine days' time." They got very quiet.

"You're doing what? When did this happen?" Mum asked. I didn't have the courage to tell my dad that I'd been lying to him for the last two weeks, so I just said, "I gave my notice two weeks ago, and those two weeks were up yesterday."

Finally, I said, "Just don't be disappointed, Dad." He looked at me and said, "I'm not disappointed, Son. I just want you to know if you're going to do something, do it properly. Life goes by like *that.* I'm proud of you and what you've done, but just do things properly."

Mom started to babble overprotectively: "When do you leave? Have you packed everything? Don't talk to strangers. What are you doing with your apartment?" I tried to tell her that talking to strangers was the whole point, but what young man can argue with his mother?

Nine days later I boarded a plane for Singapore. I was finally doing it! I didn't know if I would succeed as a professional or not, but I only knew that I did not want to come home a failure.

Lost in Translation

By the time I got to Paris and went through customs, I was frightened to death. I wished I'd tried to learn some French during my ten weeks with Kevin a few years earlier, because I didn't speak a word of it. I was standing in Charles de Gaulle Airport without any idea what to do next, so I bought a copy of *220 Triathlon* magazine, flipped to the back page, and saw a race in Orange, which is down in Provence. It was Thursday and the race was on Saturday, so I said, "I guess that's where I'm going." I booked a ticket on an overnight train to save on accommodations and I was off.

I got off in Orange, booked into a hotel, did the race, and won five hundred francs. There was a race in Avignon the next day, so I went to that and won some more money. But I needed a home base. Back in 1993 when I had raced for the French club, I had lived in a town called Embrun, in the Alps just southeast of Grenoble. I'd stayed there for five days back in 1993 and done the toughest race I'd ever done in my life there. That's where I decided I had to be. I caught an overnight train packed with people, and I became paranoid that the blokes I was sharing a cabin with were going to steal my bike box. I was dying to sleep but I kept waking up to watch them, until finally I decided this was ridiculous and I got off at the next stop, a town called Gap.

This is where destiny comes in. It was Sunday, I was tired and dirty, I had a big yellow bike box, and I was walking through the train station when a man came up to me. I remembered my mother warning me not to talk to strangers—I was still just a kid, really—so I was wary of this guy. But he saw that I had an Australian flag on my bike box, so he spoke English. "You're lost," he said. I wanted him to leave me alone, so I just said, "No, I'm fine," and kept walking. But he stayed with me. I went into town looking for the Office du Tourisme to find out if I could rent a cabin at a caravan park or something so I could live in this area. All the while, we had this running dialogue that went something like this:

"You look lost."

"No, I'm just trying to find a place to stay."

"You all right?"

"I'm all right."

Then he told me it was Sunday and everything was closed. With that, I didn't know what to do. I didn't have my French club contacts from three years earlier; I had been hoping that I would go to races like I had in Manchester and a team would see me and say, "Oh, this guy's good, we'll pick him up." That hadn't happened. As they say, hope is not a success strategy. I turned to my new friend and said, "I'll just wait right here. I'm fine, mate. I'm trying to be a professional triathlete. I'm trying to find a cabin to stay in for a month or so. I just need to get settled so I can start commuting to races."

He suggested that I come to his house so he could help me. Now I was really paranoid. All my friends had told me that the French were mean and unfriendly. What did this guy want from me? Finally, because I realized I had nowhere else to go, I went with him back to his house. I figured if things got dodgy I could always outrun him.

Well, my paranoia proved to be totally ridiculous. The guy's name was Phillip, and he had spent about fifteen years in Aspen, Colorado, selling real estate. He made a lot of money and then moved with his girlfriend, Stephanie, to the Alps, where they were semi-retired. It turned out that Stephanie had the same doubts about me that I'd had about Phillip. Who was I and would I try to murder them in their sleep?

In the end, I stayed with Phillip and Stephanie for about five weeks. They were wonderful to me. We became friends and still are. Phillip would take me on beautiful rides and I taught him about triathlon. I would go for training rides in the mountains and listen to Alanis Morissette's *Jagged Little Pill* on my Walkman (this was before iPods). I must have listened to that album five thousand times. Now I had a home base, and I was training and doing races.

There's an International Triathlon Union (ITU) World Cup series of races that I wanted to compete in, but your national team has to choose you for them, and I wasn't on the national radar. But then things started to look up: the Montpellier Triathlon Club picked me up and asked me to come and live in their training area, a small city on the French Mediterranean Sea. So I thanked Phillip, packed up my things, and moved to this tiny studio apartment in a tiny village called Juvignac.

In club racing, you don't train together if you don't live in the same area. I was racing for the club but training alone. I have never felt more homesick in my entire life. No one lived near me, I had no transport, and I knew nobody. Sure, I was training for this club, but I only saw my teammates on race weekends. After two weeks of no one speaking English and nothing to do but train and sleep, I was ready to pack it up and go home. After the warmth and hospitality that Phillip and Stephanie had shown me, I was lonely. I couldn't watch TV because it was all in French. I had no books. I didn't even have the Internet.

Time goes very slowly when you're alone in a foreign land and don't speak the language. I'd race on a Sunday in the Pyrenees, and there might be some guys from England or someone else who spoke English. I'd hang with them as long as I could, but then the race would be over and they would go back to their clubs. So with Monday came the low of lows. I would say to myself, *Next week, please let there be some people at the race I can talk to.*

At least fifty times, I must have packed my stuff and said to myself, *I can't do this, I'm going home.* But I couldn't bear the thought of having to sit down with my father and mother and tell them that I'd failed, and to hear them say, "We're sorry, Son, but we told you so.

Now come back to the real world." To go back to life in a cubicle! I just couldn't do it. I was too proud to go home.

I envied other athletes who trained close to their homes. Some of the French guys who were riding with the team had parents in Paris; they could go home for the weekend, catch up with their friends, see their girlfriends. I would've killed to do that. But being alone made me mentally tougher. I had to keep going every day. I couldn't sit around in the mornings feeling sorry for myself.

If you're in that situation, you have to fight the desire to quit every day. The process makes you stronger. *Deal with it, mate. Deal with it.* Every day you wake up and repeat that. *Get over it or go home.* Those are your two options. If you're not going to go home, then train. That becomes the simplicity of the whole experience.

If you can survive that as a young person, it creates a hardness in you. It breaks many people. Many Australian guys I knew went broke and went home because they couldn't deal with it. It's so easy to give up. You go to the train station, buy that ticket and it's Easy Street. You're on that nice 747, being fed recognizable food by people who speak English, and you're going back to comfort, family, and friends. It's the end of the dream.

I finally said to myself, *Man, people wait their whole lives to do this! Just enjoy. You're in France. Snap out of it. Go out for a ride. Go for a ride and enjoy the scenery.* So that's what I did. That bleak period in France made me a better triathlete. For one thing, I was so bored that all I would do was train. I would go for five-hour training rides just to kill time. I was learning to endure the loneliness, the strange food, the cold conditions, and the language barrier. I was becoming a warrior.

There's no secret to being a triathlete. Anyone could do what I did. The formula is simple: passion, commitment, repetition, a lot of hard work, and a refusal to fail. I didn't know anything about professional coaching methods or training blocks. I just decided on a routine, threw myself into it, and kept going. There is no reason you cannot do the same.

World Cup

All that extra training and racing had a purpose: I wanted to race the 1996 ITU World Cup in Paris. Finally, the national federation called me and told me I could do the Paris race because there were no other Australians. *Beautiful.* The ITU World Cup is the premier series of short-course racing, and on a big stage like that, a good showing against the best athletes in Europe would put me on the international radar.

My French club said okay, so I made my plans. But after getting to Paris, I realized I was risking everything. As you know if you've ever traveled there, Paris is incredibly expensive. After four days, I had nearly blown all my money. I had no choice but to perform in the race or I was done. I would have to go home broke.

Fortunately, I had a decent day and ended up finishing seventh. Once again, nobody knew this Australian who had come out of nowhere. After the race, a fellow named Les McDonald came up to me and said something like, "Who the hell are you?"

I said, "My name's Chris McCormack." I didn't know who this guy was, but I tried to sell myself. "I did the Junior Worlds in '93 and finished fourth. Now I've finished college and I've been here in France for nine weeks. I've trained for this race and I had a good day."

He asked me what I was doing the following week.

"I'll go on back to my club in the South of France and race for them."

I recall him saying, "Well there's a World Cup in Canada. Have you thought of doing that?" Of course I had. The World Cup race in Drummondville, Quebec, would attract the best of the best in short-course racing. I wanted badly to be there. But I said, "My federation has to pick me, and they've already picked the eight best athletes in Australia to race. I've got to try and cut my teeth here."

He said something like, "Well, I'm Les McDonald. I'm the president of the International Triathlon Union. I'm going to give you a wild card entry to Canada if you want to come."

I still didn't get it. "My federation will never allow it. I need to ring them and get clearance."

I remember that Les said, "No, I don't think you understand. I'm the president of the ITU. I'm giving you a wild card to do the race if you want to come. That is all the clearance you need."

Bonus! You know how you get to a party and someone says, "Let's go to another party." You just go. I had all my stuff in Paris, so why not? I said, "Okay, but how am I going to get to Canada?"

He smiled and reminded me that I'd won two thousand US dollars that day.

Two thousand bucks! I'll never work again! Les told me if I decided to come, they would dock my prize money for the cost of a ticket on Lufthansa and find me a Canadian home to stay in. I thought for two seconds and said, "Let's go to Canada." I flew to Drummondville and got picked up for my home stay. Now the whole Australian team—all the best triathletes from my country, including Miles Stewart, Troy Fidler, Lach Vollmerhaus, Shane Reed, Chippy Slater, Greg Bennett, and some others—started cross-examining me. Their attitude was "Who the hell are you? You haven't played by the rules here. We're the best in the country. You can't just come to the World Cup. The Federation has to pick you."

I was trying to be friendly, but it was awkward. I said something like, "Oh, I met Les McDonald." But that didn't wash. These guys had been on the circuit for years in order to get an invitation to the World Cup; I had been in France for three months and here I was. I wasn't staying with the team. I definitely felt like an outsider. This was another example of my unconventional way of doing things in my sport.

Alone, I went sightseeing and rested for most of the week. Since I had done all this massive training to combat my boredom and loneliness in France, the rest turned out to be exactly what my body needed. Rest is terribly underappreciated in our sport. On race day, it paid off. Only two Australians had won a World Cup at that point: Miles Stewart and Brad Bevan, another Aussie who's one of the best short-course racers in history. I got out of the water in the middle of the pack, rode like a freight train, and ran away from everybody. Boom. Ten thousand dollars, just like that.

The global triathlon fraternity was speechless. There are only nine World Cups in a year and the tenth race at the World Championship. I'd just won against all the best triathletes in the world. I remember thinking, *Did I just win ten thousand American dollars?* When I crossed the line, it was the first time I had ever been in front of a TV camera. The interviewer asked, "How do you feel?" and I said, "Can someone please give me a phone? I have to ring my mum. I've just won ten thousand dollars!"

Back with my host family, I was jumping up and down, singing, "I'm rich!" I used to make $32,000 AUS as an accountant, and I'd just made $10,000 US in one day and $2,000 US the week before, which was about $20,000 AUS at the exchange rate, all in seven days. Beauty!

My ride had been like a rocket. One minute I was a lonesome nobody in France, and fourteen days and two races later I was a World Cup racer. I certainly wasn't going back to France. I went to Bermuda, because I was now on the World Cup circuit as part of the Australian national team, and I stayed with the Butterfield family, who are still close friends today. I took sixth in Bermuda and made another two grand. I was thinking, "This is easy!" But it was only easy on race day.

Even though I was on the World Cup circuit, I was definitely an outsider. The other athletes—including the guys on the Aussie team—treated me with some animosity, an attitude of "Who's this bloke? He's only won one fluke race." It was hard, because I had intense respect for them. But I was like the new kid at school who comes in and starts getting perfect scores on all the exams. I had been training in France on my own, by the seat of my pants and without a coach, mostly to alleviate my terrible boredom. I figured I needed to swim, bike, and run a certain distance each day, so I chose the distance and did it. My finely tuned nutritional plan was to eat whatever I could afford, mostly baguettes and olive oil. Yet here I was, landing in the top ten.

What made it even harder was that because I had won a World Cup race at Drummondville, Triathlon Australia had to give me a spot on the national team. That meant dropping another athlete, which didn't win me any friends. But I had been getting consistent results—a sixth, a first, and a sixth—and I had my own money now. They pretty much had to deal with me.

It was really amazing. I had quit my job in April 1996, and by September I had won a World Cup and I was a part of the most powerful short-course triathlon team in the world. I was obviously doing something right, and now I needed a place to live somewhere between Bermuda and Cleveland, where the 1996 world championships would be. The rest of the Aussie team had gone to training camp, but as a recent addition there was no spot available for me, because the plans had been made long before I had appeared out of nowhere. I knew that Boulder, Colorado, was a haven for triathletes, so I went there. I had $14,000 in my pocket, rented a student apartment for $800 a month, trained in Boulder, and communicated with my teammates through e-mail.

Training with the Greats

Then came the 1996 ITU World Championship in Cleveland, Ohio. I got my ass handed to me by the best guys in the world. That was probably a good thing because I was getting a little cocky. I came in twenty-eighth and thought, *Wow, these guys are fast.* But while I was in Cleveland, I got to know Miles Stewart, an iconic Australian triathlete who won the world title in 1991. Everybody in the triathlon fraternity knew Miles. Out of all that older brigade, he was the one who befriended me. He was actually only a couple of years older than me, but he had been competing for years and had unbelievable talent. I remember thinking, *Wow, I just had a talk with Miles Stewart.* I called Sean back home and said, "Guess who I'm hanging out with?"

It got better. The 1996 season was over; the ITU ranked me ninth in the world, and I'd had six top ten finishes. Miles said something like, "If you come home to Australia this summer, why don't you move to the Gold Coast and train with me?" Miles wasn't stupid; he was the greatest short-course tactician in the sport but not a terrific runner. I think he saw that I was a great runner and he figured he could learn from me. I was blown away: one of the biggest names in my sport was asking me to come and train with him! So I flew home, saw my mom and dad, and then surprised them with the news that I was moving to Queensland, to the Gold Coast.

Miles invited me to his house immediately, and I started training under his father, the legendary Col Stewart. It was the first time that I had ever trained with a group, and this was the best in the world. The funny thing was, Col never had a set plan. He always changed things up. Col's archrival was Brett Sutton, who is probably the most famous triathlon coach in the world. Sutton's program was German-style: strict scheduling, extremely hard work, never deviating from the program.

But Col seemed to have no training structure. He would always be surprising us with different training blocks, different timing, and different types of power and speed work. He would focus less on volume and more on form and improving performance for the specific needs of a race. If you know anything about fitness training, you know that the best way to keep yourself from plateauing and keep getting results is to surprise your muscles. Col constantly kept us guessing, which also kept the training interesting.

I would ask him if we were training enough, and he would say things like, "Training is about winning races, not training the most." He was a hard man but a fair man, the philosopher of our sport. When I expressed doubts, he would say, "Chris, are you winning?" I was.

Col did things his own way. He believed that the swim should be the second session in the day, not the first. He was the first coach to have video of the race cued up so we could watch it and break it down afterward. Col trained me to be a *racer*. The focus was on quality, not quantity. The working dynamic was everything:

twenty-five guys working together, feeding off each other. I thrived on it. I had a great coach, an iconic athlete to measure myself against, and camaraderie with a group of athletes who were all Australians. That fed everything I wanted from the sport. From that point on, I dominated the Australian season.

By May 1997, I started to feel tension from Col and Miles, and I ended up leaving the Stewart camp. I don't think Miles realized how much I was going to take from the group — how much of their methods I would make my own. Col was the coach of the most powerful training group in the sport, and they weren't used to having people ask questions. The group was really set up to make Miles successful; the other athletes were more like role players. When I went head to head with Miles using what I had learned and beat him, I think it was a shock.

There was no animosity at all from Col or Miles, though by departing I created tension between me and Miles that would persist for more than a decade. I just knew that I had learned all I could from them. They had shown me that success in triathlon was about engulfing yourself in the sport — breathing it, sleeping it. It was no longer fun and games; I couldn't race hard and party hard like I had in the past and excel. They taught me what it takes to be a professional athlete.

In 1997, things got even better. I took what I had learned from Miles and Col — prepare, study past races, focus on quality training blocks, adapt your work to how you're feeling and to your goal — and I won my first two World Cup races to take the world number one ranking, which put me in a great position to make the team for the Sydney Olympics. I had four more podium finishes that year. Then, on November 16, I took my first ITU World Championship in Perth, Australia, beating Hamish Carter (a New Zealander who won the gold medal at the 2004 Olympics and who was probably my biggest rival in short-course racing) by thirteen seconds. In 2005, the Australia triathlon community voted that race as the biggest win in Australian triathlon history. It really changed the sport and heralded the arrival of a new generation. I beat all the big names, including the great Simon Lessing, a three-time world champion who hadn't been beaten in three years, in what was probably the most stacked World Championship field ever.

That year, I became the first man in history to win the ITU World Championship and the ITU World Cup Series *and* be ranked number one in the same season. No one has matched that achievement since.

The Sport Goes Global

That was an important time for triathlon, because I was part of a generation of younger athletes who were changing the sport and preparing to take it to a global stage. When I won in Perth in 1997, the sport was just beginning to bubble. The World Cup was becoming quite respected, and triathlon would be in the Olympics for the first time in 2000. But back when I started competing in 1992, it was still pretty much a Mickey Mouse scene.

Triathlon has a tradition of hardscrabble, old-school competition. It wasn't created as a glamour sport. Remember, the runner-up in the first Ironman in Hawaii in 1978, Navy SEAL John Dunbar, ran out of water to run the marathon and drank beer instead of water on the course! Triathletes were supposed to be badass. Back in the early days of European racing, you had to be. The courses were hard and the competitors were hard, especially at the pro level. The bike course might be hilly and 44k instead of 40k, but competitors didn't care. The challenge was the bait. It was kind of a Wild West frontier attitude.

In 1993, when I first told people I was going to make a living as a pro triathlete, they looked at me like I had gone stark raving mad. It was a fringe sport back then. It's probably the same reaction you would have gotten twenty years ago if you had said you wanted to make a living as a professional poker player. Well, the guy who won the main event at the 2010 World Series of Poker won $9 million, so things change. By 1995, the International Olympic Committee announced the sport would debut at the Sydney Games, and that brought government-funded programs in Europe.

The moment things really changed was when Les McDonald, head of the ITU, took Juan Antonio Samaranch, president of the IOC, to see his first triathlon in 1995. Samaranch was appalled that the athletes got out of the water, got on the bikes, and the spectators didn't see them again—and then the same thing happened when they started the run! He told Les that if this was to be an Olympic sport, they had to think about the spectators and television. Also, the arcane no-drafting rules, in which an athlete could win the race but then drop down to third because he'd gotten a drafting penalty on the bike, were unacceptable. Samaranch wanted clear winners in his Olympics, not gold medalists who suddenly became bronze medalists because of some petty infraction!

This was the origin of loop courses and draft-legal racing in short-course triathlon, which helped it become an Olympic sport faster than any other. In 1995, the draft-legal World Cup series started, national federations got funding, and the sport blossomed. In 1997, the IOC began implementing changes to racing gear, safety rules, and an Olympic point system that would qualify each nation to send athletes to the Games. Greg Bennett (an Olympian and Lifetime Fitness Grand Slam winner who was known as Mr. Consistency) and I traveled around the world earning points for the Australian team and competing for world number one at the same time.

When the IOC got involved, the courses had to be precisely Olympic distance, 1.5k, 40k, and 10k, not "about 1.6k," 48k, and 11k. It was more exciting. The Olympic distance had always existed, but now it was enforced. Now there was a clear way to measure my performance against that of other athletes. Now we had legitimacy because we were going to be in the Olympics. I said, "Cool, there's going to be a triathlete who has the same medal as Carl Lewis." Before, I would tell people what I did and they would say, "Huh?" Now I could tell them and be proud.

I was there at the start of all of this. I saw Swiss triathletes in national uniforms driving Volvos because they had Federation money behind them. So I can definitely say that I straddled the hardscrabble, old-school days of racing and the newer, richer, corporate- and government-sponsored days. Between 1993, when I competed for my French club as a junior, and 1996, when I won in Drummondville, the sport exploded.

So, triathlon went global. It's a product of the Olympics and the Ironman brand. Ironman has its wave of marketing and its tour of events, and then there's the Olympic distance that the World Cup races. Ironman is the premier long-course series in the world; the World Cup is the elite short-course circuit. I was the first athlete in the draft-legal era to cross over from short course to Ironman and dominate in both.

The Rift

There was also a major rift in the sport between the old guard and the new Olympic sport. The old guard was the Bud Light Series in America—the old-school, non-draft-legal, six-city tour that started back in 1982. Back then, the sport was mostly American: Mike Pigg, Mark Allen, Scott Molina, Dave Scott, Scott Tinley, Lance Armstrong, and the like. They were the pioneers. I've told you about Mark and Dave, and you know Lance Armstrong. Mike Pigg is an American who dominated at the Olympic distance, winning four national championships in the 1980s. Scott Molina is a former Ironman Hawaii winner known as "the Terminator." Scott Tinley is a two-time Kona winner who's now a teacher.

Greg Bennett, Hamish Carter, Simon Whitfield (the Canadian who won the first Olympic gold in the sport in 2000 and ranks as one of the best short-course triathletes ever), and I came out of the first wave of the Olympic movement, and we were the first ones to experience many of the changes that the ITU guys see today: draft-legal racing, short circuit, multiloop courses, big loop courses that were more spectator friendly, uniform guidelines. But the Bud Light pioneers rebelled. They said things like, "This is bullshit. This ain't triathlon."

There was definitely a rivalry between the old-school Americans who wanted the sport to stay rough-and-tumble and the newer, global sport competitors. Triathlon had started in Kona and San Diego, then spread from there. But when the international federations tried to get the Bud Light race directors to become part of the larger international circuit, the race directors basically said, "Up yours. Our races will stand on their own." Athletes would say, "I'm not buying into these IOC rules where we have to wear a national uniform." The race directors had their turf and they wouldn't let anybody else play. They didn't like that the World Cup was a professionals-only circuit. It was really about making money, and as far as they were concerned, they were the sport. Pro racing was a crock.

For a while, the three styles fed the sport. But eventually, the ITU and Ironman races started to make the older circuit irrelevant. For example, the Chicago Triathlon was famous; it was on The List that Sean and I wrote. But when you talked with other athletes and said, "I won Chicago," it didn't matter. That race had become irrelevant from an international standpoint. The Ironman and ITU circuits were more spectator and sponsor friendly. The standardized distances and rules meant that if you wanted any credibility as a short-course guy, you did World Cup. If you wanted credibility as an Ironman, you had to do an Ironman-sanctioned race. You're only as good as the people you compete against.

Now you have this Olympic distance short-course ITU system, and the athletes that are coming out of that system now are phenomenal. The old school guys say, "It's draft legal, so it's not real triathlon. Triathlon is individual." That's rubbish. I grew up as a runner and fell into triathlon; these kids grew up straight into it. We're starting to see a wave of kids who have been groomed to be triathletes from the time they were seven years old. They're swimmers for their national programs, and then when they get old enough they join the

ITU junior circuit. The old school guys grumble and say things like, "Well if they raced in my races," and I just respond, "Mate, they would run rings around you."

I'm the only one who has done the old-school races and beat the best in the world in a global sport, and let me tell you, these kids who are on the way are going to break every record. The future is in very good hands.

MACCA'S 1993 SEASON

- Diahatsu Wollongong Triathlon—FIRST junior male
- Daihatsu Canberra Triathlon—SECOND junior male
- Quit for Life Perth Triathlon—FIRST junior male
- National Park Triathlon, Sydney—THIRD overall, first junior
- Geelong Australian Triathlon Championships—FIRST junior
- Isle of Pines Triathlon, Gold Coast—SECOND junior
- ITU Triathlon World Championships, Manchester, England—FOURTH junior
- Vendome Triathlon France—FIFTH
- Triathlon De Lyon—THIRD
- Dijon Triathlon—SECOND
- Triathlon Auch—SIXTH
- Triathlon Le Ferte Bernard—THIRD
- Triathlon Montlucon—FIRST
- Triathlon St. Quentin—FIRST
- Nepean Triathlon Australia—THIRD
- Moruya Triathlon Australia—FIRST

Season Statistics and Interesting Facts

- Flight miles accumulated: 13,790
- Countries visited: 4
- Days away from home: 94

Training miles for the year

- Swim: 405 miles
- Bike: 8,475 miles
- Run: 2,080 miles

3

Racing for My Mother

If you've seen me race, even on television, you've probably noticed that apart from my official competitor number I always have the number 19455 on my singlet. Many fans, fellow athletes, and journalists have asked me about it, and the story is simple: that's how many days my mother, Theresa, a woman of aristocratic Maori descent, was alive on this earth. Her story has become my story, in part because I've found that to have a long career where you defy the odds and keep performing at a high level for years—not just in sport but in anything—you have to have a purpose that's bigger than yourself. Believe me, when you've trained and suffered and traveled and missed your family for as long as I have, the prospect of winning just isn't enough to keep you hungry and working hard. You can't just race for yourself; you have to race for something or someone else.

I race for my mother.

When I was growing up, my mum was the anchor of our family. Every night before bed, she would say the same three words to my two brothers and me: "Dream, believe, succeed." My father was the one who drove me to races and did all the heavy lifting that comes with having sons in sports, and he and I still have a very, very good relationship. But, as I've told you, he was a "sports are for the weekend" guy.

For Dad, it was all about getting a steady job, making a good living, and being productive. Dreams weren't on his radar.

Mothers are different, especially mothers and their sons. Mum was soft. She'd say things like, "Come here, sweetie, you broke up with your girlfriend? Well, I never liked her anyway, darling." If sports teaches you anything, it teaches you how to fail. I failed a lot, and I always turned to my mum after the failures. She was the only female in our household, and with three boys always in one punch-up or another, she'd be there hitting us with pans and trying to pull us apart. But for all three of us, our mother made us feel like our dreams were within reach.

Despite being terribly nervous in 1996 about her little boy going off to big, bad Europe when I left my job to compete in France, she also became my biggest fan. She always told me how proud she was of me, especially after I won the world championship in Perth in 1997. She was even prouder, she told me, that I was surely going to go on to represent Australia in the Sydney Olympics in 2000.

Since my Perth win I had pretty much dominated the sport. I'd racked up five ITU World Cup victories, won the World Cup series, and been ranked world number one by the ITU for seventeen months. However, I didn't get an automatic spot on the Australian Olympic team. There were three qualifier races—two in Japan and one in Sydney—that we had to do. The Federation would pick the "shadow squad"—the squad of athletes who would then be eligible to qualify for the Olympics—from the top finishers in those races. Making the shadow squad was *imperative*.

I was preparing to go to Japan in April 1999 to do the first race in Ishigaki. I had just finished second at the Australian Championship, losing out to my old training buddy Miles Stewart, who outkicked me in a final sprint to take the title. It was a classic finish. By that time I wasn't training with Miles anymore; I was on my own, training in Sydney and doing things my own way. So I felt good. I felt poised to tear it up in Asia and come back with an Olympic spot, which would really have been the culmination of my career to that point.

Mum's Courage

In February of that year, in the middle of my most intense training, I got some bad news. My mother was diagnosed with breast cancer. But it wasn't the earth-shattering event you would think, at least not then. I'd known other people whose mothers had been diagnosed with cancer and beat it. One mate told me, "My mum had cancer, she got chemo, and she's fine now. She had cancer eight years ago." My other friend said, "Oh, my mom had cancer four years ago." So it's easy to think it's not really such a big deal. Medicine is good now. You get some chemo and you're good. Mom would be sick, and I knew it was serious, but you never think your mother is going to die.

I wasn't living with my parents, but I went home to see Mum whenever I could spare the time in my training schedule. I would trade off with my brother taking her to her chemotherapy appointments. It was a strain on her, but Mum never complained. She would tell me not to worry about her and to keep training. "I'll be all right, honey, I'm fine," she said again and again. I began to believe her. Then one day she told me, "After Japan, you put yourself in this Olympics, honey. I know you'll go and win the gold medal." That was it for me. I had thought about skipping the Olympic qualifiers after my mother's diagnosis, but now I knew that wasn't an option. I was going to make the Olympic team, win a gold medal, and bring it to my mother.

Only that's not what happened. My mother's cancer was much worse than any of us ever knew. I don't know if Mum knew herself how serious it was, but I suspect she did because the doctors have to tell their patients what they're up against. If she knew, then putting on a brave face for me and the rest of the family was the most courageous thing I have ever seen. Winning Ironmans, winning world championships—all that pales in comparison to Theresa McCormack smiling and cheering me on while never breathing a word about the disease that was killing her.

I had my mission, so it was off to Japan for the first race in Ish-igaki. I finished fourth—the second Australian—which was okay but not great. But that race wasn't the one that mattered. It was a prelude. The next two—Gamagori, Japan, and Sydney—were every-thing. I rang home and said, "Mum, I got beat. I can't believe it, I thought it was going better than that. How are you?" Her response? "I'm fine, sweetie. You go off to Gamagori next week and you have a good race." Everything would be fine, I told myself. She was doing well. Nothing to worry about.

I flew to Gamagori and spent the whole week in Japan. This was a World Cup race, the race that mattered most, and in a blinding, tor-rential rain that made it one of the coldest races I have ever done, I won. I had made the shadow squad. Now I just needed to do the Sydney World Cup race in order to tick off all the boxes for my Fed-eration. What I didn't know was that, thousands of miles away, my mother was dying.

19455

I rang home after that race, ready to share my great news. No one answered. I left messages asking my mum or Steve, my younger brother, to call me. Finally, I reached Steve. He was the baby, which meant he was always the mommy's boy. When I talked to him, he was in tears. That alarmed me, because Steve had always been too proud to cry.

"You need to come home right away," he said, and I could hear the fear in his voice.

"What is happening?" I asked. Come home? I couldn't come home! I was going to another event in Korea the next week before heading back to Sydney. I was going to bring Mum a medal! "You need to come home," he repeated. "Mom's really sick." That was it. To hell with the race and the Olympics.

It was the longest ten-hour flight of my life. My father picked me up at the airport and we went directly to the hospital. I went into the room and there she was, Mum. Drawn and sick looking, but still Mum. "Hi, honey," she said. "You won. I'm so proud you won. I couldn't ring you. I've got no phone in here." Just like my mother! Her first thought was about what I had done. She had been in the hospital for four days, but hadn't let my father or brother tell me because she didn't want to distract me from the Gamagori race.

My vigil started that day. Every day I'd go to see her and she'd be worse. We talked with her doctor and he said that in seven to ten days, she would be gone. When you are told that, it's natural to lash out at the doctors. *Bullshit. My mates' mothers are still alive, why is mine different? You're not working hard enough, Doc.* The day after I got back, I blew up at my father and brother and accused them of being selfish for not telling me sooner. Finally, Dad put his foot down and said, "It's not the time to point fingers and argue. Your mother needs you guys right now."

My brother simply lost it. I coped by spending every minute I could with my mother, as though if I didn't leave her side she wouldn't have the nerve to die. Part of the reason was that I felt horrible guilt. I'd been away in 1996, won the world championship in '97 and become a superstar, and I had spent most of the last three years traveling around the world. I went home when it was convenient. All I could think during that awful week by her bedside was *Damn it, I'm such a selfish son. I run around the world trying to be Mr. Triathlete, chasing girls, and meanwhile my mother's dying.* I did plenty of pointless second-guessing and self-recrimination. I hadn't taken this cancer seriously enough. I should have taken her to cancer chemo everyday, instead of asking Steve to take her because I had a training ride.

I said things like, "I'm sorry, Mum, I should have been here more. You're going to get better. I promise I'm taking you to chemo every day. You've got to fight this, Mum."

Her calm in the face of her own death still amazes me. She said, "Son, I've had a beautiful life. I've got beautiful boys. You've made me so proud." She paused to gather her strength and then she said something I'll never forget. "You've chased your dream. Do you know how much — how proud I am as a mother that you've gone on to chase your dream? Watching you as a little boy turn on that Hawaii Ironman and tell me that you're going to go there and win that thing. Now you're the best in the world at this sport. I'm so proud of you, darling."

Before she got sick, I would say things like, "Mum, I'm going to be the greatest ever. I'm going to win the Olympics." But now, with tears streaming down my face, I knew that it wasn't about me. "I promise you, Mum, I'm going to win everything. You've got to stay around for this. I'm going to win this. You're going to live. I haven't done it all. I'm going to win the Olympics. I'm going to win World Cup races. I'm going to be the best triathlete that the world's ever seen. But you've got to hang around for it. Come on. It's a fight. It's hard. I know. You've got to fight this. We're going to go to the Olympics."

"You can be anything you want to be, honey," she said, smiling. "Don't do it for me, sweetie. Do it for you. You can be anything you want to be."

Those were some of the last words she said to me. During the last two days, she couldn't even talk. The cancer had eaten away her vocal cords. She died on April 26, 1999, at fifty-two years of age, less than five weeks after her initial diagnosis. The disease had burned through her like a bush fire until there was nothing left. She had lived on this earth for 19,455 days.

A Rampage of Racing

Steve shut down completely. My father was broken in a way I had never seen and couldn't even imagine. I just fell into a haze. Mum died just three days before the Sydney World Cup, the final race I needed to make sure I'd be on the Olympic team. But I was grieving and skipped the race. The papers read, "Has Macca blown it?"

Two weeks later came the 1999 Oceania Championship, a major race for the best triathletes in Australia and New Zealand. This was an important race if I wanted to satisfy the Federation and still make the Olympic team. I felt pressured to go, but I didn't want to. Even worse, the race was on Mother's Day, but I went anyway.

When the race began, I was suddenly on a mission to win. Greg Bennett and I blew the field apart on the bike and it looked like I might have a chance to win. Then when I was trying to catch him on the run so we could finish one-two, someone yelled, "Macca, do it for your mum!"

Instantly, that shattered me. I stopped running, sat on the ground right where I was, and started sobbing. The TV cameras caught me sitting on the road, falling apart.

It was the fans who came to my rescue. In one of the most moving things that's ever happened to me in a race, some people from the crowd came over and picked me up off the ground. I walked the rest of the way and still managed to finish in the top ten. Technically, I should have been disqualified, but people couldn't believe I had been there at all.

However, I was done. That race broke me. My Federation knew I had lost the will to compete. I ended up missing most of the rest of the 1999 ITU season. I contemplated retirement. Basically, I did retire. My world rankings started falling. I said, "I'm a loser, I'm done." It took six or eight weeks for Dad, Mick, Sean, and others to say, "You know what? You've got to get on with your life, mate."

My sponsors were saying the same thing. They had cut me a ton of slack, but now they were telling me things like, "Mate, it has been a while. Are you coming back or are you done? We're very sorry your mother died, but it's time to get over it and move on, mate." That shook me a little. I was acting like the entire world had stopped turning when in reality it was just leaving me behind! I shook myself and went to Europe for the World Championship, but I was just going through the motions. I didn't really want to be there.

Then the Olympic trials came around. This was my second chance to make the team, even though I'd missed the last qualifying race. As number one in the world I rated consideration, but I sleepwalked through that, too. I finished second and third Australian in these races, and everyone could tell that my old fire wasn't there. My federation wondered if I was really done. "He does not want to be here," they said, and they named me first reserve, which was a polite way of saying they were leaving me off the team.

I was shocked. I'd needed a dash of ice water in the face to wake me up, and that was it. Not on the Olympic team, mate? I'd dreamed about that for four years and promised my mother that I would win the gold! Now I was being left off because I had spent so much time wallowing in guilt and grief. I was angry and resentful.

During this time, Australian triathlete Michellie Jones invited me to come and stay with her and her husband, Pete, in America. It was a generous gesture. Michellie had made the Olympic team, and in watching her prepare for the Games like the true professional that she was and watching her win the silver medal, I felt my passion for the sport returning. She and Pete really brought me back to the life that I loved. After Michellie won her medal, I rang her mobile phone and shouted, "I have never been so proud of anyone in my entire life!" It was an honor for me to be a part of her journey. Miles Stewart taught me what it took to be a professional athlete. Michellie Jones showed me how to act and live like a professional in everything she did—her training, preparation, sponsorships, everything. She remains the consummate pro in the history of the sport, male or female.

Emma-Jane

For the first time since my mother's death, I felt ready to get back into competition. Now I had something to prove. But something else motivated me, too. The night before my mother died, my friends took me down to the pub to support me and get me out of my apartment. I walked up the stairs, and I saw this tall, blonde girl and it was

BAM. I thought, *Wow. Who is that?* I had never seen this girl before, and it was my local pub. I walked straight over to her and started chatting her up, but she was very standoffish. I bumped into her later and she told me she worked at a dress shop nearby and if I came by, she would give me her number.

Mum died the next day, and I never popped in to get her number. But fate works in funny ways. My mother was assistant coach for the national netball team. Netball is the biggest women's sport in Australia and New Zealand. It's like basketball, but you can't bounce the ball. My mum was the guru of the sport and was very well-known, so when she died she made the local papers.

I met this girl, Emma-Jane, on a Sunday. Mom died Monday night and her funeral was on Friday. Afterwards, my cousins and I went out to celebrate her life and I bumped into Emma-Jane again, walking out of this club just as I was walking in. Later, I realized that my mother had put this woman into my life, because I met her the night before Mum died and ran into her again after her funeral. A minute earlier or later and I might never have seen her again. She said, "I'm so sorry to read about your mother."

I said, "Thank you. Are you leaving?" I invited her to join us for a drink, and that was the beginning of dating Emma-Jane, who is now my wife. Poor thing, she was my shoulder during the months that I was dealing with Mum's death, missing the Olympics, and generally spacing out on life. I was a little needy. Okay, I was a *lot* needy. Our first fifteen months of dating must have been tough for her but she really showed that she loved me.

With Emma, Sean, Mick, Michellie, and others helping me, I realized something: I had a year's worth of sponsorship contracts left and I still had a passion for my sport. They suggested—rather firmly—that I get off my ass, go to America, and start working my way through all those races that Sean and I had put on The List. Emma said, "You told your mom you were going to win all these races, and all you've done since I've known you is mope around and cry 'poor me.'" Ouch.

I retorted (still in self-pity mode) that I was a total, abject failure; that I couldn't even make the Olympics for my mother. Emma said, "So what? You failed. Once. Look at you. I've never seen someone love their sport so much. Why don't you go to America and just race the rest of the year's contracts, and if the sponsors don't want you back, retire." She was right (she usually is). I had nothing to lose, so off to America I went.

That was the beginning of an absolute rampage of racing in 2000. I went to the States with a chip on my shoulder the size of the Sydney Harbour Bridge, out to show the Australian Olympic officials that they'd made a terrible mistake. *Wrong bet*, I intended to say to them. *You bet on the wrong team. I'm still the best and I proved it to you for years and you turned your back on me.* I wanted to humble them and make fools of them, and I would do it by winning every race that I could run.

I smashed everyone. I won Mrs. T's Chicago International Triathlon and the San Diego International Triathlon, two of the events on The List. I won the Escape from Alcatraz Triathlon, eight events on the North American Triathlon series (formerly the Bud Light series) and the inaugural Los Angeles International Triathlon, which at that point had the richest short-course purse in the sport. From 2000 to 2002, I won thirty-two consecutive races and was undefeated in the United States for almost three years. In 2000, I became the first tri-athlete in a decade to capture the US Triple Crown. In 2001, I was Global Triathlete of the Year and smashed course records at nine of the fourteen races I competed in. The only time before this that I had raced in the United States was 1998, when I had beaten Greg Welch (an Aussie who won the triathlon "grand slam," consisting of the ITU Triathlon World Championship, the Ironman World Championship, the ITU Duathlon World Championship, and the Long Course Triathlon World Championship) at Escape from Alcatraz. Now it was "Macca Mania." People were going, "Who the hell is this guy?" Take that, Olympic committee.

But the powers that be do not take lightly to being embarrassed.

While I was still in America, the talk among the Aussie pros and the Federation became that sure, Macca had beaten all these guys in the United States, but they were focused on the Olympics. They went into those races in training phase, not to compete, so of course Macca beat them because they were focused on tuning up for the Olympics. It was how they justified it to themselves. Then the Federation upped the ante: they asked me to come back for the Games . . . just in case! I had one question: "Am I racing? No? See you later."

The worst humiliation for the Federation was that we were supposed to win in the triathlon. But the men failed to capture a medal, and Miles Stewart's sixth-place finish was all they had to bank on. Greg Bennett—who they also left off the team—and I had amazing years. The Federation had played politics with the Games and lost. I drove the knife in a little deeper by going back home after the Olympics and destroying all the Australian Olympians on the Australian circuit. Whenever I had a microphone in my hand, I said, "Hey, you know you bet on the wrong team." I made a point of targeting all the guys on the Australian team and racing them. I would beat them and then in the postrace interview, say things like, "Yeah, so-and-so was in the Olympics. It felt great to beat him by five minutes."

People in the sport started muttering, "What is wrong with this guy?" No one had ever done what I was doing—openly reveling in embarrassing other triathletes. I wasn't winning myself any friends, but I didn't care. I was angry that just as I had gotten back on my feet after my mum's death, I had been left off the Olympic team. I felt that Triathlon Australia wasn't listening, and they weren't. I felt that I had let my mother down. That put a giant chip on my shoulder. I would go to races and say, "I'm going to smash it today and I hope my Federation is watching." It wasn't that I wasn't good enough to be on the Olympic team, but they had felt I wasn't ready. *Not good enough?* I thought. *Take that!* People either said I was intense, or an idiot, or both.

I started to believe in myself again as an athlete. Instead of thinking,

Oh, jeez, I need to do X amount of training, I began accepting that I had a gift. I wanted to create an image that would strike fear in other guys. I knew I could talk trash and back it up, so while I was always politically correct at the microphone and praised the other guys, I never backed down from calling out other competitors' weaknesses or pointing out my strengths. It was the beginning of my mental game. I was beginning to understand how identifying and highlighting the fears and insecurities in other athletes could give me an advantage in the later stages of a race, when mental toughness was everything.

It was also the beginning of a new stage of my career. I was done being under someone else's control. I was not going to put my life in the hands of a federation that could pick me or say no to me at will. I was going to run my own destiny.

Ironman

At the end of 2001, after having mud on their faces for too long, the Federation contacted me and said, "We're planning for Athens. We know you want to go to the Olympics." I flew to Surfer's Paradise in Queensland and sat down with National Performance Director Bill Davoren. He told me they wanted to put me in the Olympic program. I said, "I'll tell you how you put me in this Olympic program: put me in the Olympics, now. Put me on the team."

He said they couldn't do that. I replied, "You know me, Bill. You know my results. How have I not proven myself after all these years? If you let me focus on this event, I will deliver. But don't make me jump through hoops because you've got to justify your job."

He talked about training camps and putting me on the selection squad, and my patience finally ran out. They just weren't getting it. I said, "You know what, Bill, thanks very much. You just made my mind up for me. I'm going to Ironman. See you later." It wasn't that I couldn't do both; there's no rule against competing in World Cup and Ironman races at the same time. But I was done with the national program.

Bill thought I was bluffing, because I was the most dominant short-course guy in the world. But I registered right then and there for Ironman Australia, which was in April 2002. No one could believe it.

Ironman Australia and Ironman Hawaii were on the list I'd made with Sean, and I was determined to win them and Challenge Roth in Roth, Germany. Ironman Australia was the dream race in those days. As kids, it was the only race we had access to. Sean and I would drive for three hours and watch the guys come in. Pauli Kiuru had won it four times and raced against Mark Allen; he was a god to us. So when I went to the start line, I was just happy to be there, I didn't think I would win, especially since it was my first Ironman.

I didn't have a strategy. I just did what I did in short-course racing but did it four times longer. But there I was, leading on the marathon! When I was ten kilometers (six miles) from home, it was the longest run of my life. Then, when I was about two hundred meters from the finish, I started walking. When Sean and I would watch the race as kids, we would watch guys sprint down the finish chute and both say, "Man, if I ever win that race, I'll walk down the chute and savor it!" So I walked. I had my hands in the air, and I was a stunned kid. My brain screamed *I'm about to win Ironman Australia!* over and over.

It was the first time in twelve years an Aussie had won the home race. It was spectacular. One of my good mates who was training with me at the time, Jason Metters, knew I was a good short-course guy but didn't think I could win. We sat in the hotel afterwards and celebrated. After an Ironman you're totally destroyed inside, but happy as a kid at Christmas. We looked down over the race course and the age groupers coming in and Jason said, "You're the real deal." Later, we got Sean on the cell phone from Hawaii, and he said, "Chuck [that was Jason's nickname], you're just realizing that?"

I would win Ironman Australia every year from 2002 to 2006.

I came to own the race at Roth as well, breaking the magic eight-hour mark in 2004 (7:57:50), 2005 (7:56:13), and 2007 (7:54:22). Breaking eight hours was once thought to be impossible, but at Roth, you have 300,000 spectators on the course, and they push you and push you. There's nothing else like it. When you're having rough patches, you feed off that energy. In 2004 at Roth, when I came down the chute and saw the finish and saw "7:56" on the clock, I was shocked. I started sprinting. I was the first non-European to break eight hours. That was legendary territory; only a handful of athletes have done it. I was ecstatic. I was a sub-eight-hour Ironman guy!

That was the wave I rode into Kona.

Finding a New Purpose

I've told you how I failed at Kona for five years before finally winning in 2007. Coming down Ali'i Drive that year for the win, I should have felt jubilation. I had finally broken through and ticked off the last race on The List. Sean had died by then, so I felt like I was carrying him across the finish as well. But all I could do during those final few hundred meters was think, *I wish my mum was here*. If you see any coverage of that race, you'll see me looking up to the sky, just kind of spaced out.

After the race, I went back to my hotel and thought about how I felt. By that time, Emma-Jane and I had two young daughters of our own. I was sitting there watching them play. Everyone was celebrating, but I was thinking, *I should feel more elation than this. I've done it. I should be happier. I should feel fulfilled.* Instead, I felt ready to retire. I'd attained every goal in the sport, and now I felt like a mountaineer who's reached the summit of Everest and suddenly realizes there are no higher mountains to climb. I loved my sport, but what was left?

That was when everything came together. My mum had been on my mind all day. She had died of breast cancer. I now had two daughters. Having a grandparent who had died of breast cancer before age sixty gave them a 75 percent greater chance of developing the disease themselves. I wanted to honor my mother while doing something that my family could get involved in and that would benefit my girls.

That was when we started the Macca Now Foundation. I took the 19,455 days that Mom was alive, multiplied it by 140.6—the number of miles in an Ironman—and got $2,735,373. That's how much money I intend to raise for breast cancer by racing.

I can't tell you the effect this had on me. My whole purpose had been to finish that list of races—to honor Sean and keep the promise I had made to Mum. When I finally did it, it was like the air came out of my balloon. If not for the foundation, I probably would have retired after 2007. Instead, I had a new purpose. I also wanted my daughters to know their grandmother, someone they've never met, someone whom this disease had taken from them. I thought this was a fantastic way of doing that while doing some real good.

Together, Emma-Jane, my daughters, and I started raising money. I used my platform as a champion to raise awareness and donated the prize money from my races. I met with breast cancer groups to find out how I could help them. Auction a jersey to raise money? Done. It

---

MACCA'S (W)INSIGHTS

Find a purpose for your racing

Training and competing in something as punishing as a triathlon takes unbelievable discipline, making it easy to slack off when you get tired or discouraged. My solution: race for a purpose larger than yourself:

- Raise money for a charity.

- Honor a friend or relative who's passed on.

- Earn publicity for your business.

- Keep a promise to your children.

- Complete your own personal list.

...or anything else that keeps you motivated and refusing to quit!

was very informal at first; I would race, and we would deposit the prize money in an account that went to breast cancer research. I never envisioned starting a formal nonprofit like LiveStrong. It was just a McCormack Family thing. That was what I wanted to do for the rest of my career.

A Different Person

That cause has become my greatest motivation to keep training and racing. I had lost the hunger, but now it's back because there's a larger purpose behind every mile I bike and every stroke I swim. I'm racing for my mother now. I can make a difference in the world that's bigger than me being ranked number one or winning the World Cup. Today, we've raised more than $500,000 US for breast cancer—and that's going to increase, because word has gotten out. People want to know how they can help.

When I began the foundation, the racing world saw a different Macca. I had been labeled as this angry racer with a chip on his shoulder, and now I was soft and kissing babies. I was running around with women in Singapore wearing a pink shirt. They said, "Macca's working on his image. He's trying to be like Lance Armstrong." I think people assumed that I was using the foundation as a gimmick to build my brand.

In reality, I was discovering more about myself than I ever had before. For one thing, I realized that when I had been racing to keep my promise to Mum and tick off all the events on my list, I had neglected my girls, Tahlia and Sienna. When I realized that, it shocked me. I had done the same thing to my mother in the years before she died—so caught up in being Chris McCormack, World Cup superstar, that I had neglected what really mattered.

Starting in 2007, I took a step back. Today, my family is involved in every step of my career. If you're going to have a long career as a triathlete in a sport that consumes so much time in training and travel, you have to involve your family. My wife has just as much input in when and where I'm racing as I do. She's been around the sport now for eleven years. She knows just about as much of triathlon as anybody. She's become a tactician. Our pillow talk is usually of the "Do you remember the last time you raced Raelert you did such-and-such?" variety. "This is what you need to do," she says.

In the process, I've been able to become a different athlete in front of the camera, in the magazines, and on the social networking platforms. I've been able to tell my story and soften the perception of who I am. Instead of people simply writing what they think is true about me, they've been able to get to know the real me.

Best of all, I'm the bridge between two different generations of women. My daughters are able to learn about their Nanny. They know who she was and what she still means to me. Now we go into functions after a race, I've got the pink ribbon on, and we're giving a local breast cancer organization a check. One of my daughters hands the check over and says, "My Nanny raised this because she died of breast cancer at fifty-two." That moves me. It's given me a real sense of purpose.

Whether it's raw talent, your ability to train like an animal, or something else: if you want a long career, to be a champion and transcend your sport, you need to understand what makes you good. It can't be just because your coach tells you you're good. You need to get in your own head and break it down: "I'm good because…" What makes you tick, mentally as well as physically?

Once you understand that, your purpose becomes clear. You might be good because you're trying to prove something to someone. You might be good because you love to break down your sport like a mechanic taking apart a car, then put it back together to run even faster. You need to figure out *why* you do what you do. If you don't, you will eventually lose your way as I lost mine.

I lost my way after my mother died because her death exposed the truth: I had no idea why I was a triathlete. I didn't know what made me good. After she passed I had the same level of fitness and same strategic knowledge as before, but I didn't win races. I had lost my way. When I decided to defy the governing body of my sport so I could complete The List for me and Sean and keep my promise to my mother, I found my way again.

That experience showed me what makes me good: my willingness to take the unconventional route in order to keep a promise. Every stage of my career has been about fulfilling a promise. First, it was a promise to myself that I wouldn't go into a cubicle without spending a little time seeing the world. Then it was an unspoken promise to my parents that I wouldn't come home a failure. After that came a promise to Mum to win every race on my list, and to her and Sean to finally win at Kona.

Now my promise is to my wife and daughters that I will help make the world a better place for them. Now I race for my girls, for breast cancer victims all over the world, and for the men who love them. It's no wonder I still have the hunger to compete and win. I have a whole world inspiring me.

MACCA'S 2000 SEASON (A RAMPAGE OF RACING)

- Australian Triathlon Championships—SECOND
- Australian Olympic Trials, Sydney—THIRD Australian
- Australian Olympic Trials, Perth—FOURTH Australian
- Missed Olympic team; flew to the USA
- Byron Bay Triathlon—FIRST
- Honolulu International Triathlon—FIRST
- Oceanside Triathlon, US—FIRST
- San Diego International Triathlon—FIRST
- Arizona International Triathlon—FIRST
- Carlsbad Triathlon—FIRST
- Encinitas Triathlon USA—FIRST
- Escape from Alcatraz Triathlon—FIRST
- San Jose International Triathlon—FIRST
- USA Pro Sprint Triathlon Championships—FIRST
- Mrs. T's Chicago Triathlon—FIRST
- Rock 'N' Roll Cleveland International Triathlon—FIRST
- Las Vegas Triathlon—FIRST
- Los Angeles International Triathlon—FIRST

Season Statistics and Interesting Facts

- Flight miles accumulated: 51,985
- Countries visited: 8
- Days away from home: 251

Training miles for the year

- Swim: 680
- Bike: 14,907
- Run: 2,090

4

Mind Games

Back in 2000, I developed a bike strategy that made me very dangerous. I needed to develop my bike because Simon Whitfield was running so fast. I was a brute runner; he was about finesse. He was a gazelle as a runner. Other athletes, trying to keep up with him, had become almost as strong as he was. Simon changed the look and style of the World Cup athlete.

At my best, I knew I couldn't run with Simon and these other guys, so I needed to make my bike lethal. Historically, I had always swum with the front group, stayed with the pack on the bike, and then done the fastest or second-fastest time in the run. But now, these new runners were too fast.

So to win, I needed to start making the other athletes fear me on the bike. Because drafting was legal in short-course racing, other athletes tended to coast, letting the guys in front break the wind resistance and neglecting to push on the bike. So I changed my training. I brought strength efforts into the equation, riding big gears uphill. I did motor pacing, riding behind a motorbike, maybe riding forty or fifty miles an hour. I did short time trial sessions of prolonged effort: attack, attack, attack, and then break away. In this way, I developed a higher rev range (a faster pedaling cadence) that would let me attack and break the runners on the bike. I became able to set a varied pace that I knew would be very difficult for the other athletes to match.

By the end of 2000, I was starting to dominate on the bike. When the 2001 season started, the athletes had no idea what hit them. The bike ride became a weapon to the point where I could now dictate when the real race started. They now had this huge hole in their game and I started winning everything: the World Cup, the Goodwill Games, and more.

In 2001, I began deliberately telling everyone how I was going to beat them on the bike. I wanted them to realize how confident I was. In press conferences, I'd say things like, "Simon Whitfield is the best runner in the sport at the moment, no question." I always praise the other guys, and then go in for the kill. I'd say, "But it's no secret that I'm going to swim with these guys. I'm a five-minutes-better bike rider and I'm going to unleash that tomorrow. Then it's up to me to hang on and for the guys to catch me in the run. I'm happy with that situation. I'm not sure how the other guys feel about it."

People would say, "Why are you telling them how you're going to race?" But the guys already knew how I was going to race. That wasn't the issue. I wanted them to be worried about me, not focused on their own strategy. But I was the only one saying these sorts of things, and that was the beginning of the belief that I'm cocky. *He's an angry racer. Don't piss off Macca.*

I had never shoved my success into anyone's face, not even Triathlon Australia, who had disrespected me so badly. I was dominating the circuit and they needed me much more than I needed them. Yet they had used me for four years. I had raced all over the world, won events for them, grabbed the world number one ranking and qualified our nation for three Olympic spots, and then I was left off the Olympic team. If I'd cared enough I would have rubbed their noses in my success, but they weren't even part of my life anymore.

I've always respected the other athletes. I've never said anything that I didn't believe to be true. But nobody likes a truth teller.

Nobody likes to have the secret fears that they harbor in their hearts laid out for all to see. I was only highlighting what was happening, and everything I said was substance, but nobody had said those things before. If you're in an environment with a few dozen of the most ferociously competitive people on the planet, everybody hates the guy who always wins — especially if he tells you exactly how he's going to beat you.

So the chatter began. People started saying I must be on drugs. They wondered if I was cheating. They said I had to psych myself up, which was ridiculous when I was dominating almost every race. Reporters and bloggers wrote things like, "He's too confident. How can someone sit in a room and say, 'This is what I'm going to do'?" The press loved it. They called me a quoting machine and printed everything I said because it got attention.

I had found a huge weapon that I would use from then on because I could see the athletes' fear. I was like the little boy in "The Emperor's New Clothes" who cries, "But he's got nothing on!" Everybody made fun of the kid...until they realized he was right. Well, everybody thought I was just psyching myself up until I kept winning. Between Europe, the United States, and Australia, I was on a record winning streak at that point. Clearly, I was doing something right.

It's Win the Race, Not Make Friends

To this day, some athletes can't stand me because I speak candidly and on the record. I guess that's why a lot of people in the sport regard me as cocky. But in reality, I'm not cocky at all. I'm smart. I also know that winning in my sport is about much more than who has trained harder than whom. If there's a magic bullet to my success, beyond any doubt it's my ability to dominate in the mental game. Above all else, that comes down to learning to manage fear: my own fear and the fears of my opponents.

In endurance racing, whether the race is two hours or eight hours, the biggest limiting factor is fear. The reason you get nervous before a race is that you doubt your ability to perform when it's all on the line. The mind game that takes place before the starting gun ever fires is really the critical point of a race. It's when all your insecurities bubble to the surface. It's when you have that good angel on one shoulder and a bad angel on the other. One is saying, "You can do it, mate!" The other is whispering, "Why are you here? You can't win!" The angel you decide to listen to will determine whether you are competitive or an also-ran.

When I've broken in a race, like I did in Kona in 2002, after the event I always end up cursing myself for listening to the dark side. Because there's always a voice in everyone's head saying, *You haven't done the work, mate. You know that track session you missed? It's coming back to get you on this hill.* That's what holds you back. Each race is a new war against that evil angel. Sometimes you're going to listen to it even if you don't want to, while other times you're going to find the discipline to shut it out. There have been races where I've been in agony, but I've chosen to listen to the positive side and won. Like anything, you can train to get stronger and take down opponents who haven't done the same work.

Mastering your own self-doubts is half the battle. The other half is learning to leverage the other guy's doubts. Once again, this is where I'm unique, because I don't think any other athlete in my sport plays the mental game in quite the same way that I do. Other athletes lash out at me about it, which I don't understand. If you're a professional, shouldn't you want every edge? We're professional athletes. In the same way that Rafael Nadal will grunt when he hits a forehand to throw off his opponents, I'm going to use whatever psychological tactics I can to get an advantage over mine. As long as you obey the rules, honor the sport, and respect your fellow athletes, the rest is fair game. If you don't like it, be an age-group racer.

Fact One: Races are won or lost in key moments.

Fact Two: Success in the sport is, above all else, about enduring suffering.

My goal is to make my opponent doubt his ability to suffer when one of those key moments comes. If I'm running side by side with someone, he might be thinking, *I'm going to kill you. I'm going to do this, this, and this.* But if I've told him his weaknesses before the race, I'm under his skin. When he's facing the pain and facing the decision whether or not to endure even more pain for the chance of winning, he's more likely to think, *Macca's right. I'm not very good on the bike. I'm losing another minute to him. Oh, man, another minute. Uh-oh.*

The mental game is about getting other athletes to buy into the dark side of the force — to catch them when their bodies are screaming for relief and make them doubt themselves just long enough to decide that the punishment isn't worth it. Then you've got them. I've used that strategy many, many times over the years, and it's won me a lot of races.

The Fear of Losing the Streak

I study athletes. I learn their trends. To find a trend in an athlete, you need to look at his last seven races, at a minimum. Well, I look at more than that. I watch tape, break down races step-by-step, and find the patterns, just like a football or baseball player. When you have experience in how races play out, you can find a lot of places where a strong mental game will give you an advantage.

I started doing this in 2001 for a simple reason: the fear of losing. As I said, starting in 2000, when I thumbed my nose at the Australian triathlon officials and went to America, I got on an incredible roll of winning races — thirty-two in a row. I wanted to keep it going, but I knew someone was liable to beat me at some point. I'm big for a triathlete, and I hadn't always performed as well as the 140-pound guys in hot, humid conditions. I knew I was beatable, but I wanted to extend my dominance for as long as possible.

I had already gotten away with winning a couple of races that I shouldn't have won because guys were looking over their shoulders and assuming I was unstoppable. Meanwhile, I was in agony, thinking, *Thank God for that.* But then I realized something: *I had won those races because of other athletes' doubts!* I had all this doubt about myself, but I hadn't thought about their doubts. I realized that if I wanted to dominate the sport, I needed to find a means to create—and capitalize on—the doubts that other triathletes had about themselves.

At the elite level, the physical difference between athletes in any sport is microscopic. In an Ironman, every pro out there is a strong swimmer, biker, and runner. What separates the people on the platform from the rest is what they do with their minds. I didn't appreciate this as a youngster because when you're twenty-four, you're thinking with your balls and not your brain. You want to be the biggest badass on the block and run everyone else into the ground. But as you get older, you start to realize that you can get better results with less effort, and the key to that is mastering what's in your head.

I started to realize the power of the mind game when I was locked in a rivalry with Simon Lessing and Craig Walton, an Aussie Olympian who became a world-class coach after retiring in 2008, then announced his surprise unretirement in 2010. In my short-course career, I had really struggled to beat Simon. I think I beat him five or six times. On the other hand, I beat Craig at will, but Simon could never beat Craig. It was weird. I didn't think the reason was physical, so it had to be psychological.

Now, the consensus in 2000 and 2001 was that Craig Walton was the best swim-biker and probably the best nondrafting triathlete in the world. He was my nemesis. But in interviews, I would say, "No question, Craig is the best swimmer in the world and has a lethal bike leg. But to call him the best swim-biker in the world is a bit rich. I don't think I've done a race this season where we haven't jumped off the bike together. Swim-bike is two parts of the triathlon. Being the best swim-biker won't win you races. You have to cross that finish line first, and that means running as well." You see how I said that? No talking trash. No beating down my opponent. No disrespect. I give him credit, but then tell everyone how I think it is.

From Craig's perspective, when he read the articles or watched the interviews, he was probably starting to think, *You know, he's right. My swim margin is the only advantage I ever have on him. He rides as good as me and catches me on the run.* I knew that Craig knew I was a better runner than him. I wanted him to know that I was sure about that and didn't fear his strengths in any way. I had created a doubt and fear, highlighting his weaknesses and creating an excuse for him to quit when he was suffering.

The proof that my gambit could pay off came at the 2001 Escape from Alcatraz. All the Australian Olympic guys were there, including Craig. In the buildup to this event, I started to tell people how I was going to beat them. I would say things like, "I'm going to swing close to these guys. I'm going to be really aggressive on this event, really distance myself, and hold Craig at bay. I'm a much better runner than Craig. I'm going to pick him up. Hopefully he doesn't have too big a margin so I can hold him at bay. I'll be able to run him down and hopefully it'll give us some distance on the guys behind."

Nobody had ever said anything like this before a race. The talk was all about being humble and "training hard" and "just being happy to be here." But I was thinking about Craig's confidence on the run. I wanted to undermine it even more.

On race day, I didn't have the bike ride that I thought I would. I had assumed I would be within seconds of Craig, but instead he had a minute and a half on me. It took me a lot longer to catch him because he was running very well. But then I started to realize, looking back over my history with Craig, that if I caught him he broke every time. That was the reason I could beat him when Simon couldn't. If I caught him, his will to suffer went out the window. So my goal was get across to him as quickly as possible. Because I was telling him all the time that he was a bad runner, he didn't believe that he could beat me.

In the race I was taking no time out of him. We got to Baker's Beach, which is almost the halfway point, and it was a two-man race.

Baker's Beach is your first chance to see each other. It's an out-and-back section on soft sand. You run on the water's edge because the sand is harder. After Craig made the turn and was coming back the other way, I yelled across to ask him how far behind me the guy in third place was. The impression I wanted to make was that I was doing this real easy. He was a minute up, but I saw the look in his eyes. He knew I was there. I said, "Keep at that pace, and I'll be there in a minute, and we can go one and two!" I wanted him to think, *Good grief, I'm running my ass off, and he's asking me to stay at this pace!*

After Baker's Beach, you come to the critical part of the race called the Sand Ladder. It's a half-mile run on sand—straight up. You usually walk it. Craig was only thirty feet in front of me at this point, and I was thinking, *Gotcha!* We ran together at the top, and then I made a surge and set a blistering pace. Over my shoulder I said, "Stay strong, mate! You've got third covered!" Then I took off. The race is run on narrow, winding trails, and if you get 150 feet ahead, you disappear. I wanted Craig to think I was going to maintain my pace all the way to the finish. I didn't want him to be thinking, *Hang with Macca, hang with Macca.* I wanted him to be looking over his shoulder at the guy in third. That was how I broke his spirit.

After the race, I thought, *Dude, you had me today. I played a game of cards with you and you got bluffed.* After the race he said, "I was gone." I didn't say, "Oh, no, you had me." Instead, I played it cool: "Yeah, I just felt good up there. I was just making sure that you and I got one and two. You had a great race today, mate." Part of the mental game is seeming invincible.

It was clear that Craig had a mental block with me that he didn't have with Simon Lessing. In turn, I had a mental block with Simon that I found very, very difficult to break. When I finally broke it, I started beating Simon at will. That was when I realized that you create the boundaries for what you're capable of doing. You have to identify exactly what they are in order to break them down.

Knowing the Athletes

After that experience, I realized that the same thing must be applicable to every triathlete. If that's true, then why not create fear and doubt in all of them? That could give me a critical leg up in an event, and if they can't deal with it, that's their problem, not mine. Finding ways to break down my opponents mentally became my new between-race occupation.

I started scouting. I watched races on video. I read magazine articles. I followed and logged the swim, bike, and run times of all my key rivals: Miles Stewart, Hamish Carter, Peter Robertson (an Aussie Olympian and three-time ITU world champion), Simon Lessing, and Simon Whitfield in the ITU; Craig Walton and Greg Bennett in the American races. Overall, there were about ten marquee guys that I really focused on because I knew I would be racing them a lot. You want to get a feel for how the other guys at your level race. After a while you start noticing differences: We swim the same, or this guy bikes harder. This guy does such-and-such late in the marathon. You discover their Achilles' heels, and then you start hammering on them in public to plant those seeds of self-doubt.

I created mental dossiers on every one of my rivals. I would study someone like Miles Stewart until my eyes hurt. Miles taught me a lot, and because of that I was able to change and adapt to his main strength. Miles was a master tactician, and you needed to apply pres-

MACCA'S (W)INSIGHTS

Creating scouting reports

If you're an age-group racer, you're probably less concerned with beating another athlete than with finishing or setting a PR. So rather than create dossiers or scouting reports on athletes you want to defeat, create reports on triathletes you admire so you can emulate things they do well. Some ways to do this:

- Watch old races on television or online.

- Attend races and watch them unfold live.

- Watch or read interviews with athletes and note their tricks and secrets.

- Talk to pros and age groupers and ask questions.

- Ask coaches to break down what other athletes do well.

- Read what other athletes write on their blogs or Facebook pages and ask questions.

Determine what weaknesses or problems you've been having, find athletes who seem to have solved those problems, and become experts on them so you can do what they do to improve your performance.

sure on him early or midrace, because he was a sprint finisher. He is a phenomenal athlete, but I was a much stronger bike rider than Miles—he knew it, I knew it. And I'm a good runner. So it was up to me. If I got rid of Miles midrace, I had him. We both knew that.

In interviews I would say things like, "You know, Miles Stewart is a great swimmer and a brilliant tactician on the bike. He's a guy I've trained with and know very well. I grew up as a triathlete with him. Miles taught me a lot when I was an apprentice. But now, I'm no longer the apprentice." Makes me sound like Darth Vader talking to Obi-Wan Kenobi, doesn't it? "Miles is a kick finisher," I would add. "If I can apply pressure midrace, I've got him. Just look at his last three races." It wasn't vindictive talk; it was straight talk. His response was an "I'll show you" attitude that added to the typical tension of the prerace week.

Now, imagine that you're Miles and you've read all the stuff I've been saying. In the middle of a race, when you should be focusing on your own strategy, what are you probably doing instead? You're watching for me to make my move. So you're playing my game, not yours.

I started doing this with all my major rivals. For instance, at the live press conference before a big race against Craig Walton, I'd say things like "As far as I'm concerned, Craig is the most difficult guy I'm going to have to face tomorrow. He just won this race, this race, and this race, you know?" I'd always start with the positive for the athlete, without question. But the trick is to then move into the things that undermine confidence. "But," I would begin, "for those three races, without sounding arrogant, I wasn't there. He's a minute ten ahead of me on the swim, but I've done a fifty-one, fifty-two, and fifty-three for my last three splits on the bike, so that makes up the deficit. And I think I'm a better runner than Craig in this situation. So Craig has to have improved his run, which I don't think he's had the time to do. Otherwise, he's going to have some difficulty beating me."

Of course, Craig was right there down the table, listening and probably thinking, *He's right.* Either that or he was getting angry with me. Both emotions are positives for me. Anger makes you do things you shouldn't; fear makes you question what you can do.

That's when the muttering started. *Macca's overconfident. Macca shouldn't be saying these things.* Some people didn't like what I was saying, because it just wasn't done in our sport. But as I kept saying to my wife, I want to win! We're all adults here; if you think I'm talking trash and you're offended by it, then play the game back! I was informed, confident, and honest about each opponent. When it started to filter back to me that people were not happy with my comments, I thought, "Good. I'm creating fear." Behind closed doors, I might be tense. But as they say, you never let 'em see you sweat.

Taking Them Out of Their Game

A month before a race, I study the people I know are going to be tough. I sit down at the start of every year with Mick, my coaches, and my wife, and we go down the list of people we've got to look at.

What's changed for them since last season? Have they gotten faster? Slowed down? Why?

The early season is the most difficult, because you're basing your strategy on last season's results. You don't know what a given athlete has done in his off-season, so you've got to be really attentive in those early events. But, in general, I find it pretty easy to predict how an athlete will approach a race. Ours is a very conventional, conservative sport. Most triathletes are afraid to change things very much. That works in my favor, because I can plan on the assumption that they will replicate the racing strategy that they used the year before. Most triathletes are slaves to routine. That's why I don't have a routine in my training or my races. I adapt. In our sport, it's an advantage to be unpredictable. If you have a routine, the routine owns you.

For example, if you have a hard time getting going in the morning and your first workout of the day is always swimming, that might hurt your swim performance. So you change the timing of your swim workout to later in the day when you're more alert, right? Maybe. But if you're a slave to routine, maybe you don't. Thus, your swim never improves.

Many triathletes find it difficult to trust change. It's like lifting weights: if you get bulging biceps and triceps in the first two months, you're probably going to think, *I'm not changing a thing!* But the body craves change and surprise. If you don't alter your workout, you plateau and the results stop. Any sport is the same way. The great ones are always adjusting and finding new ways to surprise the field. But if you're a triathlete who just had a great season and someone says, "I think next year we should try something different," you're likely to to say, "Hang on mate, we've had a great season—why change now?" But just as the body gets used to a workout routine, the other competitors in a triathlon get used to your race tactics. If they know exactly what you're going to do in every race, eventually they're going to "hack" your strategy and beat you...even if you're the strongest athlete in the field.

Knowing athletes' predictable patterns gave me plentiful ammunition for mental warfare. For example, before a race, I might think, *What can I say about Normann Stadler* [the German 2004 and 2006 Ironman world champion and one of the strongest bikers the sport has ever seen] *that would give me an edge over him? He's a better biker than I am and his swim's a weakness, but I'm a better runner. He needs to get a margin of error on the bike to beat me in an event. So how do I attack Normann without seeming arrogant and crazy?*

At the press conference, I'd say, "You know, it's going to be an amazing race. It looks like Normann's going to have to work on his swim, because you know, last year's swim was not good for him. He has an amazing record, but he's got just one arrow in his quiver, and he's going to have to get a margin of error to win this race. He pulled it off last year, but it's a very difficult way to race. It's lonely, hard, and difficult to know you're losing time all day. You have to ask yourself, is he prepared to go there again? Norman knows the answer to that, I don't."

With the right words you can even turn a spectacular performance into an albatross around an athlete's neck. Take Marino Vanhoenacker, a Belgian former duathlete who won Ironman Austria five times. He did an incredible 7:52 at the 2010 Ironman Austria. It was the third-fastest time ever. Well, when somebody puts in a performance like that in Europe, I'm the first person the European press comes to for comment. They asked, "What did you think of Marino's 7:52?"

I always give credit where credit's due. Marino had a fifty-minute swim, an incredible performance by a phenomenal athlete. So I gave him that. But then I said, "We're going to see how Marino recovers from a performance like that. The third-best Ironman of all time has got to tax the body. Jeez, you know, that's a career to some people."

When I say things like that, I'm trying to get my opponents to do one of two things:

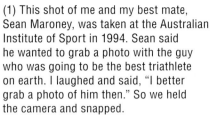

(1) This shot of me and my best mate, Sean Maroney, was taken at the Australian Institute of Sport in 1994. Sean said he wanted to grab a photo with the guy who was going to be the best triathlete on earth. I laughed and said, "I better grab a photo of him then." So we held the camera and snapped.

(2) This photo, taken at Christmas 1998, is the last photo my mum and dad ever took together. Shortly thereafter she was diagnosed with breast cancer. She passed away the following April.

(3) Me and my dad at my graduation from the University of NSW in Australia in 1995.

(4) Running with my good mate Nathan Brown in the Australian Junior Championships 3km final as a seventeen-year-old. I won my second Australian title with a time of 8:21:42.

(5) Pictured here before our annual New Year's Eve party with Sean and my good mate Luke Powell.

(6) ITU Triathlon World Cup 1996, Drummondville, Canada. This is my first ever World Cup win. I ran away with the victory and beat the best triathletes in the world.

(7) Triathlon La Ferte Bernhard, France, September 1993.
This was my first race after telling my parents I was deferring university, and I flew from Manchester to France to compete for my new team. I finished in second place and was hooked on European racing.

(8) Sydney World Cup.
The ITU World Cup race in Sydney in 1997 was a prelude to the Olympic Games. The course was just amazing and finished under the Opera House. Here I run head to head with legendary Brad Bevan and Paul Amey.

(9) ITU Triathlon World Cup, Auckland. Draft legal racing changed the entire triathlon game as the world knew it, and with it came tight group runs after swimming and biking. In this photo Jamie Hunt (NZ) leads me, Miles Stewart, Hamish Carter, and Shane Reed. In a three-way sprint for the title, Miles would edge out me and Hamish.

(10) Swimming as a sport was always foreign to me. I grew up as a runner and had to dive in headfirst to build up my swim. I swim about fifteen miles per week on average.

(11) ITU World Cup Victory, Gamagori, Japan 1999. This was the victory that put me onto the shadow squad for the Australian Olympic team for Sydney. I was on top of the world at this moment. With me in this photo are Reto Hug and Craig Watson.

(12) Using my bike as a weapon in draft legal racing became my calling card. Attacking as hard as I could and taking chances on tight circuits was what won me many races.

(13) ITU World Championships Australia, November 1997. My first ever world title. Only eighteen months after turning professional, I was able to run away from Olympic champion Hamish Carter and four-time world champion Simon Lessing. At twenty-four years of age and in front of my mum and dad, it was the most special day of my life.

14) Triathlon as a sport has exploded around the world, and the challenge of it attracts many people. Here I got to hang out with the amazing Cindy Crawford at an event in California.

(15) In my spare time I work tirelessly with the Challenged Athletes Foundation to help handicapped individuals achieve their goals. It is one of the most inspiring things in the world.

(16) Quelle Challenge, Roth. In a race I would go on to own, my only defeat at this event was in 2003 in a sprint finish with good friend and five-time champion of the event himself, Lothar Leder. We raced head to head all day, and I lost to him by three seconds.

(17) My Ironman debut at Australia in April of 2002, which I won. The race was held on my twenty-ninth birthday, and it was a great birthday present, as I became the second man in history to win an Ironman at his debut.

(18) At my Ironman Hawaii debut in 2002, I abandoned the race at mile marker 12, after cramping and falling apart. The press had a field day with it. This picture was sent all over the world and shown in every magazine.

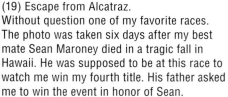

(19) Escape from Alcatraz.
Without question one of my favorite races. The photo was taken six days after my best mate Sean Maroney died in a tragic fall in Hawaii. He was supposed to be at this race to watch me win my fourth title. His father asked me to win the event in honor of Sean.

(20) Australia dominated the short course triathlon circuit for many years. This is one of my favorite photos of all time, as I'm running with my idols, Greg Welch, Brad Bevan, and Miles Stewart. It reminds me of the beginning of it all.

(21) Scott Fairchild and I have been a team for more than a decade. Without question he's one of my best mates and a great agent.

(22) Dr. Susan Kraeftner is my mind coach and one of my closest friends. She has been a part of my team for about eight years. We have an amazing synergy, and she really helps me get inside my head to work out ways of dealing with my fears and ultimately believing in myself and the way I am as an athlete.

(23) Emma-Jane came into my life and my world just opened. This is Emma on our wedding day, August 17, 2003. She is my partner in life, and I love her more than the world.

(24) Without question, Mark Allen inspired me to be a triathlete. I watched him on TV as a youngster and wanted to emulate everything he did. He has been a huge part of my success—a mentor and icon in my life.

(25) Raising money and awareness for breast cancer as part of the MaccaNow Foundation is a big part of my life. Here in Singapore I was able to spend an evening with breast cancer survivors. We did a spin class together and raised more than $25,000 for the disease.

(26) My eldest daughter, Tahlia, has grown up on the triathlon circuit. We did our first race together in 2008, and it was one of the most memorable days of my life. She just loved the entire event. Awesome!

1. Surrender.

At a critical point in the race, I want them to succumb to their own self-doubt. I want them to wonder, *Have I done enough to prepare? Do I have what it takes?* Every race is a war between the part of you that's saying, *You can do it. You can do it!* and the part that's screaming, *Why are you making me hurt like this, you bastard?* There's always a tipping point where you've got to pick your path. If you start to question yourself, you're giving yourself an excuse to quit. If at that critical moment, that little voice says for just a second, *Maybe he's right. Maybe I can't do it,* you lose a step and you're gone.

I know, because I've been that guy. I've surrendered. Back when I started racing Ironman, I was much cockier than I should have been. Remember, I melted in 2002, and then walked across the finish in 2003, which was humiliating. Well, that was nothing compared to 2004. I was in fifth place and carrying it toward the Energy Lab, but I was in agony. I had been suffering for more than ten miles, cramping and dehydrated. Well, with nine miles to go there was a sponsor car waiting, and I just stepped into it. My agent and team were freaking out, shouting, "What are you doing? What's going on here?"

I said, "I'm out, mate, I'm done, I cannot do this race, I retire." I cringe when I think about the conversation now. I had given up, and I had my excuses ready: *I'm too big for this race, I'm not built for this.* Well, who do you think was in the car? Mark Allen. The legend and my idol. He was training Peter Reid, who had torn up two Ironmans that year.

I said, "Of all people, Mark, you would have to be in this car." Then I said, "Can you take me back to transition?" And Mark replied, "No. I'm watching my athlete. You can watch this race."

So I sat there, feeling like a coward and a failure. But it got worse. An age grouper named Christian Sadowski came along, carrying his trashed bike over his shoulder. He was absolutely covered in blood and had a terrible road rash. I found out that he had been hit by a motorcycle near the Energy Lab and had his rear wheel crushed, his frame wrecked and his left fibula dislocated. But he was determined to finish the stage by carrying his bike over his shoulder; he wouldn't accept any assistance because he didn't want to be disqualified.

The sponsor car pulled up next to him and the driver said something like, "Do you want a lift back to town?"

Sadowski shook his head, and I recall him replying, "Absolutely no chance. I'm finishing this race."

God! I was looking at this guy covered in blood and meanwhile, my pain was gone and I was in an air-conditioned car. Then he glanced in the back of the car and said, "Oh! Macca!"

I've never felt so small.

All I could think was, *You're a warrior, mate, and I'm a wimp.* He actually made it the seven miles back to town without any water, beat the bike cutoff time, and finished in under seventeen hours. He won a Cannondale Bike award and made the race coverage. People were calling him a hero, which he was. And I had retired fifteen minutes before.

Well, I unretired then and there. I said to myself, "I am *not* going out this way." I realized that my bravado was empty. I wasn't a hero; I was all smoke and mirrors. I was scared of the race, but I was talking like I wasn't. I was trying to suppress my own fears by talking like I had none. But I was hollow. I had never confronted my demons regarding this race, so when I faced them on the racecourse, they won. I had a great year in 2004, but the truth was that at Kona, I really didn't believe in myself. The race had scarred me. I had surrendered. What I needed to do was work out solutions to win that race so when my moment of truth came, I would keep pushing.

2. Let ego make them inflexible.

Pro athletes in every sport have enormous egos, and triathlon is no different. In this case, I want to make my competition angry with me so that even though I've shown them the holes in their race, they'll refuse to adapt to beat me. They'll say, "I'll show Macca. I'll bury him my way." They should change their game plan for the specifics of the race, but because I bruise their egos, they won't. That's to my advantage.

Take Craig Alexander. He performs so well because he's an aggressive, angry racer. He's one of the hardest men to ever do the sport, and he can suffer with the best of us. But his limiting factor is his bike strength, so his ego is out to prove everyone wrong—to prove that his bike *isn't* a weakness. Instead of being recognized as Craig Alexander, the best runner in the sport, he wants to be recognized as Craig Alexander, all-around superstar. That's why I tease him: "Ah, he's a crap biker." I want Craig's ego to respond, *I'm a crap biker, am I? I'll show you.* That makes him vulnerable, because his ego could prevent him from adapting in a race.

But I would never use that strategy with Andreas Raelert. He's confident in what he's recognized for. He's a finesse athlete, like Roger Federer. With Andreas, I have to use a different approach. He's very calm and cool, so making him angry isn't going to achieve anything.

Normann Stadler is a bully. He's like Mike Tyson. He's at his best when people fear him and he's trying to prove something. I get in his face and let him think I'm crazy, because like all bullies, if you stand up to them, you find the fear.

The key is to understand, with each individual athlete, where that fire burns. What drives them? Is it anger? Fear? Calmness? Once I identify that, I use it to attack their performance. You have to study the athletes not just physically but to learn their characters: watch their interviews, see how they hold themselves, find out what drives them to get out there and suffer.

Folders in the Brain

Think about Tiger Woods. Nobody wants to come down the back nine on the last day of a tournament with Tiger two strokes back. They know he's never lost a playoff. His mental game is just ruthless. I saw an interview with him after he won at Torrey Pines in California. One reporter asked, "Tiger, how do you do it? You've never lost a playoff. Don't you ever feel any pressure?" And Tiger just got this icy stare and said something like, "Why would I feel any pressure? I've never lost a playoff. The other players should feel the pressure." They do, and they surrender before Tiger's even swung a club.

I try to do the same thing: give my opponents as many opportunities as possible to self-destruct. I can't count how many times I've been running side by side with a guy and I'm in agony. I feel like I'm about to quit on him, when—surprise! He's gone. Somewhere along the line, I set him up to rationalize dropping out or dropping back. Maybe Marino is thinking, *I've already had a great season* because of his Austria race. Maybe another guy thinks, *I don't want to hurt myself because I have race X next month.* Maybe another guy is thinking, *It's no problem to come in second to Macca.* When you open the door to those rationalizations, they start stacking up. Everyone has a reason to back down. Eventually, the athlete can deliver his own knockout punch... and he never finds out that I was as close to breaking as he was!

Every triathlete, pro or amateur, no matter how fit, reaches a point in *every* race where he has to decide whether he will endure more suffering. It's very simple. Either he will or he won't. You will get there. The only question is how you'll handle it.

I handle it by creating folders in my brain. Think of your mind as a computer desktop. In it, you have folders with various labels. As I'm training, I'll come up with folders labeled things like "Kona Lava Fields." Then I fill those folders with the thoughts I want to be thinking if I start to find myself in trouble in those circumstances. If I'm running the marathon in the lava fields in Kona and I start to cramp, I can mentally click my "Lava Fields" folder and know exactly what to think to keep myself going.

The file in that folder might read, *You've hydrated and have the nutrition strategy to deal with this, so don't worry.* If I work out a solution to other problems such as hydration, heat management, or nutrition, I want to put that in one of my mental folders so that when I meet that friend called Pain during a race, I can click on a folder and think, *Aha! That's right. That's what I was going to do if this happened.*

You need instant access to your folders, because thoughts about blowing up and falling apart appear at the moment when the pain comes. You don't store them prerace. At that moment, you start remembering negative things that happened before. But those thoughts are easy to delete if you have something that can wipe them away. If you're not prepared with these folders, you have nothing but empty hope.

During those years when I blew up at Kona, my mental folders were filled with toxic things like, *You sweat too much,* and *You're cramping because you're not built for these races.* That's why I've spent the last few years working really hard to fill my folders with positive ideas. At Kona in 2010, I knew that I would be riding with the front pack, so I filled my folders with positives that applied to that race.

MACCA'S (W)INSIGHTS

These are some of the ideas I put in my mental folders for Kona in 2010:

- "You had that great hill training session; you can do this."

- "Have some Coke and water and you'll be right back in the game."

- "You're such a strong rider, mate, and now you don't have to ride hard. You can save it for the run."

- "Your heart rate is slow, so you're not going to lose the sweat. You're going to be racing with a full tank."

Those were all reminders that I could draw on when things got ugly. You don't always have control over where your mind will take you when you're hurting. If you fill your head with positive ideas, you reduce the chances that you'll click on a folder that will make you want to quit.

On race day, I ran out of transition feeling awesome. But it was probably one of the hottest days that Kona has ever had. I was asking myself, *How good do I feel?* Even when you are feeling strong, your mind's still ticking. You're trying to control everything you can, but you're still uneasy. But that's still a huge improvement over an inner monologue based on fear and saying things like *It's hot, it's hot, be careful. Careful. Remember. Remember you're not good in heat.*

As the race gets more frantic and you get more emotionally and physically drained, controlling your inner voice becomes incredibly important. That's when you have to make it as difficult as possible for your mind to take you to that dark, negative, defeated place.

I also try to create folders in the brains of my opponents. I want to be Chris McCormack, computer virus. If they're side by side with me in a race, I want the folder in their head to open and them to think, *Man, Macca's in control. I don't think I can go head-to-head with him.* Even sweeter: *Macca called it. He predicted this!* If they think I know something they don't, that's a huge edge for me.

Of course, it doesn't work every time. If it did, I would have won every race. However, I'll wager that 10 percent of my victories since 2001 have come more because of my mental game than because I physically outclassed my opponents. Now, the entire pro community sees me as the sly fox taking on the young rabbits: the pure athletes versus the *smartest* athlete. Everyone knows that I do my homework, and they're starting to give me credit for being clever.

Fear of Being Judged

Why aren't more athletes playing the mental game that I play? Because they want to be liked and adored more than they want to win. We are extroverts. We're performers, and every performer wants to be applauded and loved. Too many athletes want to be the good guy as well as the winner. They think I'm the bad guy, but that's only because they haven't worked up the nerve to do what I do. I really don't understand why, because it works. This information is lying out there for anyone else to use, and nobody is picking it up. It's crazy.

It all goes back to ego. The athlete's ego tells him that he owns the relationship with the fans. That's a lie. I have been there when people jumped on my bandwagon and when people jumped off it. I learned at an early age that people's perception of me is changeable.

The foundation of our sport is the access that the amateurs have to the stars. In many ways, our sport belongs to the age groupers. If I was a Formula One car driver, you wouldn't be able to get close to me very easily, and you certainly wouldn't be able to race me. You might line the streets for the Tour de France, but you're not in the race. But in our sport, the amateurs stand on the starting line with me. They're walking up to me in transition. There's very little distance between the elite and the weekend warriors. If I have a bad day, an amateur could beat me. So they feel like they can be more vocal, and that gives many pros a terror of being judged.

You don't have to choose between being liked and being a winner. You can have both. As long as you're not disrespecting the sport or your fellow athletes, you can be a black belt in the mental game, and the people who matter—the people who know and care about you for who you are—will always love you. And as long as you compete hard and exhibit class, everyone else will at least respect you.

MACCA'S 2001 SEASON

- Australian Triathlon Championships—FIRST
- Oceania Triathlon Championships, Australia—FIRST
- ITU Triathlon World Cup, Japan—FIRST
- Oceanside Triathlon, US—FIRST
- Wildflower Half-Ironman, US—FIRST (half-Ironman debut)
- Escape from Alcatraz Triathlon—FIRST
- San Jose International Triathlon—FIRST
- San Diego International Triathlon—FIRST
- Carlsbad Triathlon—FIRST
- Encinitas Triathlon—FIRST
- Credit Suisse Triathlon International, Geneva, Switzerland—FIRST
- Credit Suisse Triathlon, De Nyon, Switzerland—FIRST
- Credit Suisse Triathlon, Zug, Switzerland—FIRST
- Switzerland Triathlon National Championships—FIRST
- ITU Triathlon World Cup, Lausanne, Switzerland—SECOND
- ITU Triathlon World Cup, Toronto, Canada—SECOND
- ITU Triathlon World Championships, Edmonton, Canada—DNF (crashed bike while leading the race)
- Los Angeles International Triathlon—FIRST
- Goodwill Games Triathlon, Australia—FIRST
- Triathlon Pacific Grove, US—FIRST
- Lawrence Memorial Triathlon, US—FIRST
- Treasure Island Triathlon—FIRST

Season Statistics and Interesting Facts

- Flight miles accumulated: 98,769
- Countries visited: 7
- Days away from home: 264

Training miles for the year

- Swim: 722
- Bike: 14,380
- Run: 2,017

5

You Can't Lie to the
Person in the Mirror

I'm willing to change and adapt based on what I learn about my adversaries and myself. Some triathletes can't do that. If they aren't getting the results they feel they should, they decide it's because they need to bike more miles or log more hours in the pool. But simply stepping up training is not the solution to every problem. We should always be taking a hard look at our strengths and weaknesses so that we can make adjustments over time. Ego prevents many great professionals from being even better.

Ego. There's that word again. We all have egos, but your ego can either serve your purpose or work against you. Sometimes, the most difficult things to face are your own failings and weaknesses. We don't like to go to that side of the brain. It's human nature to want to please yourself all the time.

After all, people cheer us because of our strengths, not our weaknesses. They're shouting, "You're the best! You're the man!" They're not shouting, "Your swim sucks!" No athlete wants that kind of negativity around him. But I've been buried by positive bullshit before—surrounded by people who just want to be near me, telling me, "You're the man, Macca!" If you're smart and self-aware, you think, *Mate, back off a little bit. I'm not as good as you think I am.*

Every competitor has to strike a balance between positive encouragement, blunt but constructive criticism, pure negativity, and smoke blown up his backside. You have to have people around you who will assess you candidly on a performance level without being negative for the sake of being negative. It's the difference between someone saying, "You need to get some glucose in you for the next hill," and "Man, you look like a truck just ran over you!" One is informed and helpful. The other is just stupid. *Yeah? Thanks, mate. If you think I look bad, you should feel how I feel.*

But too many athletes fall victim to the idea that they should never even acknowledge their shortcomings. They surround themselves with yes-men who hide their weak spots from them and fill them with empty positive chatter. Deep down we're all afraid of losing it. We're all aging, and with age comes the need to think and prepare differently. You can't compete at thirty-five like you did when you were twenty-five. That's why some triathletes retire at thirty; they can't face the fact that they are no longer the young bucks on the block who can race, hit the pubs that same night, go to bed, get five hours of sleep, then spring to life the next morning and run twenty miles.

It's not just about aging, either. Some competitors can't own up to the fact that they haven't done the work or that their plan wasn't right for the race, so they're not prepared to win. Whose fault is that in the end? As an athlete you can blame your coach, your training partners, or the man in the moon, but you're the one in charge. If you haven't logged the volume or hydrated properly for a hot-weather race, that's on you. There are people who simply can't take responsibility for their mistakes out of insecurity or arrogance. It doesn't matter; the effect is the same. The truth will set you free. If you can't face it, you'll be left in the dust.

I'm still winning races at thirty-eight because I am willing to face the truth. If you lie to yourself about your training and your weaknesses when you're down at the water's edge, you're not going to be prepared. If all that matters is what other people think of you, then you don't know who you are, and you're done. If I could give one piece of advice to triathletes at all levels, it would be this:

Don't lie to the person in the mirror.

You've got to be honest with yourself about your weaknesses and surround yourself with people who will tell it like it is and not insulate you from the truth. That's the only way you find out what needs to improve, and it's the only way you become stronger in body and mind.

Empty Words = Empty Results

The trouble with lying to yourself is that after a while, you start to believe it. That can get you into trouble. I remember a prerace interview that I did before Ironman Australia in 2004. I had won the race the previous two years, and my goal was ultimately to get the record of five wins in a row (which I did). There was a really strong Australian contingent of emerging talent that year, including Luke Bell (who had finished fifth in Kona) and Chris Legh, who's very famous and was a successful Ironman before me. But what made it even more fun was that they're from Melbourne and I'm from Sydney.

There's definitely a rivalry between the two cities. At the time, the triathlon magazines and the powers that be were based in Melbourne, but I always felt that the talent was in Sydney—like Las Vegas is the promotional capital of boxing, but the best fighters are training in the Bronx and Detroit. Athletes from the two cities enjoyed popping off and talking a little smack to each other.

However, at this prerace press event I was very polite. I had been dominating the Australian Ironman race, so I knew Chris and Luke were going to be gunning for me. I was looking forward to racing them, but I really wasn't out to provoke them. I said, "It's going to be a great day. It's going to be difficult to win again, but I feel pretty confident because my training's been good." Pretty bland stuff.

Then Chris spoke up and said something like, "It's going to be a different story this year."

My ears perked up. *So you want to play my game, do you, mate?*

I recall Chris continuing: "Me and Luke are training together, and McCormack's never been pressured here. We think if we pressure him at this race he's going to crack. Hawaii shows that whenever the pressure's on him, he cracks." I had to try so hard not to grin. I thought, *Mate, I'm happy to play this game. I love this shit.*

Then Luke started in, saying something like, "Yeah, well, I finished fifth in Hawaii last year, and I beat Macca up. This is a changing of the guard. I've stepped up and see this race as a platform to show that." The press corps ate it up.

Later on, we all appeared on the program *IronmanLIVE*. I was sitting in the middle with Chris and Luke on either side of me. Now they would have to listen to *my* interview. They had their Melbourne entourage with them, all their people and their coaches. On my side, it was just my wife and me. I thought, *This is where I'm going to get you guys.*

The interviewer said, "Macca, how are you looking at this race?" I will never forget my response. "I own this thing," I said. "I've never been challenged. And there's a reason I've never been challenged: because when it comes to racing in Australia in April, I'm unbeatable. All this bravado at the press conference and all this talk means nothing." I was rolling; Chris and Luke were just staring at me like I'd lost my marbles.

I kept on. "These guys—now they're listening and pretending not to—on Sunday morning they're going to walk down to that swim start and I'm going to be there," I said. "It's show time now. The main event is on and I've dominated this race. They've fired everything they had at me for the last two years and I've beaten them. When all the hangers-on go back to the hotel and they wake up in the morning and they look in the mirror, they're going to know one thing and I'll tell them right now what it is: I'm ready, I ain't scared and I'm here to win."

The room went silent. I remember thinking *Did I say too much?* The interviewer asked, "Do you think you can win?"

"One hundred percent," I replied. "It's going to take a mountainous effort for anyone to beat me. I am swimming incredibly, I am biking far superior to anyone in this field, and if they try and tag me on the bike, I'm going to smash them on the run because my run's stellar. So it's going to be a great race." I wanted to put it into their heads, because I really felt that their talk was all empty bravado. Not with me. I never make a promise about a race that I can't back up, not after my embarrassments at Kona. Bottom line: they tried to chase me on race day, they exploded, and I ended up beating Chris, who came in second, by nearly ten minutes.

That's a perfect case study of big talk not being backed up by self-knowledge and honesty about where you're weak and where you're strong. That may work with other athletes, but not with this sly fox.

MACCA'S (W)INSIGHTS

"The way I look at it, you're the CEO of your one-person company. It's your responsibility to put in place everyone and everything that you need to perform at your best."

Chief Executive Officer

You're the CEO of your one-person company. It's your responsibility to put in place everyone and everything that you need to perform at your best. You cannot do that if you lie to the person in the mirror. What makes you good at what you do? What are you not good at? You've got to be constantly checking your reflection.

It's difficult to face weakness, because we fear our limiter, the thing that says, *You can go this far, no farther.* But our real limiter is our refusal to face our flaws. Opening up to your weaknesses actually frees you, because you gain the power to break them down, figure out what causes them, and do something about them. You can't cure a disease that you refuse to diagnose.

Ego is all wrapped up in this. Ego gets us here. You don't become an elite athlete (or an elite anything) without believing that you're pretty awesome at what you do. But the irony is that even though you need a big ego to believe in yourself and get you to the top of your profession, to stay there you need to be humble. For instance, one of my weaknesses is that I'm motivated by anger, but it started out as an edge. My pal Mick once told me, "You broke up with your girlfriend and you won a world title. You weren't put on the Olympic Team and you smashed everyone. People said you could never win Kona and you did. You're a champion when you're angry."

He's right. An "I'll show you" bell goes off in my head when I feel slighted. But that has also been a weakness in the past. It's led me to be sloppy in my thinking, directed by anger as opposed to smarts. Because of that, I came to Kona for the first few years full of big talk but woefully unprepared.

People think that because we train alone, this is an introspective sport. It is, but not in the way that I think of introspection. If you're in your own head during a 200-kilometer (120-mile) training ride, it should be with a purpose. You should be breaking down what you're doing, thinking about the unique ways to manage a certain racecourse, how to handle your nutrition, confronting your weaknesses and thinking about ways to neutralize them. That's strategic introspection. If you're just navel-gazing on those long rides, that's wasted time.

Another important aspect of being your own CEO is surrounding yourself with the right people. My biggest strength is that I put people around me who are brutally honest with me. That keeps my ego under control. The process starts with my wife, Emma-Jane. She has no problem telling it like it is. The minute I start to buy into the "You're the man, Macca" garbage, she's there to pull me back to reality. She has an outsider perspective on the sport that I can never have.

My father is the second person I count on to talk straight to me. He's just a really honest guy. He doesn't know a lot about the sport, but he doesn't have to. He knows me and my character better than anyone else. My mate Mick, my close friend and psychological advisor, Dr. Susann Kraeftner (the smartest woman I've ever met, a brilliant psychologist who specializes in mental illness, which makes her a perfect fit for me), and my agent, Scott Fairchild, are the people who pull no punches when it comes to training and sport.

At the beginning of each season, we'll have a barbecue back home, sit down, and dissect my performance and the season to come. That's when the honesty comes out. For instance, Emma will say, "You just didn't seem to be in that race this year. Your head was in another place." I might protest, but I have to listen because I want to know. There's definitely friction when there's absolute honesty. If you want to benefit from it, you accept that as part of the price.

Then Susanne will chime in: "Very interesting, Emma. What makes you think that?" Then Mick will add, "Physically, you were doing things great. The times were there. How do you think you could improve?" Once that's on the table, we'll start breaking down the problem step-by-step. That's facing yourself in the mirror. It never gets easy sitting around a table with three or four other people telling you everything you're doing wrong. You need people who don't judge and don't bring their own agendas.

That's why the single most important choice a triathlete can make is who his coach is. Now, coaches can be a problem in this sport. If you're successful, you can do a lot for a coach's career. Coaches want to be listened to and praised for having a great plan. An egotistical coach will do whatever it takes to keep a top triathlete around so he or she can keep getting accolades. But brilliant coaches are brilliant communicators. They wear many hats. They understand not just the physical side but the characters of the people they're coaching. If you're a really great coach, you're a mentor and a friend as well. That's why my team is very, very good.

Another reason the dynamic works is that the planning process is ultimately up to me. I've been in this game a long time. I'll sit down and go, "This is what I'm going to do next year. What do you think?" Then we'll start talking about family commitments, sponsor commitments, training, and so on. Mick will hit me with "Well, you're thirty-eight. You're not twenty-five anymore. You've got 160 hours this year in airplanes. How are you going to deal with that?" We'll all

MACCA'S (W)INSIGHTS

Choosing a coach

Few decisions will impact your experience or success as a triathlete as much as who you choose as your coach. Keep these factors in mind as you move toward that important choice:

- Your coach should be about you, not his or her ego.

- A good coach should have a long-term plan for optimizing your performance that's based on your unique abilities and limitations.

- A good coach will customize a plan to those abilities and limitations, not force you into a standardized "one size fits all" training regimen.

- Make sure the coach complements your personality. If you are a laid-back person who sometimes needs motivation, an intense, demanding coach might be what you need. But be wary of choosing a coach whose personality conflicts with yours.

- Find out how many athletes a potential coach is working with. If he or she has a hundred athletes, you're probably not going to get much time.

- Your coach should be up on the latest equipment and training strategies.

- Choose a coach based on your goals. You might not hire the same coach to get you to the finish in an Ironman as you would to help you win your age group in a sprint race.

- The best way to find a coach is through referral. Ask other athletes whom you respect to recommend a coach. When you get a few names, research them by learning who they coach and talking to several of their athletes.

throw things on the table, and slowly the plan for the season takes shape. Everyone has input, because everyone knows that I want them to be completely honest. They know I'll listen.

This is not a solitary sport. Even when we're on the course, we're not out there alone. We depend on a whole team of people. Being a triathlete is—or should be—a collaborative experience.

The Young Buck and the Old Fox

For a triathlete, honesty is never more important than when you're talking about age. I'm the oldest winner of Kona, and my age was on people's minds during the 2010 showdown with Raelert. It was the young buck taking on the old fox. Would the young legs take down the old man? Or would the experience and savvy of the veteran win the day? Most people underestimate the power of strategy and the mental game in our sport; I think they figured I was running out of gas when Andreas caught me and that he just fell apart. They didn't know until after the race that I baited him and controlled the finish.

But getting older is a reality. We all will eventually age out of the sport as professionals. Your performance is eventually going to suffer because of age. So is mine. But that's not something we can change. The question is, what are you going to do to compensate and keep yourself performing at your peak for as long as possible? To do that, you've got to admit that as you get older, you can't do things the same way you did when you were nineteen and full of piss and vinegar.

I'm lucky. Mick, who I've known for fifteen years, is fifty-one, and—I say this with nothing but love—he is incredibly vain about his body. He's a sports physiologist and probably the finest personal trainer in Australia, and he's got a physique that most twenty-five-year-olds would envy. He's fascinated with the human body because he wants to make his own body look better. He'll stand in front of the mirror, flex, and complain that he doesn't have perfect

symmetry. He's obsessively attentive to his body and records everything that he does. Ever since I turned thirty, age has been part of
our discussion.

When I hit thirty, I started talking about how old I was. Guys
retire at that age, but Mick would say, "Mate, you are nowhere near
done at thirty. You are heading into the strongest years of your
career." A lot of guys around the sport said he was nuts. But Mick has
been *right*. He's been saying to me for years, "Chris, knowing you
for this many years, knowing how you work, and knowing your body
shape, you're going to be ridiculously powerful at thirty-seven and
thirty-eight." And today, right now, I'm the strongest I've ever been.
After Kona, the first thing he said to me was, "How old are you,
mate?" I had to laugh. He said, "What did I tell you?"

I've learned that as I age, I can be just as strong and powerful. It's
injuries that could limit my ability, and injuries come about primarily
because of fear-based overtraining. A twenty-year-old athlete might
be convinced that he has to do a certain training volume—a
200-kilometer (120-mile) bike ride four days a week, for example—
to have the confidence to race well. It's a security blanket protecting
him against failure. But such big workloads can't continue with age.
At thirty-five, he can't do what he did at twenty. Even more important, he has to admit that he can still deliver the same great performance in a race when he's older, *but he has to prepare differently* and
to recover more. Youth forgives errors that age punishes.

As you get older, look at your training volume. Did you overtrain
when you were younger because you feared you would fail otherwise? Did you wind up injured due to that overtraining? Could you
have done one hundred kilometers on the bike instead of two hundred and still gotten the same results in races? With age should come
self-awareness of your fears and habits. You can't afford denial if you
want to remain competitive.

With my team, I faced the fact that I needed to change how I did
things because of my "advanced" age. The goal became to extend my
peak as long as possible. As an athlete, if you peak in your twenties,

MACCA'S (W)INSIGHTS

Avoiding overtraining

Overtraining comes from a lack of trust—in your natural ability, in the work you have done, in your coach's program, or in all of the above. You fear that you won't finish your race, so you add bricks on the bike or in the pool to give yourself a security blanket. But overtraining is a ticket to injury and exhaustion. Here are some ways to avoid overtraining:

- Listen to your body. Nothing is more important. If you hurt, stop. If you're tired, cut a session short. If you're exhausted, take the day off and sleep.

- Listen to your coach. A coach's first responsibility is to help get you fit for your race without injury. If he or she tells you to take it easy, take it easy.

- Get plenty of sleep. Set a firm time to go to bed each night and a regular time to get up.

- Hydrate while you're training to prevent cramping and injury.

- Train for your age. If you're forty-five, don't force yourself into a training routine designed for a twenty-five-year-old. With age, you need more recovery time and more warm-up time.

- If you do get injured, don't be a hero. Give yourself plenty of time to recover. Coming back too early can worsen your injury or cause you to injure something else because you're changing your gait to favor the injured leg or hip.

your peak might last ten weeks. Bang! It's gone. If you want to peak in your thirties, your training has to be tailored to your older body. Mick would talk about how when he was in his twenties, he could take a week off from the gym and still look like a million bucks. But when he hit thirty-five, his muscles would start to sag if he didn't get to the gym, even though he was lifting the same weight. Your body changes, and you've got to accept it.

There's no reason why you can't win as you age if your training is more precise and targeted. But at the pro level, there's a sort of institutionalized denial of that. It's a Catch-22. If you admit that age is slowing you down, that becomes a ready-made excuse for failure. But when you don't face it and make adjustments, your times are going to worsen. You'll give people a reason to age you before your time and label you a dinosaur. I've been there. From that point it's a short distance to "If I'm that old, why should I train so hard?" Over and out.

For the general competitor or age-group racer, the most important thing you can do is to listen to your body. If you're not a professional earning your living racing, you can afford to be honest with yourself. There's a lot less at stake. If you hurt, back off your training. Talk to a coach about a program that focuses on your strengths. Most important, get some perspective. You're a triathlete. That's an extraordinary thing no matter how old you are—whether you finish an Ironman in eight hours or slip over the finish line at 16:59. It's worth accepting your age and your limitations if it means you can keep training, keep competing and keep being part of such a fantastic fraternity.

Be Yourself

The third way that triathletes lie to themselves is by trying too hard to be what they think a triathlete is supposed to be. Terenzo Bozzone is a young superstar out of New Zealand. He was a multiple-time junior world champion, and he stepped up in 2008 to win the Ironman 70.3 world title, which was his first professional world championship. I'd heard about him for years before I actually got to know him. But I took a liking to him because he seemed to get the same "Who's *this* guy?" hard time that I did in my country. There was a lot of jealousy because he was getting all the attention, but it was only because he is such a huge talent.

Over time I met many of his training buddies and asked them,

"What's Terenzo like?" They all said the same thing: "Hard worker, hard trainer, super talent." I decided I wanted to meet this kid. He'd been left off the Bejing Olympic team because of politics. We had a lot in common.

We finally met at the 2008 Avia Wildflower Triathlon in California. Terenzo had won in 2006 and broken my course record, so I figured he would be on a rampage in this race. I'm thinking, *Of all people I have to face here, it's this kid.* But he just blew it. He was there to prove a point, but inexperience and bravado ruined it for him. He ended up blowing up. I remember passing him on the bike. He finished fifth.

Later on, he came to my home. He's the most polite twenty-three-year-old kid you will ever meet. Full credit to his parents. After dinner I was thinking, *Dude, stop cleaning the dishes and cooking. You're making me look bad.* He's a perfect gentleman and a killer athlete. We kept in contact and he started looking at doing Ironman. He signed with Specialized, a sponsor of mine. Another connection.

So now I had a kind of doppelgänger on the circuit. I got to know Terenzo and started training with him. He worked out *hard*—much harder than I did at his age. I never bought into his workload, but it seemed to be working for him. In 2010 he did five 70.3-mile half-Ironmans...and won them all. He was one of the marquee athletes of the season. But I was watching his workload and getting concerned. He was racing everything.

I didn't want to step over the line and offend his coach, so I tried to mentor him and get him to think about the big picture. One time I said, "Mate, when I was your age I didn't want to be that old guy, but I am now. I'm telling you, don't rush things. You're it. You're the next king. Only you can blow this. Remember that. Start learning, man. Start watching and learning. Don't have tunnel vision. Take those two 70.3s you've won, rest a bit, and rebuild. Have faith in your talent; it's there. You don't need to force it."

He insisted he was here to learn.

I said, "You're doing a lot of work."

"I need it," I recall him saying.

"You don't need it. You're a V8, mate." And he didn't need it. But he was training like he did. I watched him doing his swim sets (he was already a better swimmer than me) and started to worry a lot. Then I trained with him for Kona. We spent a lot of time together. To be honest, between the weight of his season and his training block, I've never seen a human being endure so much training. It was remarkable. I started questioning the intelligence of his training plan.

We'd wake up on a Monday and do a 200-kilometer ride, then I'd run for twenty minutes off the bike. I'd run until my legs felt good, then I'd go home and sleep. Done. Back it off. You've done a seven-hour day. But Terenzo would get up, do the ride with me, and then run an hour and a half off the bike because he wanted to get his endurance work. I'd remind him that it was a brick set (training on two disciplines during the same workout). The bike was his endurance work. But he'd say, "Let's go swimming."

He'd already done an eight-and-a-half-hour day, and he wanted to add another hour to it? I asked him what he was doing tomorrow. "Tomorrow I'm going to do a two-and-a-half-hour run." The next day, another brick. It was a barrage of work. His mind-set was, *It's Ironman, more is better.*

Finally, I said to him, "You realize we're in Kona, don't you? Remember on race day it's going to be 100 degrees and 100 percent humidity. Don't leave your race in training camp. This island can scar your soul. Don't force it. Conditions are hard here." I wanted to say a hell of a lot more than that, but I couldn't. It was not my place to. I wanted to say, *Mate, you're going to ruin this, you're going to blow it. You should be on the podium in Kona. You're everything Andreas is, you're everything Crowie is. You're just doing way too much.*

Well, Ironman 2010 came and Terenzo had a terrible race. I swam with him quite comfortably when he should have been leaving me behind easily. He got off the bike with the runners' group and fell apart in the marathon. He finished twentieth. An obvious thing about Kona that nobody thinks about is this: It's the last race of the season. You need to be fresh for it, and it's hard to do that when you've had a season like Terenzo had. He added the crazy work at camp to his season and it finished him.

The postrace was difficult to watch, because I've been where he was: wanting the event so much and having a bad race. He was the future; he'd blown it, and he had the whole winter to think about it. We had a celebration at my house, and he was emotional, but I got him to sit down for a chat.

I had finally realized that all this time, Terenzo had been trying to live up to some fictitious Ironman ideal. Instead of thinking about the race, he was trying to be what he thought he was supposed to be: tough as nails, and training with huge volume. He had that kind of talent. But he didn't have the experience, and that made him train as hard as he *thought* he had to in order to fit this ideal.

I said, "Dude, be yourself. Open your eyes on the journey. Learn on the journey. Don't just be coached, and don't believe the hype. Watch and ask questions about everything. I've spent my career annoying people because I ask so many questions. You're a special athlete. Remember that."

Terenzo needs to go on and learn to look at himself. If he does, he can be the next superstar in this sport. He's got that much talent, and that much character. Talent and character is an unbeatable combination.

6

Every Race Is a War

Back in 1996, when I headed to Paris for my first big World Cup race, I was worried about money. What I haven't mentioned is how completely *fascinated* I was by the European racers. My first race in France had been down in Orange, which I knew because members of the band the Cure lived there, and I was a huge Cure fan. But even in a small race like that, I was enthralled by the architecture and just the age of Europe. Australia is a very young country. Europe is *ancient*.

In some of these races I would ride through vineyards and passes in the Alps; it was incredible. But as different as the landscape was, the differences between the European and Australian athletes were really starting to catch my attention. The Europeans tended to be bike/run savvy. If they had a weakness, it was the swim.

Australians were the opposite. Most Aussies grow gills by the time we're seven years old, so the swim is natural for us.

But I had never seen guys who were so powerful on the bike—and the machines they had! At that time I rode an American-made Cannondale, which is a nice bike. But the Europeans rode bikes from companies like Campagnolo, the cream of the crop. Where I came from, those were only for the wealthy people! It's similar to the fact that in America, driving a Mercedes is a symbol that you've made it, but in Europe, the taxis are Mercedes-Benzes. To the Europeans, riding a five-thousand-dollar bike was routine.

One of the strangest differences was that there were a lot of safety precautions for the swim that I had never seen in Australia, especially for the amateurs. Some of these guys just couldn't swim very well. They had showers and buckets to wash your feet when you got out of the water before you put your bike shoes on, which I found bizarre. But the best thing about the swim in Europe was that there, I was suddenly a front-pack swimmer. In my first few races, I got out of the water in the front three or four, which never, ever, happened back home. Of course, then the freight train of Europeans on the bike would come and pass me like I was standing still. It was an education in every way.

I learned more during that trip to Paris than I had learned during the previous months combined. I saw how the talent system worked: the best athletes were identified out of the club system, picked up by the national federation, and put in World Cup races. I saw that there were Europeans who could swim. I had my first experience with a sprint race in Europe, which is a 750-meter swim, 20-kilometer bike, and 5k run, finishing on the cobblestones under the Eiffel Tower. Riding that fast on cobblestones was an experience!

I took seventh that day. A Swiss athlete, Olivier Marceau, whom I had run away from in the 1993 Junior World Championships, got a very emotional win. He would go on to be one of my biggest rivals in Europe. A Frenchman, Stephane Poulat, took second. Both raced for a superhuman triathlon, soccer, and cycling club called Poisse, near Paris. The club threw a lot of money at its athletes, and they were considered the class of the sport in France. But one thing about the French guys that I noticed was that even as they got older, they always looked like a million dollars. They had physiques like Greek gods. We Aussies were always a little pudgy or something; we didn't have super-human bodies like these guys. What were they doing to be that fit?

I was noticing more and more differences and stashing them away in my memory bank for later.

Dressed for Laughs

But it wasn't until I boarded a plane and flew to Canada for the ITU race in Drummondville that I started to really understand how many differences there were in how triathlons were run in different parts of the world. For one thing, the Americans and most Australians didn't come to Paris because the world championships are in the United States. So they would all be competing in Canada. Miles Stewart was there. Brad Bevan was there. You had Wes Hobson (a former US Olympic Committee Triathlete of the Year who became a stellar coach) and all the Americans. You had the Australians and the Germans. This was the big time.

It was an Olympic distance race under cool and cloudy conditions. For the first time, I realized that these were conditions that really suited my body and my style of racing. I also realized that I was completely clueless about how a world-class triathlete should look or what he should wear. For instance, I had no race outfits, because I had no sponsors. Back in Australia, everybody raced in Speedos. You had a singlet on because the rules said that you must cover your torso, so everyone would just tuck their singlet into their Speedos for the swim. It wasn't exactly a black-tie look. Then as you got out of the swim, you would pull the singlet out, put on your bike shorts and go.

Well, I only had two racing garments: bike shorts and a singlet top. So I wore bike shorts during the swim because I could tuck my singlet in more easily. But I liked the feel. I was thinking, *Far out. I've got quite a bit more room to tuck my singlet in more easily.*

Technically, they weren't bike shorts; they were tight, chamois-less bike knicks. It didn't matter. In the race footage, the announcer actually said, "Chris McCormack's wearing bike shorts in the swim." Most of the other athletes were wearing Speedos and a singlet top. I got more than a few strange looks. After the race, guys were saying, "Who is that geek and what was he wearing?"

MACCA'S (W)INSIGHTS

Getting the right gear

Your choice of gear should depend more on staying comfortable and performing well rather than on what other athletes think. Some things to keep in mind as you choose apparel:

- Swim: You'll probably wear a swim skin or a tri suit, but in a cold-weather race, a wet suit becomes an option. Base your choice on what you know about the temperature of the water and the length of the race. If you're doing an Ironman in colder water, you'll probably want a wet suit. For a sprint race, you might risk not carrying the extra weight because you're in the chilly water for a shorter time.

- Bike: This is where you want to prevent chafing. You want your gear to be skintight, so consider wearing Bodyglide or another lubricant under your shorts to prevent uncomfortable rubbing. Always wear sunscreen, especially in a long race, even if the sky is cloudy. You'll prevent a bad sunburn.

- Run: Know the race conditions and your body type. In a cold-weather race, many smaller athletes choose to wear hats on the run because they want to keep their heat, while big athletes always wear visors because they allow more heat to escape from the head. Try to wear a jersey with zippers and pouches that let you place ice or sponges in strategic areas to keep you cool.

I got out of the swim in the middle of the pack and I rode away with Miles Stewart, Canadian Lach Vollmerhaus (a top ITU racer), Australian Jason Harper, Tony DeBoom (the multiple Ironman winner who would heckle me at Kona in 2002), Shane Reed (a 2008 Olympian for his native New Zealand and a top swim-run athlete), Nick Radkewich (an American who competed in the 2000 Olympics), and Stephan Vuckovic (a German who won Olympic silver in

2000), all really strong cyclists. We worked really, really well together. We distanced ourselves from the chase pack, which hadn't been done a lot before that. This race was draft legal, so you were allowed to swap turns—one rider would be at the front taking the wind resistance for the riders behind, who would draft off him, then after a while, another rider would take a turn in front, then another.

I was able to get off the bike with these guys, and my transition was superfast. I laugh now, but it was an advantage not having any sponsors. When you have sponsors, you're contractually obligated to wear their gear in some segment of the race, so you can lose precious seconds putting on tops, hats, and so on. I didn't have to put on Under Armour sunglasses, because they weren't a sponsor yet. I just ran in, racked my bike and I was gone. It was a transition that won for me.

So I was running along and now the TV camera was on me. I was thinking, *Wow, I'm leading. No matter what happens here, at least I'm on television.* I was waiting for the guys to catch me. I figured that Miles Stewart and the others were on their way. I got to the halfway point, five kilometers in, and there was a big video screen next to the course. I had a good fifteen or twenty seconds to look up at the screen as I came through town. It showed me as the race leader, and then they panned back to Nick Radkewich, the American, in second place, and Stephan Vuckovic, the German, in third. Then Miles Stewart in fourth. I had a forty-second lead! Far out!

I hung on to win by about twenty-three seconds over Vuckovic. Everyone was in shock. These other guys were all established stars and I had jumped out of the trees. So a lot of athletes were trying to make up excuses. *I had a sore knee. I had a bad swim. My bike went down.* It was awkward. I didn't really know how to act, because I didn't want to come across as a jerk. You can't go around saying, "Bullshit, I kicked your butt." So, I just agreed with everybody and played humble: "Oh yeah, you just had a bad day."

I was sure that some of them really had experienced off days. After all, they were the elite of the sport, and who was I? But I think there was something else at work, too, and it was part of my growing understanding about preparation. I had been training hard in Europe and I had done the Paris race just a week before, so when I got to Canada, I just rested. I didn't taper. I did a home stay with a lovely French family. But I don't speak French, and I was very jet-lagged, so I slept in and spent a lot of time in my room. Otherwise, I did minimal workouts and saw the sights. I got a lot of rest, and I think my body just recovered from all the work I had been putting it through. When race day came, my body said, "Thanks." I was fully charged and tore up the field.

After that race, we went to Bermuda. Unlike Canada, everyone was out of the water together. It was pretty much the same field as the Canadian race. We got off the bike and it came down to the run. As I rolled out of transition, Paul Amey, who would become a three-time ITU duathlon world champion but whom I had never spoken to, ran past me and yelled something like, "Let's see how you run now, dickhead!" He ran past me and took off.

After that, I was running half angry. *Why does this guy hate me?* Later, I ran past him—I thought he'd blown up—and said, "Yeah, good on you, mate. So much for you being the big hero, you loser." He ultimately went past me toward the end and ended up second to Dimitry Gaag of Kazakhstan—who a couple of years later would test positive for erythropoietin (EPO). I was sixth. Not a bad performance for my first three World Cup races. Paul and I actually became very good friends after this event, and we bonded with each other over a few too many drinks at the Sailing Club in Bermuda. We're good friends to this day.

But this had been a completely different race, and it really opened my eyes. Sure, it was the same guys, but the conditions were hotter, the course was hillier, and it ran right through the beautiful old downtown of Hamilton up and down these undulating, skinny roads. It was a completely different type of racing from Europe or Canada. I saw then that if I had prepared differently for those conditions, I might have won. That was the beginning of my seeing each race as a miniwar.

Like a Military Campaign

You should prepare for every race as though it is a military campaign. Wherever you go — the terrain, weather, food, air quality, language, accommodation, culture — they are all different. You cannot go into those races with exactly the same strategy each time. Planning and customizing your approach to each race dramatically improves your chances of winning.

In my sport, there are three distinct regions — four if you include Hawaii, which is a beast all its own. First, there's North America. There are some variations in the style of racing between the United States and Canada, but overall it's very much the same. For a native English speaker, it's easy living. It's a home away from home. I can walk into a shop or a sandwich place and order. I can turn on the TV in my downtime and watch a few shows. It's very easy to slip into a routine because our cultures are very much the same.

Asia is like being on the moon. First of all, it's hot. Many of the cities are insanely crowded and busy, and if you're not into Asian food, it's a big problem. I love Asian food, but Mick, for instance, can't handle it. In some places, the air is polluted and feels dense because of the humidity, making it harder to breathe. The courses are narrow and tight in the city, and when you're out in the country, there's nothing. And there's always the potential surprise of running into a dog or water buffalo that's just walking in the road.

Europe is beautiful. I think of Europe as having gorgeous roads and many different terrains in such a confined area. One week you could be racing in Alpine mountains, the next week you're in Belgium, where it's flat. The mind-set of the Europeans, because this is a summer sport, is to embrace summer. The Europeans who do triathlons have trained through an oppressive winter, and that says something about the character of the athletes that you're racing. They're hard, hard guys. They're tough men. And when the summer comes, they rejoice. Time to show off. That's why they are aggressive racers. But the weather is nice for a bigger guy like me, especially if you take the area north of the Pyrenees.

The people are different at every race, too. Germany tends to be the mothership of the sport within Europe. That's where a lot of the stars are from. Racing there is fast, and the courses and roads are built for speed. The Germans are born racers. They're very serious people. The sport suits them because it's about obsessive preparation. They're quantitative. They're meticulous. They are extremely aggressive in their racing. They're the people who invented the Autobahn, so everything is about speed.

The French tend to be more cycling-centric. Makes sense — this is the home of the Tour de France. Many of the courses are in rolling hills, but in a few races they'll take you into the Alps and challenge you with harder, tougher racing.

All those early years on the World Cup circuit from 1996 to 2002 gave me the depth of understanding to see that if you're going to be successful in this sport, you have to know the surroundings, culture, food, climate, language, and style of racing in every place that you go. You should be ready to adjust your entire approach to deal with the challenges those factors can pose. You simply cannot excel with a one-size-fits-all approach. For instance, my racing weight is about 177 pounds. I also sweat a lot. That means that in hot conditions, I can't go into a race with the same nutritional strategy as I would for a race in the Alps, where it's much colder. If I do, I'll dehydrate, cramp, and blow up (overheat and run out of energy).

On the other hand, I'm built for cold-weather racing. The most famous cold-weather race in the world is Escape from Alcatraz. It's in San Francisco in June, and it's freezing cold. Plus, there's no warm-up. They take you out on a boat in San Francisco Bay, you jump into that cold water, and it's on. The small guys lose heat and get hypothermia. They can't warm up. In that race, smaller athletes need to do the preparation: put on arm warmers, put on headpieces in the swim to keep their head warm, pull things on during the run to keep their body heat up. But my heat issues are gone. I'm back to normal. That's why I own Alcatraz; Mike Pigg and I each have four titles. Craig Walton and Simon Lessing have done very well at that race, too. It's a big athlete's race.

When you race at altitude, you have to prepare at altitude, maybe a place like Boulder. When I did a race in Embrun, France, I knew it would be a climbing race, so I had to lose weight and get skinny. In training, I was focused on getting my body mass down. I got border-line anorexic for that race, which sapped my strength. From then on, whenever I raced in southern France, I always spent four or five weeks training to bring my weight down without losing strength, which is a very fine line to walk. Like so much else in being a champion, this demands some humility. You can't assume that you're bigger than the conditions, because you're not. You can't go toe-to-toe with the weather or terrain; they will win every time. You've also got to be prepared for the unexpected in some areas. I did a race in China and it was pure chaos. I went out to look at the course and there were cars going sideways on the street and thousands of people in shanty-towns. I thought, *How the hell are we going to race in this?* I was scared to train there. My biggest fear was that a car would come at me out of nowhere.

I took my concerns to the race director, and he told me the gover-nor was going to start the race. He didn't seem worried. Well, on the day of the race, we got out on the road after the swim and there wasn't a soul in sight. It was like someone had knocked on every door and said, "If you step outside, you are going to get your head blown off." Then as we came into these villages, the people were standing up like they were being told, "Do not move. You will stand there all day and clap until there is not another athlete left." It was like a movie set—one of the funniest things I've seen in a race.

The Pressure of the Hometown Fans

In Europe, the spectators are very passionate and the crowds are huge. I feed off of it. If you're going to suffer, you may as well suffer with thousands of people watching. In Asia, there's no crowd at all at a lot of events, which makes things tough. Never underestimate the importance of the crowd in keeping a triathlete going. We all want to be cheered and appreciated.

That's why I'm so drawn to Europe. The European spectators, especially the Germans, are informed. They appreciate what you're doing, and they follow racing. I've heard people yell, "Come on, Macca! You outran him last week!" You have no idea how much it means to me that somebody knows my career well enough to know what I did the week before. It can really give me a boost. One of the great things about our sport is that we're so close to the crowd. I think because Europe is so cold in the winter, and they're all bottled up in their homes, that when they come out for the summer it's like, "Oh, I'm happy to stand in the sun all day and clap and drink a beer."

Knowing these regional differences has changed my strategy. For example, the German fans are very proud and can apply a lot of pressure to their athletes. So I use that to take guys out of their game a little. I really put it to work with Normann Stadler and Faris al-Sultan, the 2005 Kona winner and another German whom I had huge rivalries with in my early days in Ironman. In those days the German fans had a huge presence at events. I would arrive at races in Germany, and when I saw Normann and Faris, I could see how much they feared the huge expectations of the fans and the media. They were icons, and the pressure was suffocating for them. They were different people when they came to North America, because they could breathe. But at home, the spotlight was blinding. These guys *had* to win.

So in the press conferences, I would throw all the pressure on them. I would say, "You know, Normann and Faris have to win here—it's their home and everyone expects it. Anything less from these guys would be seen as a real failure to perform. I know how important it is to win at home and how you always step up your game with that kind of support behind you. You've got so many people here who have come to watch these two great champions perform, but I'm just going to see how I go against them. I feel like I've prepared very well, but I understand that you race a lot better at home, because you have that crowd support. So we'll see."

Beautiful words. Totally merciless, of course. But that is part of the strategy. The expectation of the crowd can be crippling if you take yourself so seriously that it's not enough to perform well—if the only thing that matters is winning. That's why, as I've said, it's so important to love the entire process of being a triathlete, including races where you don't get on the platform but perform well. Personally, I've never felt the pressure. I love the support from the crowd. But I'm an extrovert. I don't think Australia makes introverts.

Planning for War

The crowds are one variable you have to plan for. There are dozens. Knowing them and planning for them is what makes you successful. Before I set my season, I lay out all the races and break them down one by one. Okay, I'm going to Japan. What's the weather likely to be, based on what it was like in the past? Who's coming? Where am I staying? The next race is in France. Same questions: Who? What terrain? What weather? I'll do this race by race and region by region.

I always look at where I'm staying—how comfortable the hotel is, what the food is like. These are very important things. If my hotel is not comfortable, I'm not going to get quality rest before the race. If the food is bad, I might not get the nutrition I need. Most triathletes don't do anything like this. They'll just go to Asia and look at the races on the start list. They don't look at the conditions. They'll just go to the race hotel. Well, the race hotel just happens to sponsor the race. Sometimes, you learn the hard way that it's not necessarily the best place to stay.

Let's say I'm traveling somewhere for a half-Ironman, a 70.3-mile race. If I'm going from the United States or Australia into Asia, I'll fly in a week before so I can deal with jet lag. Before I head to the race city, I'll find training venues. I'll make sure I can access my bike and do the things I need to—swim and run. I love Asian food, but it needs to be clean. I'll make sure the food is safe where I'm staying. I'll run down the list of people who are racing and make sure I'm prepared for them. In other places like the US, where jet lag is not such an issue, I'll arrive somewhere else and then come to the venue a couple of days before the race. Scott, my manager and agent, plays the biggest part in that process and scouts all the locations.

MACCA'S (W)INSIGHTS

Triathlon variables to keep in mind:

- travel time
- time zone changes
- jet lag
- food quality and safety
- water quality and safety
- access to training facilities
- climate
- air quality
- language
- course terrain

You've also got to know the regions that suit your racing style and body and those that don't. Some styles and body types dominate in certain parts of the world or even in certain times of the year. In

South America, there's a guy by the name of Oscar Galindez, a world champion duathlete. Race him at home in January, February, or March, and good luck! You can't beat the guy. He's unbeatable in South America because it's hotter. It's peak season. He wins everything. He's like Tiger Woods in a playoff. He's made a real brand for himself within South America as a triathlete because he's beaten all the champions. Then you see him in May and think, *How did Oscar beat me back in the winter?* He's just a different athlete in May.

Some guys don't travel well because they don't take these other factors into account. Miles Stewart, from whom I learned so much, doesn't travel well. Some guys find it difficult to go away for a prolonged period of time to prepare. The unfamiliarity of the surroundings is difficult. Believe me, it's no picnic for me to be away from my wife and daughters. But over the years, I've compensated for this by creating base camps. When I'm racing in Asia, Australia is my base. When I'm going to Europe, my home tends to be in Wiesbaden, Germany, or Salon Provence in France. In both places, I know where the pool is. I know the rides. It's home. In the States, it's now Los Angeles.

I also know which races to avoid because I'm just not suited to them. For example, the French guys are phenomenal climbers and very strong bikers. So I have to look at courses and be selective. Take Ironman Nice...please. They'd have to pay me a hell of a lot of money to go there, because I just can't climb with these little guys. It's just physics. I weigh 177 pounds. These guys are 130 pounds. They get on the bike and bounce up these fifteen-mile climbs. They'll put minutes into you and you're just trying to survive. Then they descend, and they're great descenders. They're mountain goats. So they give themselves a huge margin for error and a wipe a bigger guy like me out of the equation.

Of course, they love to bait me. I can appreciate a well-played mental game. One of them will say, "Ah, Macca, you need to race a hard race."

"Define 'hard.'"

"Well, Nice is hilly."

"Those are not hills. They're mountains, mate."

This is war for me. If I went to fight in those mountains, I would have a difficult time winning. I know my limitations, and I know their strengths. I'll race in Provence where they have undulations through the hills, not where I have hour-long climbs. I'm selective. I tend to gravitate to the areas and events that suit me. You want to play to your own strengths, not the strengths of others.

People criticize me for what they see as me picking only races I know I can win. But that's not what I do. I pick athletes. I do Ironman Germany because it's the biggest race in Europe and I've had more chances to study the athletes. I can target them and develop a strategy I think will beat them. I prepare for the event, and then start picking them apart. Any professional athlete's goal should be to choose events where he has a reasonable chance to do well, but not races that are easy for him to win. If you do that, you don't grow as an athlete.

People have said, "Macca continues to go back to Germany because he dominates that race." No, I continue to go back to Germany because that's where you find the best guys and the biggest prize purses. I take the big races: the Frankfurter Sparkasse Ironman European Championship in Frankfurt, Germany, Challenge Roth, and Ironman 70.3 Austria. Yes, I have proven I can win them, but they're also the races that attract the best of the best. I've won Roth four times. I've won Frankfurt and come in third twice. So when people say, "Why don't you come to Nice?" I reply, "Why would I go to Nice? There's no one there."

Change or Die

You can't think, *The hotel and food don't matter. I'm Joe Triathlete. I can conquer any race.* Well, you won't conquer anything if you're doubled over from diarrhea on race day because you ate horrible food the night before. You've got to be willing to humble yourself and control every factor as much as you can in order to give yourself the best chance to perform well.

But it's also just the culture of the sport. Many athletes just don't think about it. They don't even consider that athletes might all look the same but think differently. Look at any American who's ever won in Hawaii, like Mark Allen or Tim DeBoom. They're opportunists. Patient. Not aggressive. On the other hand, German triathletes are aggressive racers and very fast; that's why they win in Europe. They are changing this sport. Ironman was built on patience, but the Europeans' aggression is changing the game. In the future, Kona is going to be a race from the beginning. In 2010, we saw the first year of attacking on the bike and not settling in. This is the European way; it's the only way they know how to race.

Physically, nothing has changed. It's all mind-set. People take off their blinders about what's permissible and go, "Wow, I can do that and this and that!" That's what I did years ago. Other guys have learned this the hard way. In the past, Dave Scott and Greg Welch dominated in America, but every time they went to Europe, they got steamrolled. Because they won Hawaii they would say, "I wasn't really preparing for that race."

Bull. Of course you were prepared. For one thing, the money was huge. One race in Europe back in 1997 paid the winner $100,000— four times what they were paying in Hawaii. The Europeans paid everyone's airfare, so everybody went and they got handed their heads on a platter. They were prepared. What they didn't understand is that these races are a very big deal for the European athlete—much bigger than Kona. They get more recognition, live TV coverage, and more money. Guys like Dave Scott, even with all their experience, didn't understand that. They needed to prepare differently. They needed to realize that the bikers were going to dominate. Sure, they prepared, but they didn't prepare the *right way*. They treated a European race the same as a race in Kona, and they're different.

When I'm preparing for a race in Frankfurt as opposed to preparing for a race in Australia, for example, I know the swim will be solid, but nothing I can't handle. The water is usually around 25 degrees Celsius (77 degrees Fahrenheit), so it will be a wet-suit swim. That requires different swimming prep, and I need a lot more training in my wet suit, so I prepare that way. If it turns out not to be a wet-suit swim, I can adjust.

I know the bike ride is going to be intense. You're riding twenty-seven miles an hour. The European athletes know the swim is their weakness, so now they're comfortable on the bike and they are used to being aggressive. I know there will be perfect roads without a dimple in them and tight turns through little villages. That means I can put a lot more pressure in my tires and I can run a rear disc wheel. On European roads, you can run a real sleek setup on your bike. The weather isn't as hot, so you don't have to carry as much nutrition. I know that the crowds will make some of the athletes push, so I work a lot more speed into my bike sessions to compensate for this. You have terrain that is up and down, and much more technically difficult courses. I also have to be more alert, because the athletes are much more open to taking risks. They're more willing to blow up, because they get their fifteen minutes of fame on TV.

When I'm in the United States, I'll do more time trial sets just above aerobic threshold. I know I'll be riding on a bumpy surface. I'll do more strength work, because I have to control the bike with more vibration. The surface is going to hold me back from the speed I can get in Europe. The athletes are more conservative, and the pace is often consistent and steady. The courses are open and straightfor-ward, with few difficult sections.

In both places the runs are fast, with lots of crowds. But in Europe, you have to prepare for a fast run from the outset. Preparing for races in the US, you anticipate that you will have to build up to your full speed. Either way, the key is to make no mistakes in your preparation.

I may be wrong, but I seem to be the only triathlete who prepares by keeping all these factors in mind. I think it's a mind-set that's just embedded in the culture: success is all physical. For me, the war mentality has been a matter of survival as I've gotten older. So many of these European guys are aggressive racers. They're risk takers and they're fast. I need to have a different strategy to beat them. They respect the fact that I respect them enough to prepare like I do.

Finding Allies

The other part of treating each race as a war is finding allies. Once you've identified the war you're about to fight, you have to identify a strategy to win that war. And with most wars, two or three people are with you. Again, most people don't think this way. They go solo.

I'm friendly with some athletes and not so friendly with others. But I look for people who could benefit from my strategy. I always make the assumption that everyone's there with the same desire as I have: to win the event. I gravitate to athletes in Europe, because I know their style suits me. They're also really nice guys. But I hang out with them and get to know them.

Take Sebastian Kienle, a young up-and-comer who won Ironman 70.3 Germany in 2009 and placed second at Roth. He has a weakness in the swim, but he's a stronger bike rider than me. So he'll spend half the bike stage catching me, and then on the back half of the bike I can work with him—which helps me. He's a good guy, and I work with him a lot. I've also become a mentor to some of the younger guys. I've become that guy they can talk to. They look up to me. I can tell how I think they should attack a race and they'll listen.

You need allies to win. The perfect example was the 2010 Ironman World Championship in Kona. In 2009, I was solo on the bike, and I fell apart in the marathon. Well, I was solo on the bike because of a bad swim. I'm a strong biker and I put myself in a position to win, but to do that I had to put in big power, and I struggled in the middle section of the marathon.

I went away from that event and said, "You know what? The strategy is right." I needed to attack in the wind on the descent from

Hawi. I needed to take people with me to keep my legs fresher, because the reason the runners were catching up with me was because they had fresher legs getting off the bike. The group dynamic keeps the pace high without you having to do all the heavy lifting.

You can't draft, but you can pace. It's easier to maintain your pace when you're with a group, because you can look at the guy in front of you, and if you were ten yards back of him and now you're twenty, you can correct. If you're alone, sometimes you don't realize that's happening. In a group, someone is always pushing. The pace just feeds itself. It costs much less energy to reach a pace and stay there than it does to slow down and try to catch back up.

I realized I needed to take allies who suited my style of racing, but also whom I thought I could beat. But that's not always easy, so then it's just a matter of weighing your options. Better the devil you know.

So in training, I'll use the media and social networking platforms like Facebook to attract allies. I'll spread the word and let it go viral. I'll write things on my blog about certain athletes, playing to the ego. Word gets around: "Did you read what Macca said about—?" I wrote a blog on the Raelerts, praising them but also posing questions like, "Why wouldn't the people coaching Andreas have him try and get away in this section of the race?" I create friends and give them a strategy I think they should adopt. That doesn't guarantee that they'll side with me, but it improves my chances, and it lets me know who's thinking my way.

I start making them think about things. The perfect example was the talk in the last few years that Craig Alexander was unbeatable. I said, "Now hang on a second, guys. Craig swims fifty-one minutes. He bikes 4:37. He runs 2:45 or better. That's Craig Alexander."

Everybody said, "You try and do it."

I said, "I've done it many times. So has Andreas and so has Eneko Llanos [a great runner who's won the ITU Long Distance World Championship and finished second at Kona in 2008]. We've gone fifteen, twenty, thirty minutes quicker than this guy."

"Yeah, bu—"

I said, "No buts. Craig Alexander does 8:19 every day of the week whether it's hot or cold. What are you frightened of? This guy's beatable. He's never gone any quicker than 8:19."

To Raelert, I said, "What you need to do is not to get off the bike with this guy. He needs confidence. His confidence is the run; that's his weapon. We need to alienate this guy. Let's bike 4:31, 4:30. Let's give ourselves a ten-minute edge and force him to have to ride the bike hard. I guarantee you he'll do 8:19 again. He's a perfect metronome."

I started saying that in every interview that I did. "Craig Alexander is phenomenal. But he's an 8:19 guy. I'm a 7:53 guy. I'm twenty-five minutes quicker than this bloke at my best. I definitely don't think he's unbeatable. I've done an 8:11 in Hawaii before, so how are you experts saying that 8:19 is unbeatable? It's unbeatable if we play the game the way it's been played the last two years and play into his strength. If we play the game differently…"

And people started listening. They did their research. And you know what? They found out I was right. I've looked at this stuff. Then I spent the season talking about that. I had to be very patient, like a spider spinning a web. Only after they see that you know what you're talking about can you start giving strategies. So when I started talking about attacking in the crosswinds on the road from Hawi, it made sense.

In cycling you never attack into a headwind because you can draft. In triathlon you always attack into a headwind. That forces the runners to put in a lot more power so they don't fall behind. The runners tend to race with power meters, which measure the wattage your body is putting out. That tells you a lot about the runner's psyche. They want to exert constant, even power. If you force them to exert more power, they watch the numbers go up and they panic. Their legs start to hurt and they start to think, *I need to save it for the run,* and they will start to back off. You're not riding the bike to the finish line, like in cycling. You have to get off and run a marathon. So when you have that mind-set, it changes the dynamics of things.

During the year I bumped into the guys in Europe whom I wanted to work with. I started tweeting about them, befriending them, and encouraging them to listen to me. I also started working on guys like Faris al-Sultan, who hates my guts and is a very easy guy to read. So I annoy him. At every opportunity, I'd say things like, "Faris is done. He's finished, I think he's cooked, he's had too many races." It was perfect. He was at Kona on the bike trying to prove a point—*We'll see who's done, champ!*—and he played right into our hands.

Cracking the Kona Code

I use whatever avenues that can get me allies. Sometimes I find allies while I'm competing. I did the 2008 Ironman European Championship with Llanos and we had a big group behind us. Eneko is a good runner and I am a good runner, and I was looking at him and thinking, *Either one of us could win this thing*. Only three months earlier, I had outsprinted him to win the prestigious Wildflower half-Ironman, so I knew he was in exceptional form.

I turned to him and said, "Hey man, let's not get too tactical. Let's put everyone else out of the game. If you want to get tactical now, then we're going to put ten more blokes back in this race. Let's be friends right now and we can fight later." So I made an ally. We put everyone else out of the game. Then he was no longer an ally. He knew that and I knew it.

For Kona, I wanted Timo Bracht, Normann Stadler, Marino Vanhoenacker, Faris, and Andreas Raelert as allies for sure. During the season I did a Competitor TV interview in Auburn, Alabama, and I looked at the camera and said, "Faris, Normann, Timo, Marino. We need to attack at Hawi. Guys, I don't know if you are still interested in Kona. If I'm talking to deaf ears here, then go there and have a holiday. But if you want to win, and you don't think attacking in the crosswinds is the thing to do, then you're nuts. If you want to beat the fast runners—Craig Alexander, Rasmus Henning, Pete Jacobs, and Eneko Llanos—we need to move at Hawi. Time to change it up boys. If it doesn't work, you can bag on me forever."

After that, I really picked my races carefully. I went to the Ironman 70.3 St. Poulten because I knew Marino and Andreas would be there. I sat with them after the race and said, "Jeez, you guys are going well. How's the prep for Kona? How are you feeling?" I couldn't look like I had an agenda. It had to come up in conversation, or it wouldn't be the right opportunity.

In that race, both Andreas and I ended up beating Marino. He was really aggressive on the bike, and after the race he was a bit bummed. I said, "You've picked up your bike this year, Marino, haven't you?"

"I have to—everyone's riding quick," I remember him saying.

I said, "You're swimming good, you're biking good, mate. You should walk away from this race pretty proud. You did the lion's share of the bike riding today. So, I felt bad having to beat you, but I just couldn't come around you."

He said it was okay.

Then I went away. That race was on TV the following week, so I messaged Marino on Facebook: *Dude, just watch your race. Be proud, mate. Best of luck at Ironman Austria. Go for it there mate, and best of luck with your prep. Don't buy into the running game. You need to get aggressive on that bike. Same thing in Kona, mate. Good luck.*

He sent me back an e-mail that was basically, "Thanks, I really appreciate that."

Score. I knew I could get him on my side.

It all came together in Kona. I cracked the code of that race by recruiting allies patiently and carefully. I didn't know if they were going to step up. After all the preparation is done, all you can do is hope. I was hoping they followed my lead, and they did.

MACCA'S 1996 SEASON

- Canberra Triathlon, Australia—SECOND
- Nowra Triathlon, Australia—FIRST
- Lake Macquarie Triathlon, Australia—FIRST
- Port Stephens Triathlon, Australia—FIRST
- Triathlon De Orange, France—FOURTH
- Triathlon De Avignon, France—FIRST
- Triathlon International La Ferte Bernhard, France—FIRST
- Triathlon Marseilles—THIRD
- Triathlon De Briancon, France—SIXTH
- Triathlon De Auche, France—FOURTH
- ITU Triathlon World Cup Paris—SIXTH
- ITU World Cup, Drummondville, Canada—FIRST
- ITU World Cup Bermuda—SIXTH
- Boulder Peak Triathlon—SECOND
- Met RX Big Bear Triathlon—FIRST
- Chicago Triathlon—SEVENTH
- US Pro Championships, St. Joseph, Michigan—FOURTH
- ITU Triathlon World Championships, Cleveland—THIRTY-SECOND
- Australian Sprint Championships—FIRST (my first Australian title)
- Gold Coast Triathlon, Australia—FIRST

Season Statistics and Interesting Facts

- Flight miles accumulated: 49,756
- Countries visited: 8
- Days away from home: 189

Training miles for the year

- Swim: 522 miles
- Bike: 10,112 miles
- Run: 2,180 miles

7

The Ali Factor

I'm a huge boxing fan. But it wasn't until I was older that I learned to appreciate the absolute genius of Muhammad Ali. When I finally did, he inspired my entire approach to racing.

Growing up, I was a Mike Tyson fan. Following him is what got me interested in the sport in the first place. When I was a kid, Tyson was at the top of the sport, but what made him fascinating was that he was such an animal. He was savage. I remember watching him beat up Michael Spinks in 1988, knocking him out ninety-one seconds into the first round. It was incredible to watch. Other world-class fighters would get into the ring with Tyson, and you could see they were afraid. I had never, ever seen top fighters look scared getting into the ring, but they did with Iron Mike. Even as a kid, I knew that when you were that frightened of your opponent, the contest was over before it started.

In the 1990s, I would hear my father talk about Ali and say things like, "Ali would kill Tyson, it would be like that," snapping his fingers. And I thought *You're typical, caught in the old days*. I told my father that Tyson would smash Ali. But I was just an uninformed kid. When you're inexperienced, you think what you see on the surface is everything. You think the biggest punch always wins.

But I started learning about Ali. Alan Jones, a very famous Australian sports radio broadcaster and respected sports journalist, had done a documentary on Ali versus Tyson and speculated about who would win. He showed old footage of Ali and talked about how people called him the "black Superman." They would show Ali, then Tyson, then Ali, then Tyson. Eventually, Jones came to the conclusion that Ali would be too smart, too big and too clever for Tyson and would work out a way to beat him.

I was offended. I remember yelling, "Bullshit!" at the television. I had watched this bloke in action, but I didn't really understand the history of Ali. I didn't know who Ali was, and the key to Ali's greatness has always been not just how he fought but who he was.

Then I met Mick Gilliam. He started out as my massage therapist, but we really bonded when we started talking about boxing. I had moved on from Tyson to Oscar de la Hoya, but somehow Ali came up in conversation. Mick was stunned when he found out that I thought Tyson in his prime would have beaten Ali in his prime. "Do you know anything about Muhammad Ali, kid?" Mick demanded. "Do yourself a favor and go read up on this man. He invented professional sport. He was the first rapper. He is the greatest athlete that's ever been."

That opened my eyes. I really started studying Ali, and in doing so I started to understand one of the reasons I had such an affinity for boxing. It is very similar to my own sport of triathlon. In boxing, you begin with a mano a mano confrontation between two athletes. And even though an Ironman might have two hundred professionals down at the water, in the end it usually comes down to a battle between two athletes. More important, both sports are about having the will to endure suffering. Late in a triathlon, you're suffering from exhaustion, dehydration cramps, muscle pulls, heat—it's hell for the body. If you watch the late rounds of a boxing match, it's the same. Both fighters might have broken noses, swollen eyes, bruises or cracked ribs, and they're exhausted. The fighter who can keep his focus and form despite his suffering is probably going to win.

So I became a student of "the Greatest." I started reading about him and watching documentaries, and I came to get some idea of the American history that he came through. I saw that he wasn't just a sportsman; he had to endure things that few other athletes had.

I also came to understand his penchant for predicting rounds—for what we would call "smack talk" today. He was creating doubt and fear in his opponents. When he first fought Sonny Liston, he told him, "You're too ugly to be champ." People thought he was crazy and that Liston was going to kill him, but it really threw Liston off his game.

But you really saw the two Alis during his two most famous fights. First came the "Rumble in the Jungle" in 1974. This was Ali the master tactician. George Foreman, younger and a powerful puncher, was decidedly favored. But Ali employed his famous Rope-a-Dope strategy—leaning on the ropes, letting Foreman wear himself out in the Zaire heat punching Ali's arms and body, clinching with Foreman and making the younger fighter support all his body weight, and taunting Foreman into reckless punches as the champ became more and more fatigued. Finally, Ali knocked him out in the eighth round, a masterful victory by a man who knew that the fight didn't hinge on who threw the most punches at any one time, but who was strongest at the end.

Then came the "Thrilla in Manila" against Joe Frazier in 1975. Leading up to the fight, Ali was very cruel to Frazier, calling him names like "the Gorilla" and saying things like, "It's gonna be a thrilla, and a chilla, and a killa, when I get the Gorilla in Manila." For his part, Frazier was outraged. He had spoken up on Ali's behalf when Ali had been stripped of his heavyweight crown in 1967 for refusing to go into the Army. Frazier went into the fight angry, and when he refused to back down, Ali destroyed him.

I devoured everything about Ali I could get my hands on. Today, I own about fifty DVDs on Ali. The more I learned, the more impressed I was. He was so charismatic, but it was more than that. He was the first athlete I knew of who had made his mind, not his body, his ultimate weapon. Now I think that if you took Tyson at his best and Ali at his best, this is how it would go down. Tyson would win the first round. But Ali would work him, exhaust him, and he would win the fight. I had sporting idols, but with Ali I found a guy who just fascinated me.

Making Triathlon a Modern Sport

I'm sure you've noticed that I'm not shy about borrowing ideas or strategies from other sports. It's one of the things that set me apart from other triathletes. Our sport can be very parochial. Because an Ironman is the most difficult one-day sporting event on the planet, many athletes and coaches have a sense of superiority about it. They don't even consider that boxers, cyclists, or pros in other sports might have secrets that they could use to perform better on race day. It's very shortsighted. I couldn't care less about feeling superior to other athletes because I'm a triathlete and they're not. My attitude is that if you're a champion, you're a champion, and I can probably learn something from you. I've taken ideas from many areas of athletics over the years in order to get to the top and stay there.

With Ali, something about the man just resonated with me. In part, it was just the way he held himself and went about his business.

MACCA'S (W)INSIGHTS

Steal from the best!

I've made some major breakthroughs by borrowing ideas from boxing, sprinting, tennis, bodybuilding, and other sports. You can do the same thing to address your own weaknesses. Find other sports whose top practitioners seem to have cracked the problems that you are facing and see what you can "borrow."

He had perfected his craft. Most boxers were brutes. Tyson was a brute. But Ali was elegant and cerebral. There was finesse, tactics, and smarts to his game. He created the mental game that I have used with such success in my career.

Of course, when I first got to Kona in 2002, I may have laid the "I am the best triathlete of all time" bit on a little thick. I had already been branded as overconfident because while all the other athletes were talking about how humble they were and how lucky they were just to be in the race, I was saying that I intended to win. It just wasn't done.

Plus, when I landed on American soil in 2000 and started winning all these races, I started speaking at triathlon clubs, which are a very big deal and hold a lot of influence in the sport. Inevitably, I was misquoted. I'll never forget a Los Angeles Triathlon Club meeting in front of 750 people. Someone asked, "You're winning all of these races, what about Hawaii?"

I said, "Hawaii is 100 percent on the agenda."

The follow-up: "How do you think you'll do in Hawaii?"

Me: "Well, my idols were Mark Allen and Dave Scott; they won six Konas. So I'd like to win seven."

Full stop. Everyone was shocked at my audacity. It was like I'd committed blasphemy, which I guess I had. The response was along the lines of "Hadn't you better win one before you start talking about seven?"

I told them that I loved Mark Allen to this day, and if anyone worshipped him and Dave Scott, it was me. But isn't it my responsibility as part of the next wave of athletes to try to do better than the wave that came before? I said, "Look, I am not out to disrespect these guys, but they've set themselves on a pedestal and they've set a mark that I would like to get to. I'm not saying I can, but that's what I'm after."

You can guess what part of that speech made it into the press: "McCormack says he will win seven!" Everyone said I was brash and full of myself. All I could do was say, "I didn't mean it the way it sounded." That was part of my crash course in how the media works.

That shows you where the sport was, and why the Ali factor is so relevant. When Ali came onto the scene, boxing was in a decline. Joe Louis was dead, and the sport was plodding and not very good for television. By taunting his opponents, building up the media hype, and winning with his own fluid, graceful, athletic style, Ali made the sport modern and dramatic. He really did invent modern sports.

Triathlon was in the same shape before 2000. At the end of 1999, membership in USA Triathlon (the main American sanctioning body) was only 19,060 people. But by June 2010, it was 134,942. Why? The Olympics, for one. The Sydney and Athens games put the sport on the map for millions of people.

But I think it was also due to greater media coverage of events, including Ironman Hawaii, the sport's glamour race. And why does the media cover some sporting events more than others? Drama and heroes, that's why. Did American audiences ever see prime, mainstream media coverage of the Tour de France before Lance Armstrong went on his incredible seven-race winning binge? Of course not. Before Lance, the Tour was just this odd French bike race. After Lance, it was *dramatic*.

It was the same for triathlon. When rivalries started appearing, athletes started talking a bit of trash, and bona fide stars started emerging, then the press coverage increased in both volume and visibility. With that, more people than ever began doing triathlons, local clubs grew, and the sport blossomed. We still don't get live television coverage of Kona, but it's coming, and I think it's due in part to some of the things that I started: playing the mind game, building up the personal showdowns, and athletes acting like real people who want to win races, not paragons of virtue who are "just happy to be here."

My Dues Are Paid in Full

My aggressive talk got the same reaction as Ali's "float like a butterfly, sting like a bee" chatter before the first Liston fight. Everyone said, "What about paying your dues?" The history of the Ironman

Hawaii shows that it's almost impossible to win your first time at the race. Even if you have the talent, you're supposed to pay your dues—which I guess means be humble and lose a lot of times before you even make it to the platform.

My response to that in one interview was, "Mate, I'm a professional athlete. I've been racing for six years. I'm paid up in full." So going into the race, it was all over the coverage: me talking about having paid my dues and saying I was going to win. When I fell apart, the prevailing attitude was, *How do you like that, rookie?*

I thought, *I haven't made too many friends here, have I?* It was humbling, but I had to wear it. That's the thing about being vocal—you say it, you own it. I thought I wore it pretty well, because I came back the following year and fought again. I got off the bike with a thirteen-minute lead, walked the marathon, and everyone was happy. Earlier in the year I said I was going to win seven, and I left busted. But I didn't run and hide. I had to wear that "cocky" label that I had pinned on myself.

I wore it again in 2003, because I came back. You try to justify your errors in your own head to give you clarity and a point of reference to start again. This time, I told myself that no matter what, I was finishing this thing. I thought I had a chance to win but I remember saying, "No matter what happens, I'm crossing that line, I'm not going to wear the flag of the quitter." And again, I was second off the bike, eight minutes in front of the chasers, and then—cramping. Always cramping issues.

So I walked to a 9:36. When I crossed the finish line, the announcer shouted, "And here he is! Macca!" Ouch. Before the race, I was on the front page of *Triathlon* magazine with the headline, "Can Macca Defy the Kona Gods and Win?" Again, I had to walk around town wearing my bravado and the embarrassment of a walking finish. It's amazing the disdain people have for you when you state your intentions—how personally they take it, as though you're implying they can't do what you can. That's where I differ from Ali: he never had to eat his boasts the way I've dined on mine.

That was when I started to have serious self-doubts and fears for the first time in my career. I worried that I would go down as the best triathlete never to win Kona. Here I would have unblemished seasons, year after year. I would not lose a race, win Ironman races, just miss world records, and smash everybody. Then I would come to the Big Island and *boom!* I'd fall over.

Then the talk started on the discussion boards and blogs: Macca is too big for Kona. He sweats too much. He races too much. You try not to grab on to those reasons, because you're searching for a reason why you're failing. But they are hard to tune out. Those were the demons that haunted me at Kona year after year from 2002 to 2006. But every year, I went back. As my dad would say, "Son, a champion keeps playing until he gets it right."

I kept paying my Kona dues in 2004 when I stepped into the sponsor car in the marathon. It was the most crushing moment of my entire career—but it was also a turning point. I realized that I was being cocky for the sake of being cocky. Ali was never cocky just to pump himself up. It was always strategic: to bait the other fighter into attacking, like Frazier had, or into exhausting himself, like Foreman had. People were saying, "He loves Ali, but he's not Ali. Ali delivered." I had won every other Ironman race I'd ever done—nine wins in nine starts—but at Kona I failed. The guys just kept letting me have it:

"Man, he can talk all he wants."

"Macca, here he goes again."

"Hey Macca, how have your Kona results been?"

"He's too big for this race. Give me another guy who weighs 178 pounds who's won in Kona. Oh, that's right. There isn't anyone."

I had to suck it up and own it. I'd invited it by running my mouth, so I had no choice but to take it. But it also drove me to find a different way to beat this race. I had been coming to Kona every year with the same strategy, and it had been failing miserably. I was trying to win the way I had won short-course events. That's why my mental game didn't work: I was trying to create fear, but in Kona I didn't have a history that anybody had to fear. Quite the opposite. I was letting the race play me. I was going against my military planning principle, in which you prepare differently for every race. That had to change. I had to adapt to Kona if I was going to change the outcome.

Washed Up?

So now I was a little like Ali after he was stripped of his title and tried to come back. Everybody was assuming I was washed up. Surely, it would be a matter of time before Macca announced his retirement or maybe dedicated himself to making the Australian team for the Beijing Olympics. I became an afterthought at Kona. And as with Ali, that told me it was time to change my strategy.

After 2004 I went home and started working. I went to the sports physiology labs to work out my sweat rate because of my concerns about my size. The sports scientists gave me this eating formula that told me how much nutrition and hydration I should take in per hour. So I went back in 2005 thinking, *Okay, I know a lot about my body now. I know how I need to tackle this race. I've got to keep my heart rate low. This "trying to ride away from everybody tactic" is not the way to do it.* I realized that I had tried to ride away from everyone because I was fearful of the marathon. I hadn't ever posted a good marathon at Kona. So I went in with a different plan…

…and spent the whole early stage of the race vomiting. Great. At the halfway point I was the furthest behind I have ever been at any race in my life. I went right to the negative, straight to the dark side of the Force. I remember thinking, *Here we go again. I'm four years into this race. I can't do it. I can't do it.* Vomiting, vomiting, vomiting. As I was going up toward the halfway turnaround, twenty minutes back, I quit. I said to myself, *This is it. I'm officially done. I am too big. Four times, four failings. I'm done.* I semiretired then and there, sitting up on my bike.

Then Thomas Hellriegel, who won the race in 1997 and rode with me at my first Kona, caught me. He had fixed a flat tire and was riding himself back into the race. He looked at me and said something like, "What are you doing man? Drink Coke and water—you've taken in too many electrolytes and carbs." The sports scientists in Australia had told me never to drink Coke because the sugar was too simple. I had to eat complex, maltodextrin-based carbohydrates and stick to this eating plan no matter what.

I heard Thomas again, "Come on. Coke and water. You have to get back to town anyway."

He was right; I had to get back to Kona. I figured I would just stay with him as long as I could and get home. But within five minutes, I stopped taking my electrolytes and had some Coke. *Click*. It was like a light went on. I felt better immediately, and I drank just Coke and water from that point on in the race. I was twenty minutes back at the turn; I got off the bike twelve minutes behind. I ran the fastest marathon of the day and finished sixth, 8:40 from the win. I ran across the line for the first time and hobbled over to do my interview. That was a good day.

I recall Peter Reid, who won Kona in 1998, 2000, and 2003, saying in an interview he did a couple of years after he retired, "I saw Macca cross the line in 2005 and it looked like a light went on. I knew that guy was going to win this race. It was like he'd worked it out." I knew I was doing something right. I'd finally posted something. It wasn't a win, but I'd performed well. I hadn't blown up. I'd come from the depths of the dead, run through the field, and I posted the fastest marathon on the island. I was being talked about as a player again.

Kona, 2006

Another important part of the Ali factor is not backing down from a challenge. When someone calls your character into question, you confront them. Most of the time, they will back down and you'll have them at a disadvantage. That's the position I found myself in after the 2006 race in Kona.

Everything changed for me in 2005. That was the day I finally got faith in my marathon. I had always seen myself as a cyclist who wasn't the equal of the top runners in the marathon. So in an Ironman-distance race, I would put out a lot of power trying to ride in the front group of cyclists and give myself a margin over the great runners, who I had always assumed would torch me in the marathon. It was a tactic born out of the fear that I just wasn't good enough as a runner. But fear is the enemy in triathlon. By giving in to it, I was burning myself up on the bike, so cramping in the marathon was inevitable. Mick had been saying, "You have to back your run. You don't need this margin of error."

Changing who you are as an athlete is hard to do. But if one thing isn't working, you have to try something else. In 2005, I realized that Mick was right. I ran a 2:49 marathon—the fastest in the field—on the hottest day in the history of the race. It finally hit me: *I'm a good marathon runner.* I went away from the 2005 race knowing that I could trust my marathon. History shows that the fastest marathon wins—*if* you get off the bike with the front group of riders. I was apprehensive about that. But that was the strategy I chose. I would stay with the top riders. Patience, patience, patience—and have faith that I was the best runner.

I went into the 2006 season with that in mind. After my first Ironman riding with a group, I remember thinking, *This is easy.* My legs felt good. I won Ironman Australia, and that was when I started to understand the importance of riding to keep your legs fresh. I went to the 2006 Challenge Roth in Germany, one of the most important Ironman races on the circuit, and stayed with that approach. I rode with a couple of guys and boom! I ran a 2:42 marathon and won. Then I went to America and won several 70.3-mile half-Ironman races. Just like that, I was a runner.

I started training to get leaner for Kona. Because I'm big and heavy for a triathlete, my size works against me in the hot weather of

Hawaii. So I wanted to maximize my lean body mass. As October drew closer, my plan was simple. I would swim with the group, ride with the group, and back my marathon.

Once the gun went off to start the swim, I noticed that Normann Stadler was swimming really well. Normann, who won the title in 2004, was an established star by then. He started out in short-course racing, but his swim was weak, so he switched to Ironman, where there's more time to make up for a poor swim. That was the first year that athletes used swim skins, low-drag wet suits designed to help you cut through the water like a torpedo. Normann was the first athlete ever to have one. His sponsor, Blue Seventy, invented it, and he wore it while the rest of us were all swimming in our old gear. Good for him; you do what you can within the rules to get an edge.

I was having a brilliant swim of my own. When I got to the turn at 1.2 miles (two kilometers) out, I was in the front group with Faris al-Sultan, who had won at Kona in 2005. I thought, *I must be having a spectacular swim, because Faris is a strong swimmer.* I got out of the water with the first group of swimmers, a fantastic start to my day. As I got on my bike, I noticed the difference inside my head. In past years, there was panic and desperation; I felt like I had to get out ahead of the group and put miles into them or I would lose in the marathon. Not this year. This year I was calm. I was going to be patient. I was a runner and I would ride like one.

I pulled out of transition with a good-sized group: Australian Luke Bell (a multiple half-Ironman winner), New Zealanders Bryan Rhodes (a multiple Ironman winner) and Cameron Brown (who has owned Ironman New Zealand), Stephan Vuckovic, and a few others. But as we rode out, I saw a rider ahead of us whom I didn't recognize. I dropped back a bit and found Faris. I said, "Who's that up ahead?"

I remember him saying something like, "It's fucking Normann," like he couldn't believe it. Neither could I. You never expected to see Normann riding up front out of transition because he was usually four minutes behind the lead group in the swim. Not today.

"Wow, he had a great swim" was all I could get out. Now we had a race. I played by my new rules. I stayed with my lead group and let them do some of the work. Even though drafting is illegal in Ironman, there is a benefit to riding with a group. It's easier to set and keep a steady pace, so you conserve a lot of energy for that looming marathon. I had never stayed with a group before, but I was doing it now.

Normann, who's a great rider, was slowly putting time into us. Even so, I knew that if as a group we could keep him within ten minutes of us, I could beat him on the run. Normann had never run a marathon in less than three hours. I had run 2:49 the year before and I knew I could run 2:45. I wasn't worried about Faris; I'd done forty-five triathlons against him, and the 2005 Ironman Kona was the only time he'd ever beaten me. I could handle him.

Into the first half of the bike stage, Faris kept coming around me and Luke Bell, riding to the front of the pack and trying to cross the gap to catch Normann. I think the fact that both men are German had something to do with it. It's a small country with two great champs and only a few major sports. They had their own intracountry rivalry going on. They didn't hate each other, but they weren't friends, either. Faris wasn't going to rest until he caught his countryman. That was fine by the rest of us. We were content to let him do all the work pacing the group.

After the halfway-point turn at Hawi, we started losing more time to Normann. Faris was really getting upset, screaming something like, "We're losing too much!" over and over. But I wasn't worried. Coming out of Hawi, Normann had about five minutes on us. If I got off the bike only five minutes behind him, I knew I would win this race. Even as Normann put in the power and gained time on us—six minutes, seven minutes—I was confident. He was putting everything he had into this bike ride; he would pay for it in the marathon. I heard Faris yelling and thought, *The guy you should be worried about isn't Normann, mate. It's me.*

My group came into Kona eleven minutes down on Normann. It

was the first time in Kona that I had gotten off the bike with the front group. I sat with the strong riders and rested my legs a bit. I played by the rules, got off the bike, and I've never felt so good at the start of a run at Kona.

MACCA'S (W)INSIGHTS

Keep your legs fresh for the run

Some tips for keeping yourself fresh while on the bike so you can deliver your best possible results in the marathon:

- If it's a draft-legal race, then be prepared to ride in groups. This is to your advantage, because you can enjoy an easier ride for some of the stage. But be sure to take your turn at the front!

- Select a gear that will allow you to maintain a cadence of around 90 RPM. This will keep you moving at a healthy pace but should not exhaust you.

- Consider your goals. If you are aiming simply to finish, then conserve your energy as much as possible, even if this means sticking with a weaker bike group. If you are trying for a personal record or competing with other athletes, you must ask whether or not hanging with a weaker group and having a poorer bike split is worth having to make up the time on the run.

- If you are a strong runner, consider riding in a lower, lighter gear so you have fresh legs and can really perform in the run. If you are a weaker runner, then use a higher gear and get more speed out of the same cadence. Even if you save your legs, you're not going to get much benefit out of it if you're a so-so runner.

- Don't automatically go into a higher, heavier gear for hills. The more time you spend out of the saddle, the heavier your legs will feel on the run. It's fine to spin up the hills.

I blew out of the transition area and immediately put distance on the guys behind me. In the first five miles, I ran two and a half minutes off of Normann's eleven-minute lead. Running south on Ali'i Drive, I ran past my old French triathlon club coach, Guy Hemmerlin. He shouted that Normann had ridden 4:18 on the bike, a new Kona record. Be patient, he said to me. Normann will come back. I was delighted. There was no way the German could put out enough power to set a record on the bike and have enough left in the tank to beat three hours.

I made the turn, ran back north into town and up Palani hill. Palani had become a checkpoint for me because that was where I had fallen to pieces in the marathon in 2002, 2003, and 2004. I was still worried about it. It's hard to shed those fears even when you know you've trained and used the right strategy. Since all I'd ever known at Kona were three failures and one so-so event, I was apprehensive. But I *bounded* up Palani that day. When I got to the top, I felt amazing. It was on.

That was the point that I really started after Normann. Guy was on his bike and rode alongside, giving me splits that told me how far ahead Normann was. I was taking thirty to forty seconds a mile out of him. If I could hold this pace, I knew I was going to take him down. *Be patient,* I told myself. *Don't blow this.* I definitely still had some fear, based on harsh experience, that I would overheat and blow up. *Be patient,* I was telling myself, words I had never used before in Kona.

I swung into the Energy Lab—nine miles from home. This was my first opportunity since mile marker five to see Normann. We crossed past each other at the turn, and I could see that he was starting to labor. It was oppressively hot in the lava fields, and I wanted to get it into his head that I was coming. So as we passed, I made sure he saw me glance at my watch, then I smiled at him. *Got you, mate.* He was smiling, but it looked more like a grimace.

But despite all my bravado, I struggled on the climb back out of the Energy Lab. It looks like a nothing climb, but it's a mile long, and after more than 130 miles of racing in that heat it *hurts*. I really felt the climb. I swung back out onto the Queen K Highway with six miles to run, and that was the first time I really felt the heat. The Lab had hurt me. I was just under five minutes down.

My team was going berserk. They said, "You have to go *now*!" I pulled off my fuel belt and dropped it on the ground. It had nothing left in it, and I was going to be as light as possible for the final assault. I went for it. In the next mile, I took forty-five seconds out of Normann's lead. I took forty seconds out of him in the mile after that. My wife, Emma-Jane, and my agent, Scott, were shouting, "Keep pushing!" I could see the television helicopter in the sky, its camera focused on Normann, and it was almost above me. I got another split, and I was two and a half minutes back. With three miles to go, I was 1:50 behind.

I was in pure agony. It was probably the most gone I have ever been in any race. It was pain beyond pain: heat, abdominal cramps, screaming muscles, exhaustion. But I heard voices in each ear saying, *Do not stop pushing. How many times have you failed in Kona? Keep at it.*

On the famous hill where the legendary Mark Allen and Dave Scott had their famous showdown in 1989, I was so close that I could read the sponsors on the back of Normann's jersey. Now there were two groups of people on the road: a bunch of Germans cheering Normann, and my team helping me. The chopper was literally overhead now, and, in my agony, the noise of the rotor was unbearable; I wished I could just wave the damned thing away.

With just two miles to go, I got another split. Forty seconds. That was all the lead Normann had left. I had been taking forty seconds a mile out of him, so I knew I could catch him. But...I also knew the history of this race. I had said to Mick earlier that I needed to be leading on Palani hill if I was going to win.

History showed that whoever led on Palani won the race. When you make the turn from Queen K to Palani, you're immediately running downhill while the runners behind you are still running uphill. You can understand why the runner who gets there first has a huge advantage. It's the literal turning point of the race. I knew that if I didn't catch Normann before he made the turn onto Palani, the race was over.

I tried...but I couldn't quite get there. Normann reached the crest of the hill, and as he made the right turn onto Palani he took a glance back at me. I was close enough to see the smile on his face. That smile said, *You know the history of this race. I got here first.*

That was an instantaneous explosion for me. I hit the wall. It was exactly the kind of psychological warfare that I had been trying to practice, and he destroyed me with it. That smile broke me. Normann was running downhill; I was still running uphill. He ran thirty seconds out of me after that, and I was lucky to get home.

I can't even tell you what happened on that last mile down Palani, through the left turn onto Kuakini Highway, the right onto Hualalai, and the final turn onto Ali'i Drive. I was on another planet. I remember people coming in and out of my vision like I was drunk. Then I glanced up and I thought I was hallucinating: it looked like Normann had hit the wall, because he was still out on Ali'i. So I started sprinting. But he'd just come back out to slap hands with the crowd. When I crossed the finish line, he held my arm up, which was good because I could barely stand on my own. Never before in my life had I taken myself to that level of pain. Normann had beaten me by seventy-one seconds.

After the race, I'd never been so exhausted in my life. I ended up in the medical tent getting two liters of IV fluids; that's how dehydrated I was. My father stood above me saying, "Son, you don't need this in your life. You've got two kids, what are you chasing?"

At the press conference, everyone was congratulating me on a great race and an unbelievable finish, but I was totally confused. I remember the doubt that crept into my head at that point. I couldn't understand it. I had done everything right—sat with the group, stayed patient, played by the rules—and this guy had still beaten me. In the past, whenever I had raced a nearly perfect technical race, I'd always won. But not this time. What had I done wrong?

Later, I found out that not only had Normann set a course record on the bike, but he had run a personal best 2:55 in the marathon. Combined with his swim, he'd had an incredible day. He took everything I threw at him. Other athletes would have folded. But not only did he beat me, he led from start to finish. That's an agonizing way to race, because you're always losing time. I had the easier job—I had a rabbit on the road that I could chase.

I learned a lot about Normann's character that day. He had always been labeled as eccentric, kind of a prima donna, hot and cold. But he was the best rider in the sport, and he was the better athlete that day. Physically, he had shown me a side I didn't know he had. What's more, he had beaten me in the area where I thought I was unbeatable: the mental game.

War

At the press conference, I tried to give Normann credit for both his physical prowess and mental toughness, but I guess I didn't say it quite right. I was trying to give him a compliment and I said, "I ran the best race of my life, but I never realized that Normann Stadler was that good." I was trying to give him full credit, but he took it the wrong way and things exploded from there.

Faris had finished third, and after the press conference, I saw he and Normann talking, which was unusual because they really didn't care for each other that much. I assumed that I was the subject of the conversation. After all, I was an easy scapegoat for Faris; he could blame his third-place finish on me, and he didn't like me, anyway. In a funny way, I think those two Germans bonded over their mutual dislike of me that day. I love when I can bring people together.

Whatever was said, it would have remained trash talk, except that Faris went public with it in his postrace interviews. He said something like, "I just don't like his tactical bullshit. Macca's a pussy." Meanwhile, I was watching and listening with my jaw on the ground, thinking, *Have you followed my career? I've been in the front longer than you've been in the sport.*

At the awards banquet and presentation the next night, I went up on stage. Normann went along and congratulated everyone, including Faris. I recall him saying to Rutger Beke, this Belgian guy who had come in fourth, something like, "You know, you're the best runner in this field." It was obviously said so I could hear it, which was weird. When Normann got to me, he sort of nodded and shook my hand but didn't make eye contact with me. I was still beaming. I'd gotten second in Kona, and I was headed in the right direction. I had performed well, shown grit and heart, and stayed with my new plan. I was proud and ready to come back in 2007 and win.

But when I walked off the stage, a guy handed me a BlackBerry. On it, I read an interview Normann gave where he called me out and said something like, "Macca should be disgusted with himself, ashamed of himself. What a pussy performance, sitting in the group. I wish Faris had got him. I hate his tactical bullshit. He should have some balls about him." Basically, he was accusing me of drafting—of cheating—even though there had been a drafting judge right by me during the entire race.

It was ridiculous—and I was boiling mad. I could hear the whispers going around: *Have you heard what Normann wrote about Macca?* I was the last one to know. Well, I wasn't about to let that bullshit go unchallenged. I hunted Stadler down at this party. There were hundreds of other triathletes, because everyone attends these celebrations. I walked around, asking, "Has anyone seen Normann Stadler?" I felt like I was back in school. Then I walked into this pub area and it was like something out of the movie *High Noon.* He was there with his entourage. I think people might have expected a fistfight, but I wasn't interested in that sort of payback.

"Normann," I said calmly, "can I chat with you for a minute, just behind the wall?" I wanted to keep it quiet, but I recall him saying, "If you have anything to say, you say it here."

Have it your way. I said, "Mate, what's with the interview? What the hell is that all about? Normann, you know me mate. Look at me." But he couldn't look at me. I remember that he finally said, "I don't respect you, man."

That tore it for me. "Don't respect me? I'll race you anywhere, mate. Pick a place."

This was playing right into his hands. He said something like, "The race was yesterday and I won. I've won two, and you've won none."

I was ready to declare war, and I did. "Normann," I said, "I didn't have a problem with you yesterday, but now I have a huge problem with you. I'm going to retire you from the sport, mate. Mark my words."

I turned my attention to the crowd around us, which had grown quite large. "I am going to retire this man from triathlon," I said to the gathering. "This man will never beat me again for as long as his ass points to the ground." I turned back to Normann. "I'm going to smash you. I'm going to find every race you do next year. No one else exists in this sport for me except you and your friend, Faris. I'm going to retire you both."

I stormed out. When I cooled off, I could have kicked myself. I had just signed Under Armour as a sponsor and I was thinking, *I should have calmed down. They probably think I'm a nut.* Then I ran into some Under Armour people and they said, "No, that was wicked! Some tension is always good for sport." They absolutely loved it.

Then I found Faris. I said, "Faris, what's your game, mate?" I tried to be calmer with Faris. He's a few years younger than me, and he had won Kona, but he'd never done anything else. "How would you feel mate," I asked him, "if someone attacked you in ten years' time about the way you race, with the career you've had?"

As I recall, he replied, "Don't talk to me."

This would be two war declarations in one day. "All right mate, you hear this loud and clear. I'm going to retire you from this sport. You will never, ever, ever, ever beat me. I'm going to kick your ass." I turned to his friend, who was sitting next to him, and said, "Did you hear that, mate? I'm going to retire this man from triathlon." Back to Faris. "You're classless, man. But have a good night."

And in 2007, I went bananas. The Ali in me came out. I was determined to take all the fight out of the people who had disrespected me. I started targeting them. Faris had signed up for a race in Dubai in January. I booked my ticket and went. I turned up and shocked him. "Hi, mate," I said. "How are you? Didn't know I was coming, did you? Game on."

People say I'm motivated by anger, and if anger helped me bury these two, I was happy to embrace it. In the race, I swam with Faris, and as I was running out of the water, I said, "Hey, come on, champ!" I rode three minutes off of him on the bike, and after I got off I ran two more minutes into him on the run. After I crossed the finish, I started my watch and waited for him to come in. "Dude, you're 4:52 behind, you joke," I said. I followed him as he walked past the line, and I said, "Remember our talk in Kona, Faris? This is only the beginning, mate. You're gone."

I started racing and winning all of these events. I went to Europe and I targeted both men. Then it was time for the Ironman European Championships in Frankfurt and Challenge Roth, the two biggest races in Germany. Everyone was trying to get all three of us to race each other again. The Frankfurt officials came to me with a contract and said, "You need to put your money where your mouth is and take on the Germans in Frankfurt." I said, "Pay me and I'll come to the race." I ended up having both Frankfurt and Roth put figures on the table. I took the biggest one. That was Roth.

I went to Roth and publicly announced that I was going to try to break the world record. I had barely missed a lot of records that season, and I hadn't been beaten all year. I crushed Roth, finishing in 7:54 and just missing the record. It was beamed live on German TV, and I knew Normann and Faris saw it. Normann was the world champion at that time, and he was running the race in Frankfurt the following week. So I got to go as a spectator, and I saw Normann doing his prerace interviews. Time to drive the knife a little deeper. I waved and said, "Hey, champ!"

He looked out from the interview area, and I said, "Got your attention now? Remember what I promised you in Kona? You can't hide from me, champ, I'm going to destroy you. I can't wait." I turned to walk away, then I turned back and said, "Good luck tomorrow. I'll be watching." I remember the fear in his face. He and everyone else knew I was talking about Kona. They probably also figured I had gone insane. Both he and Faris had terrible days. Normann pulled out of the race and Faris finished sixth.

I started e-mailing everyone about Kona. I'd write, *Thirteen weeks and counting, fellas. Twelve weeks and counting, boys.* In any interview, everyone wanted to know the hype. It was the biggest thing in our sport. The personal conflict had become the story, just like with Ali.

A Method to My Madness

I ended up having an amazing 2007 season. I just missed the world record, won all these races, smashed Faris, smashed Normann, and smashed everybody. I even got an e-mail from Faris's mother, which I've kept, asking me to please leave her son alone. But going into Kona, I still didn't have a title. Now I had to win. If I didn't, my career would be over.

My wife Emma was getting concerned about me. "Chris, you've got to calm down," she said.

But there was a method to Mick's and my madness. Sonny Liston. We wanted these guys to think I was crazy, like Liston did with Ali. We wanted them to think there was nothing I wouldn't do.

Mission accomplished. I ended up breaking both those boys that day at Ironman. Faris got to the start line and then dropped out because he said he felt sick. Normann got halfway through the bike and started complaining that he felt weak. He ended up stepping off the course. I went on to win the race from Craig Alexander. I ran through the finish with my arms up in the air. Normann greeted me, and I said, "Thank you very much." I respected that a lot. I actually have a good relationship with Normann now.

I had scared them both to death. I didn't back down before the bullies. If you stand up to a bully, they freak out and back down. I was the brash kid who had finally delivered. I had stood up to the Germans, which no one had done before. Now, that didn't change a lot of people's opinions about me; as many people hated me as liked me. But even the people who hated me were saying, "Man, this guy's got huge balls." I was that freaking nut job who called everybody out and backed it up. People were starting to warm to my style now.

There are a lot of good athletes in every sport, but not everybody has that killer instinct. Not everyone can talk it up and then come along and stick the shiv right in. Larry Bird and Michael Jordan could do it in basketball. Roger Federer does it in tennis. Tiger Woods does it in golf. By waging my war against Normann and Faris, I had established that we thought the same way. I'm a good guy, but don't mess with me. I'll rip your throat out. That was the reputation I wanted to build.

If you take a pro license, how can you be upset that I want to race you and beat you? That is what I do for a job. They took a pro card, didn't they? They said I want to be a pro-licensed holder. Well, welcome to my world. Race me. If I bump you or call you out, that's part of the sport. Poor baby. If it's too hot in that fire, there is an age-group field that you can race with. This is my job. This is how I live.

I think I come across as a very confident guy, and that takes me back to Ali. He was never shy about telling people what he thought. If he boasted, he backed it up. People perceived that Ali was a character, and they didn't confuse the Ali who was saying all these outrageous things with the Ali who was the real person. I don't think people are there with me yet. They still confuse the athlete playing the mental game with the person who's a husband and daddy. But I will *never* be the guy who does his prerace interview humble and grateful, saying, "I just hope I do well today." I do twelve-week and fourteen-week training camps so I don't have to hope.

Before my 2010 race in Kona, Mick called me. He said something I will never forget. He said, "This is your Foreman fight, mate.

Rope-a-dope these bastards. Use what you have over them. You know the race. You've got experience. Forget about those failing days, they're behind you. Just make sure that when the time comes, you can knock them out."

After my win, he said something to me that I had never, ever thought of: "I've followed your career since you were a kid, and there's not been a world championship that you've raced that you've not been the favorite for. Have you ever thought about that? In every world championship, you're the lead dog. It's, 'Can McCormack pull it off?'

"Except this one," he went on. "Kona is the one race where you've never been a favorite." He was right. In Kona, I had always been an afterthought. Nothing had been expected of me. I was a relic. There had been no pressure.

"It's amazing that you pulled it off," Mick said.

I think it was the Ali factor working. A lot of my peers think I'm just about the noise and getting the most press. Plenty of people made that mistake with Ali. But later in his career, Ali was also about getting people to underestimate him.

Float like a butterfly, sting like a bee...

MACCA'S 2006 SEASON

- Ironman 70.3 Pucon, Chile — SECOND
- Villarica Triathlon Chile — FIRST
- Kurnell Triathlon Australia — FIRST
- Ironman Australia — FIRST
- St. Anthony's Triathlon US — THIRD
- Ironman 70.3 St. Croix — THIRD
- Memphis in May Triathlon — FIRST
- Ironman 70.3 UK — FIRST
- Rothsee International Triathlon, Germany — FIRST
- Quelle Challenge Roth Ironman — FIRST
- Wein Triathlon Austria — FIRST
- Ironman 70.3 Gold Coast, Australia — FIRST
- Ironman Hawaii World Championships — SECOND
- Soma Half-Ironman Arizona — FIRST

Season Statistics and Interesting Facts

- Flight miles accumulated: 91,645
- Countries visited: 9
- Days away from home: 202

Training miles for the year

- Swim: 707
- Bike: 17,475
- Run: 3,265

8

Don't Call Me "Fluffy"

I have never been injured in training or competition so badly that I couldn't keep training or finish a race.

Let me repeat that. Since 1996, when I began competing in World Cup events in Europe, all the way to 2011, I have never been injured while training or competing.

When I tell people that, most of them can't believe it. The common assumption—not just among the general public but among triathletes themselves—is that being a triathlete equals getting injured. That's such a wrongheaded attitude that I barely know where to start correcting it. Let me start with this: if you're training and competing as a triathlete, getting injured *is* inevitable . . . but only if you're going about it the wrong way.

Injuries are the bane of a triathlete's existence. The common ones—runner's knee, Achilles tendonitis, and swimmer's shoulder—will interrupt your training schedule and reduce your fitness. Some athletes try to compensate for pain in one area by changing their form in another, resulting in further injury. Injuries can cause you to miss races, blow sponsorship opportunities, and lose prize money. Worst of all, they are a terrible psychological blow. If being successful in this sport is about choosing to persist at that moment when the suffering becomes nearly unbearable, then injuries are what make the will to persist crumble. After a while, it's just not worth the pain and frustration.

I have a reputation as being "fluffy" in my training. When people look at the reasons for my longevity and success, they always tag me with "talented." Well, sure. Natural talent has to come into the conversation, as do great coaching, great support, and some incredible good fortune. But I'm also smart, my system is right, and my way of training is the right way for me. The subtext, however, is that I win with raw talent *in spite of* my fluffy training regimen. It's symbolic of how misguided the triathlon mind-set is that people presume that if you haven't been injured, you haven't been working hard enough.

Performing at your best—not winning—is the goal. *Not* getting injured.

The mind-set of the typical athlete is that you take your body almost to the point of breaking and hold it there for as long as possible, and then you get a result. I don't believe in that. I believe that your energy comes in waves, and that you need to roll with that energy. When your body wants more, give it more. When it wants you to back off, back off. You adjust and treat training as a holistic process.

One of the biggest mistakes many athletes make is to treat their training as something separate from their regular lives. You can't segregate them. Stress is stress, whether it's physical or mental. Cortisol, the major stress hormone, produces real effects on the body. If you're working all day or fighting with your spouse, you're going to feel just as exhausted as if you'd done a 100-mile training ride. These things will weigh on your training and performance. Life adds up, and that fatigue is going to cost you. That's why you have to be more adaptive in your training. If you try to force a tough training regimen into a tiring personal life, you're going to burn out.

Rigidity in training comes from fear. Doing so many miles becomes like a talisman against failure: "If I don't do 400 miles this week, I'm dead on race day." That sort of thing. It's rubbish. I've been labeled fluffy because when people ask for my training "secret," I tell them there's no key session or magical sequence of workouts or something I've cooked up in the Batcave.

The answer is that I rest more and take time to analyze my competitors. But that's not sexy or macho enough, apparently. So they'll scoff and call me fluffy and say things like, "He's lucky that he's talented. It'll catch up with him soon."

An Anti-Rest Culture

A lot of the problems with triathletes' training arise because they don't address flaws in their training when they're younger. When they age, their training is built around that "more is always better" idea, and injuries become inevitable. You have to adapt your training as you age—not just in terms of your repetitions, but your entire approach. That's part of the advantage of experience.

It's not easy to get other athletes to try my way, though, because ours is an anti-rest culture. Heck, Western civilization is mostly anti-rest! The sport has always been fearful of the word *recovery*, as though needing to recover means you're a big wimp who can't take it. If you know anything about fitness or exercise, you know that when you work out, no matter how tough you are, you tear muscle fibers and cause inflammation in joints and connective tissue. Recovery lets those things heal. Without it, you're gonna get hurt, period.

If you are paying a coach to get you ready for a big race, then you are going to make that coach justify the cost of hiring him. So if he says, "Today, you're going to swim five kilometers and do speed training on the track, then tomorrow you're going to rest," you're probably going to lose it. "What? Rest? I'm paying you to tell me to rest?" Too many athletes feel the need to justify themselves by how much they work.

MACCA'S (W)INSIGHTS

"That's the monster that's human nature. We train to look good to other people, to look good to ourselves, to justify the cost of a coach, or as some sort of inoculation against the fear that we won't have what it takes on race day. But we rarely train for the only reason that matters: to be the best we can be in body and mind, and deliver our finest possible performance on race day, regardless of the result."

It's okay to rest. I've said this in speeches and gotten standing ovations. But in the modern world, that's just not a popular idea. Outside of sport, in business, people boast about getting only two hours of sleep and still going into work. They're stressed, they're not sleeping, and they wonder why they feel like hell all the time. It's like the less you sleep, the more hardcore you are. Translate that to the triathlete world and it's "Look at me, I ran twenty kilometers yesterday after riding for six hours."

That's the monster that's human nature. We train to look good to other people, to look good to ourselves, to justify the cost of a coach, or as some sort of inoculation against the fear that we won't have what it takes on race day. But we rarely train for the only reason that matters: to be the best we can be in body and mind, and deliver our finest possible performance on race day, regardless of the result.

Adapting on the Bike

I think many triathletes develop a training routine and then stick with it no matter what because of their egos. They don't want to adapt or use something that another athlete is using, I suppose because it will mean that they depended on someone else for a key part of their performance. Remember, this is a very macho, lone wolf kind of sport. Personally, I think that's a ridiculous attitude. If you want to win, then you send your ego on vacation and you adapt whatever you can find that works for you. That's something that I have never had the slightest trouble doing.

Here's an example of what I'm talking about. When I started racing in America, I had to turn my bike into a weapon, which it had not been before. But I wanted to start making others fear me on the bike, and in doing that, I had a fantastic asset at my disposal: the awesome cyclists I had competed against in my World Cup days. I started hanging out with cyclists. Within Australia, it was professional cyclists like Stuart O'Grady and other guys who rode in the Tour de France. Because I was the world champion in triathlon, I had the status in their eyes to ride with them and learn from them.

I started going to sports events, and if they were there, we hung out and became friends. If I was in Europe, I would look up the European cyclists, who were always so strong and tough. Eventually, I started asking questions. "If you were doing training sessions and there were five sessions you had to do to be better, what would they be?" They would give me ideas and then I'd implement them.

In this way, during the 2000 World Cup season I developed a cycling groove that worked for me. It consisted mostly of strength work, time trials, max effort intervals, and time-trial intervals ten kilometers in duration. There's a phrase, "absolute lactate saturation," that means keeping power when you're exhausted and you've exceeded your body's maximum lactic acid threshold. Those sessions would really hurt, but they were short. I would time-trial for only forty kilometers. I also did a lot of bike races, because the more time I spent hanging out with the bike riders, the more I thought of myself as a bike rider. The energy fed itself.

Because drafting (riding behind other cyclists and letting them deflect the wind resistance, making your ride easier) was legal in short-course ITU World Cup racing, the bike ride was the thing that most pros were neglecting. They'd swim with the front group, the bike ride would be very easy, and then they would run hard. There was definitely a lack of focus on the bike ride, because the more you burn your legs on the bike, the more it takes away from your run speed. So a lot of the World Cup athletes were saying, "Well, I don't want to ride too much because I can draft, and I've got to run quick, so I'll run more in training." I went with the other option. I knew I couldn't run as fast as Simon Whitfield or Paul Amey. If we stood on a starting line fresh, not coming off a bike ride, those guys were quicker than me. I accepted that. Some of the people I talked to about this—including my coaches—told me I shouldn't be thinking like that. But I'm a realist. I needed to think of another way to beat the fast runners.

Part of training smart is putting your ego second to doing what you have to do to win. You have to be honest with yourself. That's the first thing I would drill into any athlete who's looking to take something away from this book. Know your weaknesses and learn how to train to overcome them as best you can. Don't lie to yourself, because when you're in pain and agony, you can't lie.

Because I was willing to change my training philosophy, I won the 2001 Goodwill Games in Brisbane and basically everything else. It did it by riding away from the field in draft-legal races and being very, very aggressive. Nobody else was doing that. I had confidence in myself as an athlete and knew what I was doing.

MACCA'S (W)INSIGHTS

"Part of training smart is putting your ego second to doing what you have to do to win. You have to be honest with yourself. That's the first thing I would drill into any athlete who's looking to take something away from this book. Know your weaknesses and learn how to train to overcome them as best you can."

The Skeleton

I get asked all the time about my typical training week, and my answer is always the same: there is no typical training week. I build on what I call a skeleton, but the specifics are based on how I feel that week. That's why I've gotten the "fluffy" label. Everybody else thinks you set a routine and then gut through it no matter how tired you are or how much you hurt. That's not how I do things. I listen to my body, and that's why I don't get injured.

I have a certain structure I like to follow. On Monday, I'll do strength work on the bike. I tend to work off one key session per day. Think of your skeleton as one key session every day. That's the one thing you've got to do. If, after you do it, you're wiped out, drop the rest of the work you had planned for the day. The rest is fluff.

In 2010, I was looking to develop my bike strength and fix up my swim. I knew that the swim had to be rectified at the beginning of the swim session. I needed to get a good start, be fast enough, and build my lactate tolerance. So I added an extra swim set to the mix on Tuesday, something I never used to have. It was very speed intensive, and I did it first thing in the morning. Normally, early-morning swims are a problem for me. By the time I wake up, the session is nearly done. I turn up at the pool early with everybody else, get in, and just start going through the motions. I'm doing the coach's set, because I've informed my coach that I want speed from this set. I want lactate tolerance work. But by the time I've woken up I'm three kilometers in, and I only have two kilometers to be in the groove. So I started changing my sleep habits and starting focusing on that Tuesday session.

The skeleton works off the assumption that if you were to do just this as your bare minimum, you would survive and finish your race. For any athlete, you establish the skeleton based on how much time you have, what's happening in your life, and what kind of race you're preparing for. Then you build your body around it.

One key to training this way is to attach no guilt to it. You have to let go of the numbers. Stop counting how many miles you did at the end of the week! You have to train yourself to be confident that you are doing enough and stop overtraining as a security blanket.

Another key is establishing a skeleton that's suited to what you're after in your race. Are you looking at finishing? Are you trying to win? If you're an age grouper doing an Ironman, your training goals are going to be very different from mine. You might be hoping to finish in less than fifteen hours; I'm looking to finish first in around eight hours. So a strength set for me will probably be very different than a strength set for you. (Take a look at my skeleton-building foundation below and pattern yours around it with the help of your coach.)

That approach didn't endear me to sports scientists or coaches. According to them, success was all about training according to a hard-and-fast routine. I was the guy in the classroom who hears the lecture, then puts his hand up at the end and says, "That's all bullshit." In a way, I was discrediting their whole field, and to make it worse, I was winning. If a coach isn't writing programs for people, then what's he good for? But I think coaches are more important than ever, provided they can adapt along with their athletes and have a relationship with them that recognizes what's unique about each one.

For example, some coaches have sixty or seventy athletes and send out a generic training program for all of them. In light of what I've just said, that's insane. What works for one athlete might permanently damage another. I'd like to see more athletes question poor race results; you almost never see that. The coach is in the perfect position: he gets credit for the successes but no blame for the failures. The athlete always blames himself. I'd love to see athletes start asking, "Well, Coach, what happened?" Once there's accountability, there will be change.

I think this is a major reason that rest is the most underrated thing in our sport. The perception is that you don't need a coach to rest. If you're a coach, you're paid to develop these elaborate training strategies with just the right arrangement of bricks, time trials, strength work, and the rest. The thing is, a good coach knows when an athlete should rest, how much rest he should get, and what he should do coming out of a rest day. Rest, like every part of our training, is strategic.

What many athletes don't understand is that you don't gain strength on the bike. You don't gain strength lifting weights. You gain strength sitting on the couch watching TV after your workout is done. When you exercise, you damage your muscles. You repair that damage during rest and sleep. That's when the important changes happen. That's why I rest as much as I do. If you want proof that it works, look back at my Drummondville race in 1996. I rested the entire week and destroyed the field. But in the Ironman world, I get called "fluffy" because rest is not macho. I just say, look at my results.

Skeleton Builder

When you're building your training skeleton, start by planning your time. You are doing three sports. You've got to fit in a lot of training. If you're also working a full-time job, time is precious. The difference between a professional and an amateur triathlete is that pros have more time to train and rest.

Write down all the variables and everything that's controllable. Work around your family, your job and anything else you have to do. Then you start with a strategy built around your honesty to yourself. I decide on a given day whether I'm going to work on my strengths or my weaknesses. You make that plan according to your objective, and you have your skeleton. That's your mandatory work, maybe six or seven hours per week if you have a total of fifteen hours available to train. Then have your coach build on your skeleton—adding key sessions and determining the minimum that you can get away with doing.

You also plan test sets. For some people, their test is a race where the results don't matter. It's not about the race; you've predefined what you want from that event. The test might be swimming off the front of the pack or improving your bike split. You're gauging the results for the work that you did by setting targets for the race. It's basically a brick session. You can't let your inner competitor get involved and worry about the outcome.

My basic sixteen-week skeleton foundation program follows on pages 155–164. It can work for any triathlete, but it's geared toward competition at the Ironman distance. A couple of caveats, however:

- This program presumes that you start with a reasonable level of fitness. If you're not already training regularly or haven't exercised in a while, get the approval of a licensed health-care professional before starting this training.
- This is also a program designed for a professional triathlete. If you're an age-group competitor, it might be too intense or too time-consuming for you. If so, ask a qualified coach to help you modify it to suit your needs.

(*Chapter 8 text continues on page 165.*)

Macca's 16-Week
Skeleton Training Program

BLOCK ONE

Here the focus is on getting the body ready for the punishment to come. Workouts are lower intensity and strength oriented. Sets include a lot of strength efforts on the bike, twelve-minute climbs on hills with a 6 or 7 percent gradient, using the big gears with a low cadence, keeping the heart rate relatively low and putting your muscles under load. Run routes are always hilly, too. You want to force your muscles to fire. Keep in mind, you don't win or finish an Ironman in the first four weeks of training, so don't go flat out.

Week 1

Monday

- Up at 5:30. Swim 12 × 400 meters, doing five to six minutes per quarter (400-meter set) with a one-minute recovery between each. The first is a warm-up, and the last is a cooldown. There should be no real rev (heart rate elevation) to the effort, but it should start to get uncomfortable by the seventh or eighth quarter.
- A four-hour ride in hilly terrain with about forty-five minutes of climbing. Do four 12-minute climbs on a hill with a 6–7 percent gradient, using the big gear and low cadence. Spin down the hill to rest the legs and do it again.
- That's your key skeleton set of the day. If you do a recovery run, run with no pressure. If you want to walk, walk.

Tuesday

- Ride in a group with a higher cadence—a flat speed ride. Four hours through hilly terrain.
- A strength-oriented run, about 1:20 with hill repeats. Run to a hill with a 6–7 percent gradient, and do five 1,500-meter runs up the hill with good form and good control. Run just below

your anaerobic threshold. (Determine this by subtracting your age from 220 to get your maximum heart rate and then taking 80 percent of that number.) The key is not to create too much lactate, which causes fatigue and cramping. You should build your aerobic diesel engine. Run with good form: hip stability, strong core, and good biomechanics. You're not trying to get up the hill as fast as you can. Your first effort should be the same as your last. If you're slowing down at the end, you went too fast.

- If you do an end-of-day swim set, make it 3 miles of technique-oriented swimming.

Wednesday

- A 5.5-hour bike ride, hilly terrain but not obscene. You're just clocking miles.
- Jog off the bike for twenty minutes with no expectation on pace. Focus on form: running tall, hips underneath you, focused on your core, especially your transverse abdominals. You want to come off the bike feeling like a runner.

Thursday

- A long run, about 14 miles. You're running out the ride from the day before. Controlled running, undulating terrain but not overly hilly, and *always* on a soft surface. Finish the second half faster than the first. Don't use a power meter or heart rate monitor here, or for the first four weeks. This is about learning to feel when you're doing well.
- After lunch, a relatively harder swim session: 3 miles with a big warm-up. Instead of ten 400-meter sets, try doing twenty 200-meter sets. This is a swim-focused day. Pick up the pace.

Friday

- A three- to four-hour controlled ride at a fairly quick cadence, but with no pressure.
- Rest.

Saturday

- This is a big bike day, but with purpose. You might go five hours, but with an hour at the pace you would do in a race. This will evolve into your race-specific training session, where you test your nutrition and always are always in "aero position": bent over the bars to minimize wind resistance.
- Off the bike, run one hour at race pace.
- In the afternoon, replicate your swim set on Monday. Consider using swim paddles, which add resistance, keep your heart rate down, and increase strength.

Sunday

- A long early morning run, at least 18 miles, which you will build up to 22 miles. As always, soft surface and undulating terrain. Try to vary the terrain so you're using different muscle groups.
- Do an open-water swim on Sunday, if you can. If you're prepping for a race where you'll wear a wet suit, wear one. If the race is non-wet-suit, don't wear one. Swim only as long as you feel good.
- At least seven hours after your morning run, do running drills on an oval track. This is technique running. Run a mile around the oval with soft acceleration, activating your core and keeping your hips underneath your body. Work on sound running biomechanics.

Week 2

- Repeat the same workout schedule as Week 1, but move the Friday bike session to Thursday and take Friday off.
- Add 10 percent to your volume (10 percent more distance or time) to your key skeleton sessions, such as the hill work on the run and the race-pace part of the bike ride. For example, if you did forty-five minutes of hill riding on Monday in Week 1, do fifty minutes on Monday in Week 2.

Week 3

- Repeat Week 1 and add 10 percent volume across the board.

Week 4

- This is recovery week. Repeat Week 1 but reduce your volume 5 percent off the Week 1 volume.
- Take Friday off.
- The key is recovery. If you feel tired or flat, reduce your Week 1 volume by 10 percent. Listen to your body and don't be rigid. Do three hills instead of five. Ride for three and a half hours instead of five.

BLOCK TWO

This is training camp month. I'll fly out on the Thursday of Week 4 to get ready for training camp. Now, issues have started to surface and you can address them. You're aware of what needs to be worked on.

For each week of training camp, you repeat the same schedule and volume that you did in Week 3. But now there's more of a strength component, and you're pushing yourself. There's a performance expectation in your work now. It's starting to hurt.

Week 5

- Repeat Week 3.

Week 6

- Repeat Week 3 but add 10 percent volume.

Week 7

- Repeat Week 3 but add 15 percent volume (5 percent more than Week 6).

Now you're working to hit targets. You're timing your results. If you're doing your hill work, your coach might say, "I want you to ride up each of these hills in 5:40." It's about consistent effort that feels like work. If you're tired, then you might cut the overall length of a bike ride from three hours to two, but still do forty-five minutes of hill work.

Week 8

- Recovery week. Cut back to the same volume and schedule as Week 1, but no more strength work. Now it's about building speed. Instead of hills, you're riding four 10-minute sets on a flat road, accelerating and using your pace as your guide. In the run, do four 60-meter acceleration sprints.
- This is where you must start to adjust as you get older. You're building up some serious volume. You have to back off. It's okay to say "I'm dead tired. I'm going to take tomorrow off" with no guilt.
- Don't be afraid that you're going to blow up. That's the purpose of camp: to bury yourself. You should have an underlying rhythm to your training now and be in touch with your body. If you got no sleep or ate crap food the day before, cut your workout back this week. If you did a hill in six minutes last week and today you did it in 6:20, recognize that that's fatigue and know to back off.

BLOCK THREE

During this block, I usually go back home. It's nice to have a change of scenery.

The focus now is totally on pace. You'll do specific sets that are oriented toward the pace you'll do in a race. You will usually feel relatively slow in this block, because you need to find your pace and rhythm. Think of it as spending eight weeks hitting the heavy bag in boxing, and now you're hitting the speed bag.

In this block, you'll do two 2-week cycles. In your swims, you should be getting closer to the anaerobic pace you will swim in the race.

Week 9

Repeat Week 7 but with the following variations:

Monday

- A four- to five-hour ride, accelerating on the hills. This is a speed and tempo ride where you go the same speed on flats and the hills. You want to spike your heart rate.
- Swim and run like Monday of Week 7.

Tuesday

- Same as Tuesday of Week 7, but the bike hill session becomes a set, structured running track session. It's a descending session: 8 × 2k or 10 × 1 mile. Try to complete the first two in eight minutes, then the next two in 7:30, then 7:00, then 6:30, and so on. You're to get a feel for even tempo running. It's boring but worthwhile. Have your coach give you a time after each lap, so you can see whether or not you are maintaining consistent effort.
- The easy-spin ride becomes a ride with groups in town where you can swap a few turns on the front, sit in a bunch, and get the feel.

Wednesday

- Seven-hour ride. Try to come home over the last one to two hours at a race pace, with a negative split.
- Same easy run off the bike.

Thursday

- Same long run, one and a half to two hours, but with a negative split.

Friday

- Same long ride as Week 7.

Saturday

- This is a huge day: you'll do test sets.
- Time-trial bike ride at close to race distance. You might do 120k (72 miles) at race pace. Take nutrition, do it on a circuit

(maybe a 12-mile loop), so you can have someone clock you to see if you're slowing down. Your goal should be to get to race pace and stay there. This session hurts.

- Get off the bike like it's a transition, have your shoes laid out, and run forty-five to fifty minutes at quicker than Ironman race pace.
- Two miles of swimming, 100-meter sets, trying to stay below your anaerobic threshold.

Sunday

- Do a 2:15 to 2:30 run. Run at a steady state and focus on nutrition. You should have expectations now. You want to feel good.
- Open-water swim of about race length. For instance, at home I have a 2.5-mile open-water loop course I swim for Ironman. Start to push it and keep time. If you're tired, back off. If you're feeling good, push harder.
- Afternoon: A thirty-five- to forty-minute run on soft, flat ground. This run should have an upbeat tempo to it—maybe a half-Ironman race pace.

Week 10

Replicate Week 9 with two changes:

- Move Friday's ride to Thursday and take Friday off.
- On Saturday, reduce the distance on the bike to maybe 50 miles but with greater intensity.

Week 11

Replicate Week 10, but make Saturday's bike ride like the Week 9 time trial.

Week 12

Replicate Week 10 with no changes.

After your test set, be prepared for the whole program to change. After a first test set, I have changed my entire plan based on the results. If your swim is there, then just train to maintain it. You need to have that adaptability in your training program. Make your adjustments, do your next week, and then have another test set. Adjust again, and then test again.

BLOCK FOUR: TAPER

Your body will get used to your routine after a while. When you're doing an endurance routine, your body tends to hide a lot of its fatigue sometimes, and you tolerate it. Then when you begin a taper, your body sometimes says to itself, "Oh, thank God that's over," and it starts to shut down. You'll probably feel absolutely horrible when you begin to taper. So I have an easy, one-week taper during which I expect to feel horrible. Then I build up the body again with the big week, which makes me feel good again. This way, I avoid homeostasis and keep getting results.

The key to tapering is sleep. Rest, rest, rest. Don't squeeze in one more session. The hard work is done. Rest and reward yourself. Remember, no guilt. You're saying, "Thank you body, for cooperating."

Week 13

This is a replica of Week 1, but drop your volume and intensity by 25 percent. It's a whole week of pressure-free training. The only thing you can do at this point with more intense training is get hurt. But you still need to keep the engine revving. You need to stimulate your energy systems and muscles. If you're tired, do less.

Week 14

Replicate Week 12. This is the week you rev your body back up to keep everything tuned. Set time goals. Push.

Taper Week #1 — Week 15

Monday

- Off day.

Tuesday

- Overall, cut 40 to 50 percent off your Week 14 volume and intensity on this day. If you rode at race pace in Week 14, ride at half race pace.
- Swim about 4 kilometers (2.4 miles) in 200-meter sets. There's no need to force it anymore. There should still be some speed to the set, but you're not hurting. There's no need to keep testing yourself. Some athletes say, "I've got to make sure it's still there." If you've done the work, it's there.
- A two- to three-hour bike ride with a group, focusing on cadence but keeping a solid pace. If you don't feel good, cut the ride short.
- An easy run off the bike for maybe twenty minutes.

Wednesday

- Repeat Tuesday, still cutting 40 to 50 percent off your volume and intensity.

Thursday

- Repeat Tuesday, still cutting 40 to 50 percent off your volume and intensity.

Friday

- Complete day of rest.

Saturday

- Short, sharp, fast day.
- Fast thirty-minute swim, like a sprint.
- One-hour ride with about four 1-mile efforts in the big gear, going for speed and revving your heart rate.
- Thirty-minute run with some sprints.

Sunday: Test Racing

I like to do a test race at the end of my first taper week, exactly one week before the race I'm about to do—maybe a sprint event or an Olympic distance event. It's something to spark the system.

In the morning, wake up as if it's race morning. Eat your race breakfast and follow your race routines that you've set. This is what you're going to implement the following weekend, so you want to make sure you've got it down.

In your test race, swim and bike as hard as you can if it's a sprint distance. In the run, maybe run hard for the first three or four kilometers and then back off. Then it's home and complete rest. You're done.

Taper Week #2—Week 16

Monday, do nothing. On Tuesday, do a longer bike effort, 3–3.5 hours. Otherwise, follow the same routine as the week before, taking about 15 percent off the volume and intensity. For example, if you rode for two hours on the previous Wednesday, ride about ninety minutes. In the swim, nothing should be too hard. Focus more on intensity, but also give yourself a long, floating warm-down to flush out your system. You should feel good during this week.

(*Chapter 8 text continues on page 165.*)

The Last Prep

Now I start to bomb two nutritional products: a colostrum-based product called Biestmilch, which supports immunity, and Coenzyme Q10. That's for cellular energy and heart health. I take 800 milligrams a day—about four times the typical dose. That's my tapered heart rest. The heart's a muscle, too, so you have to give it a break. Coenzyme Q10 is like my reward to my heart: "You've got to give me a big effort, so here's some fuel." It always makes me feel amazing. It might just be a placebo effect, but I don't care. If I don't take it, I don't race well. If I run out, I'll freak out and make my wife run around to find more.

If you're doing a race in hot conditions, spend your last few days being attentive to hydration. Don't flush; don't just drink water. People wonder why they cramp in a race and I tell them, it's because you flushed out all your sodium and potassium, mate. But steer clear of Gatorade, which is mostly sugar. Mix your own electrolyte drinks. Be attentive to drinking, but don't force it all day, every day. I'll get more into this in the next chapter, but deep muscular hydration takes about a week. Use your taper to top up and really bring your stores up.

On the Friday I'll take the day off. I'll rest, stay out of the sun and eat. Friday tends to be the day when you're organizing things and the apprehension comes. You should be thinking about your strategy. Have a checklist and go through it. Make sure you get everything done. Check your gear.

Saturday, I do the same set I did the Saturday before. But I'll do it in sets of four: four sprints in a swim, four sprints on the bike, four sprints on the run, to spark my anaerobic system. This goes again to being willing to borrow good ideas from other sports. I had an interesting conversation with Joachim Cruz, who was the 800-meter sprint champion from the 1984 Olympics, a phenomenal runner. I asked him what he did as his warm up prior to an 800. He said he did things in fours. I asked why; I'm always asking why.

He said, "Well your body tends to work nicely with threes and fours. The first effort you do, your body will go, 'What the hell was that?' so that one's wasted. The second effort you do, your body's like, 'All right, we're running hard, are we?' Your system's now awake. Your third one you can live with, and your fourth one you deliver. Then you back it off."

That made sense to me, and it's always stuck with me. I thought, *I'll take that and apply it to swimming. If it's good enough for Joachim Cruz, it's good enough for me.* I have used that approach since then and been very successful with it.

On the morning before the race, I'll do an easy swim set—throw the arms out for a quarter mile, nice, long strokes. I might do some backstroke, maybe four 50-meter efforts with full recovery. Then boom, up to race pace. When I feel worn down, I get out. On the bike, I'll ride for thirty minutes with maybe four 45-second big-gear, race-pace efforts. Finally, I do a twenty-minute run. I'll do four 100-meter run-throughs where I'm feeling good, always in the shoes I'm going to race in. Then I slide them into the bag and go to bed.

Remember, at this point you're not trying to get any fitter. It's about feel.

What does an athlete say when a reporter asks, "How did you know you were doing well?" He says, "I felt good." You're trying to find the feeling of being at your peak.

Race Day

Sunday, race day. When you show up, you want to be fully in the mind game. You know your body is prepared, but you should also be fully in the head game. What are you observing? What do the other athletes look like? Me, I have an alter ego on race day. Outside I'm smiling. But inside, I'm looking for fear and apprehension. You don't want to play poker with me on race day, because I'm looking for your tell—that something that tells me you don't think you have it today.

I'll walk past some of my competitors and say good morning. I'm not boisterous and loud. For example, in Kona last year, I had all the press around me. I walked down to Timo Bracht and said, "Mate, can I borrow your pump?" He said, "Sorry, it's not my pump." No big deal. I didn't need his pump, but I wanted him to think I was chilled out and relaxed.

You see a lot of guys with their iPods on, and to me that says, "I'm hiding, I'm scared." I never wear an iPod in public, and I never put one on in the transition area. I never, ever, want the other guys to think I need to resort to music to hide or pump myself up. The mental game has a million little moving pieces.

I watch how guys move. I look at faces. Some guys are nervous. But I always want to look like I've been there a million times before. So I show my face—"All right guys, I'm here"—and then I disappear. I find an area and go to it with my crew. Then the iPod goes on. I warm up, always in private. I talk to myself a lot. I'm preparing to meet the pain.

You should be telling yourself, *This is good, I'm ready.* If you haven't raced a lot, some nerves are fine. Hell, if you didn't have nerves before your first Ironman you'd be a robot! But having your head on straight is critical on race day. It's easy to say, "The race is this day." But when it's sixteen weeks away, you don't get yourself mentally ready for the pain, don't know your goals, and don't have a strategy in mind. It can be daunting if you haven't prepared for that morning in your head.

When I was younger, I didn't want to be there. I felt sick. I used to come away from those races and go, *What is wrong with you? Two weeks ago, you were excited. You couldn't wait to race. You were running really well.* But on race morning, I would be panicked, saying *I don't want to be here, I can't do this sport anymore. I don't want to do this sport because of this.*

You've done all this training and in theory, that's great. But now theory is done and you have to perform—and what if all the work turns out to be wasted? That's why I say it's important to love the process of being a triathlete, not just the results. There's a fine line between excitement and apprehension. I listen to my wife's iPod sometimes while I'm warming up, trying to calm my mind and make it silent.

I don't let anyone see me until just before the start. Then I get in the water and start looking relaxed again. I start swimming, goggles on. I'll greet everybody. I'll look for marquee guys. I'll wave to Andreas: "Have a good one, mate. All the best." I do sprints in the water, and I want to be seen in it. It's all about perception, looking like you don't have a worry in the world. That is the most nerve-racking time, five minutes before the race starts. There's no escaping now. The ones who wanted to run and hide have had to put their wits on. I want them and everyone else to see me and wonder why I'm so relaxed. "What does he know that I don't?" Then the gun goes off. Showtime.

Training and Age

My basic skeleton strategy can work for any triathlete at any level— but there's a "but." As you get older, you can't recover like you did when you were younger. Full recovery is the key to preventing injury as you age, period. You have to listen to your body. You have to put your ego on the shelf and stop trying to do what you did when you were twenty-five.

Age is going to prove that I'm right when it comes to being fluffy and holistic with your training. That's because when you're forty-five, training cannot be about the numbers. If you're looking at kilometers per week, age is going to *retire* you! There are just certain workloads that the body cannot handle as it ages.

That's okay. First of all, you have to ask yourself what your goal is. Do you want to impress yourself with your training miles? Or do you want to finish on race day? Do you want to set a personal record or even win your age group?

MACCA'S (W)INSIGHTS

"As you get older, you can't recover like you did when you were younger. Full recovery is the key to preventing injury as you age, period. You have to listen to your body. You have to put your ego on the shelf and stop trying to do what you did when you were twenty-five."

Once you know that, you train smarter. You do all the strength work you did when you were younger, but spread out over a longer time. I used to do a twelve-week block. Now I do sixteen with the same amount of work. That gives you more blocks in the middle.

With Kona, my team basically added a week per year to my prep for the past few years. We started at twelve weeks, then added a week, and now it's sixteen or seventeen weeks. That's accepting and planning for the challenges of age. If I had a hiccup with injury, I had time to heal and get back to training. That also gave me some room to miss a few training days because of fatigue. If I was exhausted on a training day, I would be able to listen to my body, take that day off, and still be able to build my training block.

Now that I'm an old man, preparation is the biggest change. I have to anticipate and prepare more because I need more time to recover. I can still do exactly the same things in training and in a race; my top-end speed has gone dormant because I'm running Ironmans and not sprint races anymore. I'm not doing sprint-specific workouts.

Reduce the volume of high-intensity work as you age. If you do some intense work, give yourself an extra day of recovery that you might not have taken years before. That takes confidence and self-knowledge, but those should come with age, too. Getting older has its rewards.

9

Coke, the World's Best Sports Drink

We're athletes. We're not integers in a formula.

I learned that lesson the hard way when I went to the best sports scientists in Australia trying to figure out how I might keep from cramping in the lava fields at Kona. Cramps had done me in at my debut in 2002, and in 2003 and 2004. Even in 2005, when I had run the fastest marathon, I'd cramped terribly until I started drinking Coke. Yet the sports scientists didn't seem to have any answers. I found the answer I needed the way I always seem to: by going around the typical information sources for my sport to a different source: another athlete.

Let's take a step back. In Ironman, the usual formula is that you should consume so many calories per hour you're racing. My magic number, based on my body size, my weight, my perspiration rate, and other factors, was 400, according to the sports nutrition specialists and their PhDs. And when I first moved to the Ironman distance, I listened. I didn't know any better. When I was doing Olympic distance races, which last only two hours, I didn't know anything about nutrition. I had an energy gel and took it. When I went to the half-Ironman at Wildflower in 2001, I thought, *This is twice the*

(27) The common rule of thumb in triathlon is that you can't win the race in the water but you can certainly lose it. In 2009 a poor swim cost me the title in Kona.

(28) My second Ironman Australia win in 2003. After failing in Kona in 2002, it was sweet to come back home to Australia and win again.

(29) Ironman European Championship, Frankfurt. The bike ride has become a weapon for me in Ironman racing. The weather conditions of Europe allow me to exploit this and get very aggressive on the bike. This is the European style of racing, on the cobblestones.

(30) Ironman Hawaii 2006. I had never been in so much pain in my life. This photo was taken three miles from the finish. I was 90 seconds behind Normann Stadler at this point, after reducing the gap from 10 minutes. My mindset was: "Run as hard as you can until you black out. Forget the pain."

(31) I lost this race by 71 seconds, and was lucky to cross the finish line. I could hardly stand up at the end of this event and was absolutely destroyed. New champion Normann Stadler met me at the finish line.

(32) I attack on the bike coming back into the crosswinds toward the halfway point of Ironman Hawaii. This set up the entire 2010 race and took the pure runners out of the game.

(33) After my war with the Germans Normann Stadler and Faris Al Sultan, I flew into Frankfurt and took them on at their own race. The course record was 8:10, so a time under 8 hours was seen as impossible. I went on to win the event in 7:59:55, a new course record and a new Ironman European championship.

(34) At the Ironman European Championships, I am in agony postrace as my body starts to punish me for what I forced it to do. All Ironman races end this way, whether you win or lose. These are the photos that never make the magazine covers, but as an athlete you never forget this pain.

(35) With the fastest marathon of the day, on one of the toughest years in Kona, I was able to cross the line in 6th place in 2005. Finally a result in the world's toughest event, after the failings of the three years prior.

(36) The multi-lap spectator-friendly triathlons, brought about by the ITU, have changed the sport. Two lap swims and multi-lapped bike rides make the racing dynamic and fast. Here I am in Sydney, starting the second lap of the swim course after exiting the water

(38) Longtime rival Craig Alexander finished second to me in the 2007 Ironman World Championships.

(37) Attacking the bike rides in Europe is the key to success. For bigger athletes like myself, it's always smart to attack on the cobbled sections of the road. Here I am doing just that at Ironman Europe, in the section of the course known as "The Hell."

(39) The 2010 Ironman came down to a final match race against Andreas Raelert. Never in the history of the event has the winner been decided so close to home. This photo was taken with two miles of running to go.

(40) When I knew I had won my first Ironman world title, after all the buildup and all the pressure, the emotions flooded in. I looked to the sky and thanked the two people in my life who shone down on me that day: my mum and Sean Maroney. They sat on my shoulder all day and willed me to victory with the fastest marathon recorded on the new course.

(41) Mick, Scott, and I had the opportunity to hang out with boxing legend Shane Mosley in Las Vegas for one of the super fights. We have a close affinity with the sport.

(42) After five years of trying and a complete reinvention of the way I attacked this race, on October 13, 2007, I was crowned the Hawaii Ironman World Champion. The fulfillment of a lifelong dream.

(43) View from behind the finish line at the 2010 Ironman World Championships.

(44) Winning my second Ironman Hawaii title was better than the first. I did it my way.

(45) After crossing the line in Kona, I was told by the powers that be that the breakfast cereal giant Wheaties viewed my performance worthy of an appearance on their iconic box. Here my daughter Tahlia and I meet with the company postrace.

(46) There's no greater joy than being greeted at the finish line by the people who matter most in your life on the biggest day in your life. Here is my wife, Emma, my youngest daughter, Sienna, and me less than 60 seconds after crossing the line. My eldest daughter, Tahlia, is actually holding on to my leg, but she's not in the shot.

distance—I'll take two gels. When I went to a full Ironman, I figured I could just take four. I'd pack a couple for spares and that would be that. That was as much thought as I ever gave nutrition.

Then came my meltdown in 2002. People were stunned. "You didn't focus on nutrition?" they said. But when you don't have any nutritional strategy and you're taking six of something, you think that's heaps. People expected me to know this stuff, because I was such a dominant athlete at short course. My naïveté was shocking to them. Then my failings in Kona made me realize that I needed to access people who would give me the eating plan I needed.

Keeping the Tank Topped Off

There's about fifty minutes of stored glycogen energy in your muscles. So you need to add fuel beyond that. Usually, in an Olympic distance race of two hours (an hour and forty-five for the elites) you don't need anything. You drink a bit of carbohydrate/electrolyte mix on the bike and that's all, because by the time you hit the wall and you're falling apart, you're almost home. Nutrition is the least of your worries. If anything, you're looking for a *zap* from a caffeinated sports drink or something with sugar.

You're getting 100 calories out of your electrolyte drink and you're covering what you sweat out. You might get 100 calories in a gel, but you should always take a double-caffeinated gel, because you want that stimulant effect in a power race. But at the halfway point, the game starts to change. You're going to run out of fuel. So you need to take fuel on. As I've learned over time, your body is not like a car, where you can run it empty and then fill it up toward the end. You have to keep it topped up and let it run out at the finish line—or not let it run out at all.

The longer the race, the harder it is to fight your way home when you're running out of fuel. You can make nutritional errors in a half-Ironman and survive. If your stores run out, you can get to the aid station, get some Coke, and because you're only five kilometers from home, you can get there.

But in a full Ironman, you have no chance of winning or even finishing if you make a nutritional error. The professionals are out there for eight hours. Some of the age groupers are out there for seventeen hours. Try not eating for seventeen hours in your daily life, sitting at a desk, and see how hungry you get. When you add exercise to the equation, your body is going to run out of everything.

So in Ironman, it's all about keeping the hydration and calorie stores as high as possible, for as long as possible. Basically, that means carbohydrates. You still need to take in small amounts of protein, which a lot of the sports drinks now have. The predominant fuel source for us, early in a race, is fat. But the quickest fuel source is carbs. Your body wants a blend of simple and complex carbs.

A Race Ain't a Lab

The key to Ironman racing is teaching your body that fat burns. You do that by training your body so you can remain below your aerobic threshold, or AT, where you burn the most fat. Fat is a wonderful source of energy, and you need to burn it during such a long race. Everyone will say, "Yes, of course, we know that." That's all well and good in the perfectly controlled environment of a lab, but an Ironman isn't a lab.

Out there, during a race, you don't have any control over what your body is going to choose to burn. You can try to keep your heart rate below your AT, but when you put it under stress it's ultimately going to grab for the quickest, easiest fuel source. That is carbohydrates, the glycogen stored in your muscles.

So even if you are fat burning, you're still sucking glycogen out of your body. So you need to keep those stores topped off, because you can't take fat on when you're racing (imagine an athlete on his bike eating a bowl of guacamole or swigging from a bottle of olive oil). Fat takes too long to digest, and there's no blood in your stomach to digest it. You need blood to digest food and transport nutrients around your body. Your muscles are demanding blood to supply them with oxygen, and your body takes the blood from your digestive tract and shunts it to your quads, calves, and so on. This limits your ability to digest anything complex, which is why you see people throwing up.

Simple carbs are the only choice in this situation, but most of the carbohydrate products are maltodextrin based. That's a simple sugar, but it's a complex simple sugar, if that makes any sense. Remember, to pass across the blood barrier and be used by the cells, all carbohydrates must be broken down to glucose, their simplest form.

Now, if you break down maltodextrin, instead of getting one glucose molecule you might get five. Bonus. But the process takes longer, and meanwhile your muscles are screaming for energy. So what I do is take the maltodextrin when my heart rate is at its lowest, because my body can spend more energy breaking down and storing that energy to keep those glycogen stores up. But as my heart rate climbs and the race progresses, I simplify the sugar and get as close to glucose as possible. That's Coke, as Thomas Hellriegel taught me one hot day in Kona.

You should have seen the faces on the sports scientists when I told them I drank Coke. They were horrified. "Coke is the worst," they insisted. "The sugar is too simple, too refined." But you can learn only so much in a lab. I've listened to the athletes, and one of the most common complaints I hear is, "I have stomach problems." People have stomach issues with maltodextrin. You won't have them early in a race, because there is still plenty of blood flow to your stomach. But later in the race, as your heart rate starts to climb, the blood starts going out of your stomach. After a while, you can no longer break down those more complex sugar molecules, so not only do you have stomach problems, but you're running out of energy. Welcome to cramps, fatigue, and bonking (running out of glycogen energy) on the run. Game over.

So after my series of fiascos in Kona, I went into the lab and got exact numbers for my body. Remember, the scientists had told me all along that I could never win Kona because I was too big and perspired too much; I would never be able to keep myself hydrated in that Hawaiian heat and humidity. But I kept looking for a solution, and they gave me a formula. I was to consume 400 calories, 1.25 liters of fluid, and 800 milligrams of sodium each hour to cover my sweat loss. To keep from losing more fluid than I could take in, I needed to keep my heart rate under 152 for as long as possible in humid conditions.

I went to Kona in 2005 armed with the perfect formula. My secret weapon was a really smart guy in a white lab coat. He'd tested me, prodded me, and given me the Holy Grail. Physically, I believed I was better than everyone. So I thought, *Now that I've got this nutrition thing licked, you're all dead.*

How did that work out for me? That was the race, if you recall, where Thomas found me throwing up and vowing to retire. So much for the guys in the lab coats.

My Magic Formula

After Thomas got me to start drinking Coke and water, I ran away from the field to my best finish in Kona up to that time. I went back to Australia with my head spinning. I was an idiot! I had been forcing in food because I had this piece of paper telling me that's what I was supposed to do. When I stopped giving my stomach maltodextrin that it couldn't digest and starting drinking Coke and water, it was night and day. There was something to be learned from that.

I said good-bye to the lab. I sat down with Mick and my crew and said, "Okay, what did we take from this? What did we learn?" What we decided was that as the heat picked up and my heart rate climbed, I would take in less fuel as the race went on. So I start at 500 calories per hour, and then go down. At the same time I simplify the sugars, so as the blood leaves my stomach, I'm giving my body very simple sugars to break down—sugar that turns almost instantly to glucose and gives me the energy I need.

What I had forgotten in my haste to come up with a nutritional strategy is what worked so well for me in my training: *adaptation.* I had been rigid—400 calories per hour, from start to finish line. Ridiculous. People like rigid programs for the same reason they like overtraining: they don't have to think, and it gives them something to pin their hopes on. *If I take in X calories, I'll finish in under eleven hours.*

So next season we started testing. The night before a race, I'll wake up at 2:00 a.m. and have an Ensure Plus. I'd drink another Ensure Plus the morning of a race as a breakfast supplement. That lets me take in more calories three hours before the race to really top up the stores. Then, because I'm going to feel a little bit lethargic with those extra calories, I'll take some caffeine. Not a big dose— maybe a cup of coffee to spark up my system for the swim, but it gives me that feeling of alertness. Now, there are all these unwritten rules about caffeine in triathlon and endurance racing: don't touch it until the run, it's a diuretic and it dehydrates you, you've got nowhere to go once you start caffeine, and so on.

Those rules are a crock. Who made them up? I started drinking a coffee before races to the absolute horror of the guys watching around me. They would say, "Where are you going to go from here?" I'd think, *Right past you, mate.* Maybe one day I'll develop my own prerace coffee drink and call it Café Macca.

Anyway, the caffeine would give me the early spark, and in my bottle I would have the calorie-dense Ensure Plus. Now, when you take something like that in a race, you're going to feel shitty for a while, but it's your foundation. Even if you feel like garbage and don't want to eat, you've got the calories in you. When your heart rate is at its lowest, you want to get those calories in your body and across the stomach wall. I trained a lot on that, and it worked for me.

MACCA'S (W)INSIGHT

Rule of thumb: your carbohydrate mixture should get simpler as the race progresses. On the run, you should consume carbohydrates that are in the simplest form, as close to glucose as possible. When you're on the bike, consume denser, higher-calorie maltodextrin-based foods, as your heart rate is lower. You may feel bloated, but you can digest this food easier at lower heart rates and while you're riding. On the run, it becomes harder to digest food. Bring caffeine into the mix as the race progresses. Practice this in training.

I'll take that within the first two hours of the bike stage. In those first three hours, I'm taking in nearly 550 calories an hour just drinking out of a bottle. Ensure Plus is maltodextrin based; it's got a bit of protein in there, all the minerals, sodium—everything. Beyond that, I slowly sip my electrolytes and I keep my hydration at 1.25 liters per hour. I make my own electrolyte drink and take my own salt tablets, because I don't like the sports drinks that are offered at the aid stations. There's a lot of sugar in those drinks, and I want control over what I'm taking in. Plus, who knows what could fly into those vats and die?

After three hours of this, I feel bloated and very full, but not lethargic. Slowly, that feeling starts to subside, and from that point on I'm on a maltodextrin-based gel. I use the Clif Shot because I worked with them to develop a gel that meets the demands of a triathlete. It's a little more electrolyte in a maltodextrin-based shot. Perfect. Now my focus goes from electrolytes to hydration. I might take in 300 calories an hour, consuming three gels an hour from seventy kilometers to the end of the bike. If I feel terrible, I go to Coke.

Your body will tell you what it needs. Let me write that again: *Your body will tell you what it needs.* The danger of an ironclad plan is that you can't plan for what your body is going to tell you during an

Ironman. In a race, I don't want to hang around and wait to feel good. I want to feel good *now*. That means I drink Coke. If you're apprehensive about Coke, take a twenty-five-milligram caffeinated gel. Caffeine is good at cutting through the mental haze and making you feel better.

By the time I get to the run, I'm doing one to two gels an hour. That's for me; if you're an age grouper and you're going to be running for six or seven hours, you'll need a much higher calorie intake. Listen to your body; I can't say it enough.

On the run, you need a quick boost. That's where Coke is great. The high comes quicker, but so does the low. The sugar is simpler, so the hit is not as long lasting. So you need to consume more and more and more. Something else to keep in mind that they can't measure in the lab: by the time you get to the run, your mind-set is reward. Instant gratification. *I want to feel good.* Your body wants you to thank it so it will get you through to the end.

Whether you're planning for a marathon or an Ironman, you need a nutritional plan for an endurance run. It might be, "At every aid station, if I need to walk, I walk." That is productive walking. The focus for me in the running is electrolytes, caffeine, and carbohydrates so I don't cramp. With all that, Coke is the perfect sports drink.

I found Red Bull in Germany. I was racing and calling out "Coke, Coke!" at an aid station, but there was no Coke. I was freaking. There was a big Red Bull tent nearby, and I was desperate, so I popped one and drank it and said, "God, this tastes like shit."

But honestly, within three minutes, that stuff did give me wings. I felt great. So now I have Red Bull in my special-needs bag instead of Coke. It's perfect for a big shot of sugar and caffeine, and the amino acid taurine is good for the heart.

For most readers, the issue isn't going to be winning. It's going to be finishing. If that's you, you need to be 100 percent flexible in your nutrition. I see people all the time who say, "I threw up," or "I was throwing up and had to recapture what I lost." First of all, throwing up is a proud tradition at Ironman races. Second, let me ask you this: If you went to a buffet with your spouse and kids and your kids started stuffing food down their throats, what would you say to them? "Slow down, you'll be sick." If they started throwing up, would you say to them, "Have some more"?

That doesn't change because you're moving. When you vomit, your body is saying, "Enough." Your body can't talk to you, but it can send you clear signals, and being on your knees and retching your guts out by the side of the road is a pretty clear signal: "Back off for a few minutes."

That's why you need flexibility. No coach—no person—can tell you how your body is going to react in a race. They can only give you a guideline. You need to be armed with that information—a basic understanding of how your nutrition works, what your basic nutrition plans are, and what to do if certain things happen. Trust your body and trust your judgment.

Can We Put Chocolate in the Special-Needs Bag?

For the record, I'm not a monk or a vegan when it comes to my diet. I eat a very balanced diet, but I work off a 90-10 principle. That means 90 percent virtuous eating, 10 percent bad stuff. After all, I live in a world with two little girls who want sweet things. I travel all the time, and you know how hard it is to find healthy food in an airport.

I think the most important thing for a triathlete in day-to-day nutrition is being conscious of what you eat. If I have a couple of burgers one day, the next day I'll catch myself and have a nice, lean steak and a big salad. One of the keys to success is preparing your own food. I eat at home with my family every night when I'm not on the road. When you go out, you have no control over the fat, sugar, and sodium that ends up in your food. When you shop and cook, you know exactly what goes into what you're putting in your body.

I try to keep things interesting. I love spicy foods. I live on chilies.

Thai food, Mexican food, Indian food with hot curries—the spicier the better. I'll even grind up chilies, add olive oil and salt, and put them on bread as a spread. They're full of antioxidants and fabulous for the metabolism. They're also a wonderful antiseptic for the body.

I love healthy fast foods. I eat a lot of Asian wok food with olive oil. The wok is the main tool in our kitchen; we use it for everything. You can cook fast and healthy in it and use very little oil. I hear people complain how hard it is to eat healthy, but I disagree—I think it's much harder to eat badly! To eat healthy, just find fresh, whole foods and don't do very much to them. Add spices, combine flavors, and train yourself to love the taste of real food instead of processed flavorings and tons of fat.

This is definitely not about depriving yourself. You're already asking so much of your body, punishing it with workouts and races, that it's important to spoil it with great food and, occasionally, with treats. If you feel deprived, you're not going to stick to it. Personally, I have an addiction to chocolate. But only the good stuff, like Cadbury. I don't have a palate for sweet stuff in the mornings, like pancakes. That's when I need my protein.

MACCA'S (W)INSIGHTS

Dietary dos and don'ts

There aren't many hard-and-fast rules about your daily diet as a triathlete. But there are some general guidelines that are wise to follow if you want your body to perform at its best and resist injury:

- Eat plenty of fresh fruits and vegetables for antioxidants, which help prevent cellular damage during and after training, and also help prevent inflammation.

- Eat plenty of healthy fats such as those found in almonds, avocados, and olive oil. These also help reduce tissue inflammation.

- Consume plenty of lean protein—fish, poultry, lean beef, tofu. Your body needs protein in order to repair muscles damaged during strenuous workouts.

- Eat complex carbohydrates to give you energy during workouts. These include whole grain breads, brown rice, dry beans, and lentils.

- Avoid empty calories by avoiding anything "white": white sugar, white potatoes, white flour, white rice.

- Treat yourself to something bad once in a while. You're working hard and there's no need to live like a monk.

The general idea is to give your body what it needs to get lean, repair damage, and use food energy as efficiently as possible.

At the end of a day of training, I might say to Emma-Jane, "Should we get a chocolate, darling?" So we go down to the shop and get a chocolate. That's my reward. Too bad I can't ever see triathlon having an official chocolate sponsor. "Ironman, brought to you by Cadbury," probably wouldn't be well received.

How Bodybuilders Helped Me Win Kona

My other major issue with Kona has always been hydration. That's why the sports scientists and everybody else said I was "too big to win"—I couldn't hydrate enough to keep from cramping and burning up in the marathon. They told me I should go back to short course. And for years, they were right.

Well, after years of cramping and dying in Hawaii, I was fed up. After winning in 2007, I was seeing the race changing, and I knew my cramping problem was the only thing holding me back. But I didn't see a solution. I talked to Mick, who, as I've said, is borderline obsessed with his body and how to maximize both its health and appearance. He told me about his friends in bodybuilding: "These guys know everything about muscle health, including hydration." I was doubtful. "What the hell is a bodybuilder going to tell *me*?" I said, "I've got to run, dude. These bastards can barely walk."

Mick said, "I'm not talking about running. I'm talking about understanding what's happening in your muscles." He told me about how bodybuilders get that incredible "cut." When these guys prepare for bodybuilding competitions, they are very careful in how they use water. If you dehydrate too much, you lose the size of the muscle. But they have to get rid of the water in order to get that definition. It's a very fine line. Pro bodybuilders become like pharmacists—experts when it comes to nutrition, muscle size, and health.

What holds a lot of the bodybuilders back is that when they get up to perform, if they haven't dehydrated properly, they are cramping. It ruins their competitions. So they walk a fine line in achieving proper hydration. I needed to find a way to increase my muscles' capacity to store fluids and energy without adding mass, and my hydration strategy at Kona wasn't getting it done. So I figured I had nothing to lose by meeting some bodybuilders.

Some of the guys I met were just steroid heads, but then through sheer luck, in September 2009, I ran into a guy in France who had a nutrition company. He didn't look as big as a bodybuilder, but I got to talking to him. I'm always talking to these guys and getting their opinions. Finally, he told me that he used to be Mr. France as a bodybuilder. Talk about meant to be. I said, "Dude, I have some questions for you."

In Monaco, we sat down for a coffee. He had come to the sport of triathlon from bodybuilding and he formed a nutrition company. He told me that he came to triathlon because it's the only sport in the world outside of bodybuilding where people are infatuated with nutrition. He was right. Triathletes are obsessed with nutrition: gels, calories, carbohydrates, and so on. He told me a story about his first competition in the United States, which was also Arnold Schwarzenegger's last competition, and he was paired off with Arnold.

Finally, after some more stories, I got down to business. I said, "Tell me why I cramp, mate. I'm doing these races, and I think it's my sweat loss and my electrolytes. But I'm still unsure about this electrolyte model because —"

He stopped me. "What makes you unsure about the electrolyte model?" I recall him asking. I said, "I'm not a sports scientist, man, but if it really is an electrolyte imbalance that makes you cramp, then why are only certain muscles cramping? It's one body. It should be cramping everywhere. It has to be more than that."

He gave me a look that said, *Hey, you've actually thought about this.* I told him I usually cramped in my internal abductors. "Why wouldn't my calves be cramping?" I asked. "And my quads? Because they're all working. It can't be that only the working muscle cramps."

He told me that in bodybuilding, there were two types of hydration. Cramping for bodybuilders tends to come from dehydration at the muscular-cellular level, not the blood plasma level. He suggested that in my hydration phase, in the week or the three days before a race, when I was panicking and saying, "Hydrate, hydrate," I was just filling my plasma volume.

He explained that what tends to happen is that the blood gets full of water, which is good because you feel like you're hydrated, and you pee a lot. But the osmosis across the cell wall doesn't happen as quickly without the high intake of electrolytes, because your muscles protect themselves. They are very careful of what they take in.

A lightning bolt hit me in the brain. Of course. I was hydrating myself at a plasma level but I wasn't hydrating my muscles, which would hold the water for much longer.

He went on, saying something like, "You're training in hot weather for weeks on end, but muscular hydration takes time. Take it from a bodybuilder, we are all about muscular hydration, because it gives size to our muscle. When you get that cut about you, you're dehydrated." He told me that bodybuilders hydrate by drinking a big load of magnesium, calcium, and added sodium and potassium in solution, consumed slowly over about two weeks, so they saturate their muscles.

This was genius. These are minerals that the body finds difficult to urinate out in high quantities. Bodybuilders would hydrate at the plasma level, then start with the minerals, and the body would go, *I'm going to store this beautiful stuff,* and stick it in the muscles. Two weeks before a competition, bodybuilders look bloated because they're saturated with water and minerals. But—and this is the key—the body dehydrates from the plasma *first*! That's why bodybuilders sit in saunas for a couple of hours before competitions and suck the water out; it comes out of the skin and vessels but leaves the muscles saturated, so they look cut up like the Incredible Hulk.

This was magic. I knew this mineral-based hydration approach could be my answer for my cramping problems. It just made perfect sense to me. I would have to be careful with potassium, because too much can cause an irregular heartbeat. I was scared to try it so close to Kona, so I ran in 2009 with my usual approach and again, I cramped and cramped. This was intolerable. I had to try something new.

So I started adapting the bodybuilding strategy to my needs before the first races of the 2010 season. I didn't bomb as many minerals as Mr. France had suggested, but I was very attentive to those three minerals during the month. I started eating lots of bananas, and then started taking supplements. I was focusing on hydration but not killing myself, because I was wary of shocking my system.

Then I started chasing hot weather races in Asia early in the season. I don't know if it was the placebo effect or not, but it was working. Kona in 2010 was the first year in my entire career I didn't get even a hint of a cramp. I was able to be the athlete I am and ride hard with my heart rate above 150. *No cramps, no worries. I'm going to run hard and then run without falling apart.* I was able to execute the kind of race I'm able to do everywhere else in the world—to play my strengths and go 8:10, and win the race. And it came from a bodybuilder's advice.

If you're an age-group racer, you can follow the same course I did. Look outside the box to find something or someone outside triathlon who might be able to help you solve a problem. Trouble with stretching? How about asking a yoga instructor? Difficulty with your stride? Talk to someone who runs marathons. You probably already have access to people who can help you. You just need to reach out. You could be amazed at what you find that can help you perform better in a race.

The Heat Is On

Heat management is always a huge issue in Kona. You have to regulate your body temperature in just about any Ironman race, but it's critical at Kona, because it's usually around 100 degrees with high humidity.

At Kona, you'll see athletes constantly going through the aid stations, which are a mile apart, grabbing ice and ice-cold sponges. The average male professional triathlete generates something like 300 watts of energy per hour during an Ironman. What happens to much of that energy? Right—it becomes heat. So, in a hot-weather race where the air temperature is too high to cool your body, you've got to dissipate that heat. So we stuff balls of ice and freezing sponges in our shorts, into our tops, and under our hats, and pour ice water over our heads—anything to keep the core temperature down.

For me, as a bigger guy, competing in Kona was all about heat management. Hot races are little guy's races. They write the history books. They write the literature that we all have to read. They're like "Yeah, it's hot out there. You need to hydrate." That's simple for you, mate. You're 145 pounds. We big guys have a bigger surface area. We heat up a lot quicker, and we lose fluids a lot more. That's why I changed the strategy of how I had to race. I had to keep my heart rate low for as long as possible and keep that core temperature down. It became about cooling off the head, cooling off the extremities, and holding ice in my hands and in my shorts—anything to keep cool.

That's why we bigger guys started making our own race suits with add-ons that helped us cool our bodies. Torbjørn Sindballe (a three-time ITU world champion) was the first to make one. Everyone's race suits basically look the same, but I found the zippers to be way too short. I could get only one or two sponges into my suit, because when you're running through an aid station, you've got one second to grab a sponge. With some of the suits I had in the past, by the time I'd grab a sponge I couldn't get it down, and I'd miss the next one. I decided I was going to design a suit with a longer zipper, almost to the bottom, a little bit off center so that it would sit like a pack and hold the sponges. Then I could load up with sponges and keep cooler.

MACCA'S (W)INSIGHTS

It helps to know how the aid stations work. It's always sponges first, then water, and then ice, cold electrolyte drink, then ice, and finally sponges. So I'll hit it and boom: first round of sponges. They're wet. They go in. Grab the second one, squeeze over my head. Then drinks, drinks, ice down the pants, water, sponges, and back on the course.

I keep as many icy-cold sponges as I can against my chest. I put them there because—I know there's no science behind this—that's where my heart is. Every drop of blood in my body goes through that organ, so I want to keep that thing cold, even if it's only a placebo effect. Some sports scientist is probably going to read this and go, "What an absolute crock," but I don't care.

So now I've got wet, icy sponges that can keep me wet and moist between the aid stations. That's important because I'm a bigger guy. Then I'm at the next aid station and I repeat the process. I also always have a visor and sunglasses so I can create a dark cocoon. It feels mentally cooler. I want to feel cool. I always wear dark lenses; when guys try on my glasses, they say, "These lenses suck." That's because they're the blackest you can get. I want to carry around my own personal nighttime.

Kona is really not a level playing field because of the heat. I used to say it before I won, and everybody said, "Of course you're saying that—you can't win the freaking thing." Now as a two-time winner of the race, I can say that it's not fair for the bigger guy. It's our world championship, but I think the sport needs another championship event. Some of the best triathletes in the world have never won in Kona: Sindballe, Jurgen Zack (who weighs 178) and Lothar Leder (who weighs 181), to name a few. These guys are exceptional in Europe and some of the best triathletes to ever race in the sport. Meanwhile, some triathletes who aren't the best in the world but are just great in heat have won this race. They're going to be remembered as the greats. That's unfair.

I think the sport justifies other races now. Tennis has the Grand Slam, but what if the French Open was all that mattered? You'd say, "Roger Federer sucks," and Raphael Nadal would be the best player ever because he dominates on clay. I'd love to see an Ironman Grand Slam: Kona, Frankfurt, and a third race. Or maybe they could rotate the world championship and hold them in Kona every other year. That would be huge for the pros. You would still have Kona, but it wouldn't be given that world championship status every year. In 2011 it could be Frankfurt, or it could be in Australia. As a pro athlete, that gives you the opportunity to be a world champion in Frankfurt. It also elevates the drama and interest in the sport. "Can he also win in Hawaii? Can he be the undisputed champion and win two world titles on two different courses?" You'd have more marketing opportunities, and Hawaii would still remain an important event.

But I don't know if that will ever happen because of tradition. Hawaii is where the sport started. Imagine if things were switched around and the world championship was held in the cold. Greg Welch won in Kona, but he never liked cold-weather races. We raced the Longleat Triathlon Grand Prix in the United Kingdom, and he ended up in a medical tent because he was freezing. The same happened in Gamagori and again in Sweden. The big guys always bury the little guys in the cold. What if the championships were in Longleat and the little guys had to battle those conditions all the time? They'd be kicking up as much of a fuss as I am.

It's taken me all these years, and now that I've got the title, I look at these other big guys who struggle and I speak up for them. They're starting to adapt their training—more nutrition and Coke and discovering an eating plan that works. But a lot of the amateurs are my weight and more, so what a lot of them face resonates with me. I know how difficult it is to get a bigger body to perform under hot conditions. I'll meet amateurs at appearances and races and they'll say things like, "Macca, man, I'm six foot three and 194, and shit, Kona is hard." I say, "Yeah you're built for football, mate. You're not built for our game. But if you want to do the sport, you're like me. You need to adapt, you can't do as much volume in your training, and you need to back off your running, because you're not built to run."

The world championship needs to show who the best athlete is in any given year. In general, the biggest stages in our sport need to be more open to more athletes—professional and amateur—who have the talent and work ethic to qualify. To make that happen, it would be wise to make the weather conditions less of a factor than who has the best plan, the toughest mental game, and the best team. The entire sport would benefit.

MACCA'S 2005 SEASON

- Half-Ironman Pucon, Chile—SECOND
- Triathlon Buenos Aires—FIRST
- Brighton Beach Triathlon, Australia—FIRST
- Ironman Australia—FIRST
- St. Anthony's Triathlon, US—THIRD
- Ironman 70.3 St. Croix—THIRD
- Cleveland Triathlon, US—FIRST
- Buschutten International Triathlon, Germany—SECOND
- Montlucon Triathlon, France—FIRST
- Lugano International Triathlon, Switzerland—FIRST
- Rothsee Triathlon, Germany—FIRST
- Barcelona Triathlon—FIRST
- Quelle Challenge Roth Ironman—FIRST
- Desaru Half-Ironman Malaysia—FIRST
- Ironman Hawaii World Championships—SIXTH
- Noosa Triathlon, Australia—FIRST

Season Statistics and Interesting Facts

- Flight miles accumulated: 78,798
- Countries visited: 13
- Days away from home: 221

Training miles for the year

- Swim: 727
- Bike: 19,920
- Run: 3,003

10

My Masterpiece: The 2010 Ford Ironman World Championship

Despite my reservations about the heat, however, Kona remained the prize everyone wanted to capture going into 2010. Me, I planned to win again. Even though he was the two-time defending champion, I wasn't too worried about Craig Alexander coming into the 2010 Ironman Hawaii. He was the favorite after winning two years in a row, but I knew if other athletes attacked the race the way I had suggested, he was someone I could deal with. Then there was Andreas Raelert. He had just run a stellar Ironman European Championship in Frankfurt where he torched the field—one of the best Ironman races in history. With that came the wave of Germans saying that triathlon had a new king. The year before in Kona, Andreas had finished third in his debut, twenty seconds in front of me, which is a great performance for your first time in one of the toughest triathlons on the planet.

There was talk about the American Chris Lieto, which I didn't see because he was a good swimmer and the best biker in the field, but he didn't have the run. My main concerns were Andreas, Craig, Rasmus Henning (a great Danish runner I've mentioned before and who'd won Ironman China, Roth, and the ITU European Championship, among others), Marino Vanhoenacker, Timo Bracht, and Eneko Llanos. Those were the men standing between me and a second title. I was considered a long shot. Slowtwitch.com gave me seven-to-one odds. I loved it. No one would see me coming.

For me, the key was the swim. For the first time in Kona, I was very attentive to my swim start. I made sure I got in the water, and as I warmed up, I figured out where everyone was on that starting line, which I had never done at Kona. The math was simple: *fix swim, win race.* Plus, all year I'd been thinking about who I was going to position myself next to in the swim, and I set myself up so that Peter Jacobs, an Aussie kid and a phenomenal swimmer, was to my left, and Andy Potts, an American who's probably the best swimmer in our sport, was to my right. I was totally alert and ready, and I said, "This is my race, right here."

Boom!

The cannon went off, and four strokes in I was leading the whole field, but it didn't take long for Peter and Andy to catch up to me. That's what I was counting on; when people swim next to you, they create a wake, and if you're a weaker swimmer you can sit on the hip of a stronger swimmer and gain some speed. It's hard, but I can travel at the strong swimmer's pace until he breaks me and get three hundred or four hundred meters like that. Well, I had great swimmers on either side of me, so it was like body surfing! We went a quarter mile and I was right there with the two best swimmers in the field! When Peter and Andy left me behind, I sat on their feet for a bit and got a draft, and then looked around. I was four body lengths ahead of the rest of the field.

Fantastic.

I knew the good swimmers were going to come past me, but I was going to see who they were. I'm a solid swimmer, but I'm also usually in a group, so there's no margin for error. If I make mistakes, I'm not strong enough to make up the time. So my goal is always to swim in the front group. That was why the start was critical. I'd been casual about it in 2009 and said, "Oh, I'm always in the front group." I thought I was in the front group but I wasn't, and by the time I realized it, it was too late to make up that time. That's the value of being in a group, whether you're on the bike or in the water: it helps you maintain your pace.

Rasmus pulled up beside me, and I stayed on his hip, and I led with him—a far superior swimmer—all the way to the first turn. I was elated, because I knew it was impossible now for me to get dropped. I had the fitness and I could swim well enough to stay with the front group. I was having a beautiful day. All the fear and anguish over the year before was now gone.

I came in with the first group, and because I had been concerned about possibly having another poor swim, I had really tightened up my transition. I had a box for my nutrition so I wouldn't have to put it in bags, and I had taped my straps to my helmet because in 2007 I couldn't get them on and lost thirty-five seconds in transition. So

MACCA'S (W)INSIGHTS

Making transition count

A fast transition can be the difference between a personal record and a disappointing race. Here are some ideas for making the most of this critical interval:

- Rehearse your transition exactly as it will go on race day.

- The fewer things you need to grab, the better. Have your nutrition already loaded on your fuel belt or bike so you can grab and go.

- Don't socialize. You can chat with other athletes after the race.

- Wear a one-piece racing suit if you can so you never have to change clothes.

- Start transitioning before you reach the official area. You can remove your swim cap and goggles or bike helmet as you're running to the transition area, so when you get there you've saved precious seconds.

- Scout the transition area with your team before the race starts. Are there obstacles such as pillars or tent poles? Are there any surfaces that are likely to be slippery after the swim? Plan for any potential problems in advance.

while I got out of the water twentieth, I had such a quick transition that I was on the bike third.

Boom! I rode out of town, and I had a lot of the boys around me — Faris al-Sultan, Dirk Bockel (an athlete from Luxembourg who had placed seventh in Kona in 2009), and the like. I grinned at them and said, "Boys, it ain't 2009!" Game on.

The Ride

My plan was to be patient until the crosswinds on the road to Hawi. But Ironman introduced a new rule in 2010. To keep riders from drafting, you have to stay ten meters behind the bike in front of you. Under the old rule, if you wanted to pass, you had to pull two meters to the side of the bike in front of you, and when your front wheel drew even with the front wheel of that rider he had to drop back and you could slide into his position. But because the packs have gotten so big, the new rule meant that you had to pass the entire pack, which is tough. I thought, *This is going to be chaotic,* so my early goal was to stay in the front, not do all the work, stay out of trouble, not get a penalty, and not have any gear break on me. It's important to stay composed and not get caught up in the hype as you ride out of Kona.

As I settled into the ride and stayed with Chris Lieto, I noticed that Andreas, who had destroyed us on the bike in Frankfurt, got aggressive early. It was a hot day, and I remember thinking, *Dude, this isn't Frankfurt. You're not going to get away.* Nobody just rides away from the field in Kona. That's because the race is changing. The best bikers in the sport, the aggressive Europeans, are all there now. If you're a weaker rider, you can get behind the stronger riders and let them set a strong pace for you — even as they let the very best riders set the pace for them.

The presence of so many powerful riders is why the runners can stay near the front of the pack and stay relatively fresh. That's exactly why I knew it was so important to attack in that crosswind and take the runners out of their comfort zone.

So I stayed with guys like Faris and Dirk; they were the allies I would take with me when I attacked. Andreas was trying to go with Chris Lieto, who was starting to exert some serious pressure on the field. I saw that all these athletes were putting a lot of pressure on themselves to perform in the ride. I thought, *Andreas, don't burn your matches here, mate. You've got a good run on you.* I made a mental note to watch him for signs of fatigue later on, which would prove pivotal.

My prerace interviews with the German press had been just as pivotal. They asked me about how great Andreas Raelert was and how anyone was going to beat him. I saw this as a great opportunity to use the German press in my favor, knowing that they would be talking to Andreas. So I said, "Andreas hasn't really put together a phenomenal back-end marathon yet. Every marathon he's done, he's fallen apart in the last ten miles." They looked at me like I was crazy, but I added, "Think about it. I have his splits for all his marathons. He fell apart in Kona in 2009, he fell apart in Frankfurt that same year, he fell apart in Arizona in 2007. This year in Frankfurt he had such a big lead off the bike that he could lose all that time in the last ten kilometers. You guys are saying he eased up, but I am convinced that he struggles, and I think he knows that as well." I knew Andreas would see the interview, and I was trying to plant doubt in his mind.

My group got out to Kawaihae, where we made the turn to climb to Hawi. Everyone was still together, but some guys were starting to drop off as the heat hit us. I was about eighth when I saw Normann Stadler sail past the group and take Andreas Raelert, Faris, Marino, and Timo with him. I almost panicked. They had done what I had been preaching all this time—they had attacked. There I was, still back with the runners, and I was thinking, *You idiot! You've missed the attack, you didn't practice what you preached!* Suddenly I was thirty seconds down to a group of some of the strongest riders in the race.

My first instinct was to go for it and get across to them, but I calmed myself and realized that it wasn't the time. I knew they would push the pace but that I still had time to make my move up near Parker Ranch, in the heavy crosswinds up toward the bike turn. The five-man group had opened up about a minute lead on me, so about six miles before the bike turn at a point called Mahukona, where a strong headwind slams you right in the face, I made a proper, committed attack on Normann's group. Out of the saddle, go! A South African, Raynard Tissink, came with me.

It was hard, but we immediately distanced ourselves from the runners' group. I remember looking back at that group and no one was responding. I thought, *They won't respond.* So I had Normann, Timo, Andreas, and their group a minute ahead, and then Raynard and me, and then fifteen guys falling behind. Safety in numbers: that's the runner's mentality.

I turned to Raynard and said, "We have two choices here. Either we commit until we get across to that group or we sit in no-man's-land all day, and I'll tell you where I'd prefer to be. Let's go." He said he was in, and we hammered all the way to the bike turn at Hawi. At the turn we were a minute down on the leading group and we'd taken a minute out of the runners' group, so we were really in no-man's-land. We got our nutrition, put our bottles on, and committed to the chase.

That was the hardest part of the race for me. I was going flat-out on the bike and finally caught Normann's group back at Kawaihae. So it took a twenty-mile chase for Raynard and me to ride one minute out of them; meanwhile we had added two minutes to our lead over the runners' group, which had been my goal in the first place.

I got on the back of the group with Normann, Faris, Andreas, and the rest, and we headed back toward town. Andreas looked back, and I think he was surprised to see me; I gave him a big smile because, just like in the swim, my confidence was up. This was right where I wanted to be: the runners were alienated, and six of the seven best cyclists in the field were with me. On the push for home, I had the

V-8 and the runners had the four-cylinder. We were going to put time into them and force them to burn their legs to avoid losing even more time—just like I said was going to happen. The runners had no one back there doing the heavy lifting for them.

We kept up the pace, and I went past the group and said, "Hey guys, this is it, let's push. C'mon." It was unfolding exactly as I had told them it would, and they knew it. Each of them had come to Kona to win, and they smelled an opportunity. So they really committed and everybody started to push back into town.

Later we got a split on the runners' group: 5:30 behind. *Beautiful*. My strategy was working to perfection, so now I started focusing on the guys with me. Timo, Marino, and Andreas were my biggest concerns in the run, and of them the biggest threat was Andreas. So I put myself behind him to look for weaknesses. There's a section between Waikoloa and the scenic lookout on the Queen K Highway where you start climbing a major hill. That's where I started watching for gaps. When you're feeling good on the bike, you're constantly trying to stay out of that ten-meter draft zone. You catch yourself pedaling too hard and getting too close to the rider in front of you, and you back off so you don't get a penalty. But when you're starting to struggle, the gaps slowly open, and you're forced to get back into that zone.

Gaps were opening in front of Andreas on the climb. He seemed to be getting out of the saddle a lot and working really hard. We shot past the scenic lookout, where the road is bumpy all the way to the West Hawaii Veterans Cemetery, thirteen miles from home. There was a crosswind the whole way, and Andreas was definitely out of the saddle a lot—fighting it, grabbing fluids, and going for gels. He was doing a lot of work on the bike, and I knew that he was going to be happy to get off. So I made up my mind then and there that once we hit the cemetery, I was out of there. I wanted to give myself a margin of error over him for the marathon.

Meanwhile, Marino Vanhoenacker had made his big move at the scenic lookout and built a 400-meter lead on the rest of our group.

But what was strange was that Faris hadn't tried to close that gap, which made no sense because he knew Marino was a better runner than he was. Then I realized that *no one* in the group was going to go after Marino. When we reached the cemetery, I attacked again, and Raynard came with me.

We broke away, and when I looked back Faris wasn't coming, Andreas wasn't coming...nobody was coming. I looked over at Raynard and said, "That's it." I dug in and started pushing all the way to Kona International Airport. He committed right along with me, and we each took the lead for five and a half of the eleven miles from the Energy Lab back into Kona. We caught Marino just before transition; we had ridden his lead off him in less than eleven miles.

For a year, I had been preaching to Normann, Timo, Andreas, and the other top bike riders that they needed to change where they made the push—rethink how they spent their strength. "Look," I'd been saying, "if you do it my way you're going to have the same fatigue when you get off the bike, but you'll have ten minutes on the runners!" Sure, they would have to outrun me, but wasn't it better to have one guy to outrun instead of ten guys with their best part of the triathlon ahead of them? So I sold them on a plan I knew they would go for because it honestly gave them a chance to win.

What I don't think they counted on was my strength on the bike. When I was doing 40k short-course races, I was the best biker in the world. I had reinvented myself as a marathoner to win Kona in 2007, but I knew that in 2010 the newer runners could beat my marathon time. In this new strategy, I would piggyback off my bike strength. My plan had been to get into that lead pack, rest a bit, get off the bike with seven guys and have better legs. But with thirteen miles to go, I felt good, so I attacked, which wasn't in the plan. I think people had forgotten that I could really ride a bike. *Gentlemen,* I thought as we went into transition, *consider today's race a reminder.*

Chris Lieto had gone it alone and dominated on the bike, as everyone knew he would. But I was fifth off the bike behind only Lieto, a German named Maik Twelsiek, Marino, and Raynard. Most important, I had nine minutes on the elite runners, which was in the range I had predicted. As I started the marathon, things were unfolding as I hoped.

The Run

I had a 1:20 lead over the trailing group as I came out of transition. It was probably the fastest transition I've had at Kona. I was feeling wonderful and confident. I had been able to conserve on the bike, and I ran out with fresh legs, my fuel belt on, ready to go. But the race wasn't over.

If you've never seen the Ironman in Kona, the marathon begins and ends on Ali'i Drive, which is like the Champs-Élysées for our sport. The road runs right along the waterfront, five miles out and five miles back, the hottest portion of the race. Well, in 2007 I set a ridiculous tempo on Ali'i and it worked. Most years, people are conservative there and really start their run out on the lava fields, but I thought if I could set a punishing pace on that stretch, I could run the legs off some of the runners who were desperate to catch up with me after falling behind on the bike. I wanted to bait them.

I compare my sport to boxing quite a lot because they are both about pace, tempo, and style. If you're a young boxer, and I'm a slugger, then I don't want to box you. I want to get you in the corner and slug it out. I have to get you to fight my way. I'm older and I have experience, but what do the young runners have? Finesse, nice muscles, and spring in their step. I was going to take those away from them by making them commit to my all-out pace — play to their egos and make them chase me. Having already burned their legs in the bike stage, they wouldn't be able to keep up.

So I set a killer pace out of transition. *Catch me if you can.* Lieto, first off the bike, had a six-minute lead. Andreas, Timo, and Marino had committed to my pace. When I made the turnaround at five miles I had run three minutes off of Lieto's lead, so I knew he was done. Running north on Ali'i, I was passing the guys who were still going south, so I got to see them for the first time. Marino was in third, and Andreas and Timo were together in fourth and fifth. I figured Andreas and Timo would stick together and Marino would drop to fourth. He'd run an incredible 7:52 at a race in Austria, just missing the world record, but I figured that was his race for the year. Now I knew who I would be working against for the title, and I knew I had to keep the pace—and the pressure—on.

I was also looking for the runner group with Crowie Alexander, Eneko Llanos, and the rest. Finally, at seven minutes back, I saw them. Time for some more of the mental game. I wanted to let them know I knew how far behind me they were. So as I passed Craig I made sure he saw me looking at my watch, a move that said, "Got you covered!" I could see the frustration in his face, and at that point I knew it was a four-horse race.

I got to Palani Hill. Ali'i Drive had felt great, but Palani hurt. I saw Lieto on Palani and passed him just after the top. Over the top and with Lieto behind me, I got a split at 2:20—that was Andreas and Marino, running together behind me. Timo was four minutes back, out of the picture.

I started working those miles from mile marker eleven to fifteen, and I started losing fifteen seconds a mile. I had been running 5:45 or 5:50 miles along Ali'i, and now I was running 6:10. These guys were still running 5:55. They were coming, and I had to force the next mile.

When I got to mile marker sixteen, I was 1:20 up. I was losing exactly fifteen seconds a mile. I saw that Andreas had distanced himself from Marino by thirty seconds, and I thought, *He's coming.* This is where the experience—the ability to set your ego aside—really comes into play. I took the pressure off.

I said to myself, *Stop forcing it. He's going to catch you. Let's relax for four miles, take that pressure off, be prepared for the catch, take it down a notch, do the Energy Lab, focus on nutrition, focus on the things you can control, and as you come out of the Energy Lab, you'll have six miles to run with this guy. You've done that a million times, so let's be ready for a war, may the best man win.*

What made me make that decision? My coaches have said, "The old you would have grunted it out and fought on." They're 100 percent right. A few years earlier, fear would have driven me. I would have said to myself, *I can't let him catch me or I'm done!* But now I know better. I have experience. I've learned over the years to think several steps ahead in a race, to have an overall strategy in mind and to trust in my training, my knowledge and my plan.

Most athletes in our sport are completely in the moment—how am I feeling right now? How fast am I running right now? But I was attentive to the whole race as a process. As I knew Andreas was going to catch me, I kept saying to myself, *The race doesn't end until the pier, mate!* That gave me permission to take ego out of it, take the pressure off and stop forcing things. Instead of acting out of fear, I stayed in control of the race.

MACCA'S (W)INSIGHTS

Tips for each Ironman stage

Swim

- Be careful at the start. It's easy to get kicked or pushed under in the rush of 1,500 age groupers. Better to start a little more slowly, make sure you don't get bloodied, and then settle into a groove.

- Try "drafting" in the water by getting alongside stronger swimmers and letting their wakes carry you for a few meters. It's a great way to get a little extra speed.

- Relax and trust your buoyancy, and enjoy the scene of the swim: divers below you taking photos, sailboats and warships watching. Appreciate the fact that you're doing an Ironman.

Bike

- Take sodium throughout the bike stage. You'll need it.

- Keep your helmet on at all times. Most races are very strict about safety and they will disqualify you if they see you with your helmet straps undone.

- Pay attention in a group. You can't draft in Ironman, but groups can still be dangerous. Watch for other riders who look inse-cure or out of control, and steer clear of them. A bad fall will end your day.

Run

- Keep going. For some reason, lots of age-group racers report bursts of energy at three to four miles from the finish. Clearly, there is some sort of physiological change going on, but you don't have to know its cause to benefit from it. Don't quit if you've made it that far.

- Take advantage of downhill stretches. Don't walk them. Let gravity be your friend and make sure to coast and breathe on the downhills.

- Don't be embarrassed to walk through the aid stations. This gives you more time to get the liquid, ice, and sponges you need.

I made the commitment a mile from the Energy Lab. So instead of running past the aid stations, I took my time: water, Coke, ice, sponges. When you take that pressure off, running with the view that the person is going to get you, you feel good. Then I turned into the Energy Lab, ran down the hill to the turn, ran back, crested the hill, and got a split...and Andreas was still thirty-two seconds behind me.

I thought, *Shit, I thought he was going to get me here*. I had taken my time and done those things that you neglect when you're under pressure, like blowing through aid stations. The elation I felt! At that point in a race, when you're more than seven hours in and you're emotionally and physically exhausted, little positives become massively magnified. I had been thinking I was going to have to run hard for six miles, but if Andreas was going to take another thirty seconds to catch me, I would only have to run hard for five. Bonus! I was going to cruise for another mile.

I have to say something here about the Raelerts. The split I got coming out of the Energy Lab came from *Michael* Raelert, Andreas's brother. He gave me an accurate split on his own brother, knowing that it would give me an advantage. That speaks volumes about the class and sportsmanship of these two guys. We're going to see big things from them in coming years, and the future of the sport could not be in the hands of two better individuals.

So now we came down to it. The last ten kilometers. Down at the finish line on Ali'i, the speculation was starting: Would Andreas catch Macca? Greg Welch and Michellie Jones, fellow Australians serving as analysts, started talking about my smarts and experience versus Raelert's athleticism—the old dog versus the young buck. I think a lot of people assumed that my age was getting to me on the last leg of the race, and Andreas would catch and blow past me. When I heard that after the race was over, I had to laugh. Not only had I baited Andreas, I'd baited the fans and TV commentators, too!

I relaxed. I would only have to run five miles hard with this guy. With five miles to go, I got the split: He was eighteen seconds back. *Far out!* He wasn't catching me like he was before. I was hurting but I had another gear, and I only had to run four miles with him. Bonus! I was starting to feed my positive emotions because at this point you're running on emotion.

Again, the mind game comes into play. In a lot of pursuits, it's easy to get out of your game when you get near the finish and start to get excited. I was counting on Andreas doing that. He was fourteen seconds back when we hit the four-mile mark, and now we had people around us. There were the TV cameras on motorcycles, and cars honking, and he had a wave of Germans cheering him on. I couldn't see him, but I could hear them yelling, "Come on, Andreas!" and the like. Now, this guy has been racing for twenty-two miles and looking at my back the whole time. I know how it feels because I've been that guy. I knew he wanted to get across and catch me. So I stopped cruising and ran harder. Either he wouldn't get across and the gap would open, and he'd wonder what was going on, or he would force himself to get across and it would hurt him.

In watching the race coverage after the fact, it was quite dramatic. People really saw this as a game of cat and mouse like the famous showdown between Mark Allen and Dave Scott in 1989. Everyone was wondering what I would do when Andreas caught me. Did I have anything left in the tank?

With three miles to go, he ran up on me. But he didn't pass me. It was obviously a relief to get there; he was going to settle in. This was his mistake of inexperience: He turned the race into catching me, not being ahead of me at the finish. When you chase for so long, and the splits are dropping, you can't wait to catch the person in front of you. But when I picked it up in that last mile, he forced himself to push. Once he got there, I said to myself, *This is the pace,* and he seemed happy with it. We were still running sub-6:15 miles.

I thought, *Don't blow this, mate. Don't get excited, stay in your game.* I had five kilometers (three miles) to go, and I'd been prepared to suffer for ten. Bonus! I can suffer for 5k with anybody. We ran together for a bit, and now we had hundreds of people around us. I wanted to be the alpha male, so I stayed one step in front of him — being that annoying person you run with each morning who always keeps you just off his shoulder. Just past the three-mile mark, in what has become a much-talked-about moment, I turned to him, handed him a sponge that I'd been carrying with me, and said, "Andreas, best of luck. No matter what happens here, you're a champion, may the best person win." He said, "Macca, thank you," and shook my hand. We didn't say another word to each other.

We came up to the hill where Mark Allen made his move on Dave Scott in 1989 in what they called the Iron War. I thought, *No matter what happens, this is really cool! This is like Iron War Two!* It's amazing where your mind goes. I made a move on the hill and gapped Andreas quickly, but then I panicked. I wondered, am I making a move here because this is where Mark Allen made his move on Dave Scott, or because this is the right place to make a move? It had happened too easily, so I backed off. *We're a long way from home, so don't blow this.*

Looking back I saw that I had gapped him by fifteen or twenty meters—six or seven seconds! It took him a mile to run that out of me before. I decided that I wasn't going to hand this back to him; I'd keep the pace on and make him force his way across. I could hear the Germans shouting, "Come on, Andreas, come on!" I knew at that moment that he was going to buy into the shouting; his fans were going to make him do things he shouldn't do.

We crested Palani Hill and he caught me again. I thought, *Big mistake, dude. You rushed that.* As he caught me he took this deep, whooshing breath like he was preparing for a push, but to me he was psyching himself up. As we turned down the hill, there's an aid station exactly one mile from home. It's on the left and it's really more for the runners coming up the hill, because as we come down we hug the tangent on the right turn and stay to the right. But Andreas started yelling, "Coke! Coke! Water!"

I was shocked. He going for Coke *now*? We've got a mile to go! We're running for a world title here! But I wanted him to take that Coke and water, because if he went for the aid station, I was gone. He had to go to the left to get to the aid station, so I started pushing him across so he would have to go in close to get his Coke and water. The people stand there with the cups, and if you can grab them with a long arm reach, it doesn't take that much momentum off you. But if you're forced to shorten that arm reach, you lose some momentum. I wanted him to have to go close to grab what he needed. It was in slow motion, like waiting for a mousetrap to hit the mouse. The minute his hands went up, I hit the gas. When he looked up I was ten meters in front of him again.

This is it. This is my run for the title. I wasn't slowing down. Palani is downhill, so I knew I had to get my leg speed up. But at the bottom, where you turn left onto the flat at Kuakini, you need your own effort to keep that leg speed up, and it gets uncomfortable. But it was one mile. How many times had I suffered for one mile? It all came down to this: All the days I had been away from my kids, all the years of suffering, it all came down to this one moment. *Do not let up.*

Then I started getting stomach cramps and stitches. I put my hand into my stomach as hard as I could; I didn't care if I busted a rib. I felt like I was record-setting 100-meter sprinter Usain Bolt, though when I watch the coverage now it looks like slow motion. We were a quarter mile in, which feels like twenty when you're in agony. I was too scared to look back because of the cramps, but I saw the timekeeper on the back of an official motorbike. His name is Eric Gilsenan, and he's known me for years. He gives us the splits on a message board, but he's not allowed to show favoritism to any athlete. I said, "Eric, where is he?" Eric looked at me and shook his head. He said something like, "Macca, you know the rules, you know I'm not allowed to tell you that I can't see him." Then he went back behind his board.

Bonus!

I made the right turn onto Hualalai Road, and I couldn't see Andreas, but I didn't know how far back he was. At that point, you're still a half mile away, which is an eternity. Then I turned onto Ali'i Drive. Hallowed ground. It doesn't get bigger in our sport. As a seventeen-year-old kid, I would do training runs with my mates and the last three or four hundred yards we'd have our arms in the air going, "Ali'i Drive!" When I made that turn, Andreas had not made the turn onto Hualalai, so I knew he had hit the wall. He was broken.

So I got to enjoy that run along Ali'i Drive. I don't remember much at all from 2007. It was all emotion. I remember thinking of my mum and Sean. This time, I savored it. I remember every step of it. I still see faces in the crowd that I recognized. It was sweet. I ran under the Wheaties arch, and there was a group of Australians there who gave me a flag. I was so alert, so attentive, so full of energy. I zipped up before I crossed the line... and I didn't have sponges in my top.

In my 2007 finish photo, which is *the* thing in triathlon to have, I had left sponges in my top—that's how out of it I was at the end. So I had these "man cans" in my finish photo. That haunted me; at the high point in my career, I've got tits. So this time, I took care of business: sponges out, zipped up, and crossed the line. It's a very personal moment. Everything is flashing before your eyes. It's like an out-of-body experience. Right in front of me were Emma, Tahlia, and Sienna. The picture of me with my arms in the air screaming was taken at the moment when I saw my family. Everyone was in tears. Tahlia was jumping up and down.

These were the people who had been on the journey and had never doubted me. I had asked Emma for one more shot to win in 2009 and I hadn't done it. She had the faith in me that I could win in 2010. She gave me the green light and backed me to try one more time. I promised her that I would deliver, and I did. To have it happen the way it did, to grab my wife and girls and Scott, my agent, and the people who believed and have a family "We did it!" moment was incredibly satisfying.

Andreas came in 1:20 later, and I was so proud and happy for him. I greeted him and Marino, who came in third. Races are never easy, but after nine times in Kona, it was the best I have felt after a race. Everything from my career came together at one moment. It unfolded exactly as I said it would. Marino, who had finished fifth or sixth in past years, was suddenly on the podium saying, "Macca, you're a smart fox!" A painter or a writer spends his whole career trying to create a masterpiece. Kona was my masterpiece.

MACCA'S 2010 SEASON

- Lavaman Triathlon, Hawaii—FIRST
- South Beach International Triathlon, US—FIRST
- Escape from Alcatraz—FOURTH
- Ironman 70.3 Austria—SECOND
- TriStar Worms Germany—FIRST
- Ironman European Championships, Germany—THIRD
- TriStar Estonia—FOURTH
- Pacific Coast Triathlon, US—FIRST
- San Diego Triathlon Challenge—FIRST
- Ironman Hawaii World Championships—FIRST
- Silverman Half-Ironman, Las Vegas—FIRST

Season Statistics and Interesting Facts

- Flight miles accumulated: 103,486
- Countries visited: 9
- Days away from home: 195

Training miles for the year

- Swim: 678
- Bike: 20,480
- Run: 2,654

Stayed home a lot this year. Cut back on my racing over four hours in duration. Reduced the volume of races. Actual travel miles increased but time at home increased. We increased my flights but reduced my time away from home. Happy medium.

11

No Problems, Just Solutions

Many factors went into my 2010 win. One was stubbornness. I refuse to accept anything as just being the way it is. As far as I'm concerned, a problem in triathlon is like a safe full of money—it's worth taking a shot to try and crack it, right? For instance, I had problems for years with the heat, and I had always assumed that there was nothing I could do to train my body to adapt better to it.

Then I had some consulting sessions with Mark Allen a few years back and I asked him what he thought I should do about Kona. He thought I should run more. "What about sweat loss?" I asked. He said, "Well, I never had a huge problem with heat. I didn't like it, but I never have a problem."

So what was the great Mark Allen doing that I wasn't? It turned out that he used to train in dry conditions for a big part of the year, especially when he was training for Kona. When you train in dry conditions, your body becomes like a camel. It learns to hold water. If you train in humidity, your body becomes exceptional at losing water in order to cool you. Mark would train in San Diego or Boulder, Colorado, where it's dry and hot, and teach his body to hold on to water.

Genius.

Bloody hell, I had never even thought of that. I thought he and so many other athletes went to Boulder for the altitude and the camaraderie. It was brilliant. I had been apprehensive about Boulder, because I had been training at altitude and I didn't like how, as a bigger guy, I got weaker faster. I was losing my strength, because you just can't do as much power work when you're a mile high.

So I adopted Mark's strategy but dropped the altitude. I went back to Los Angeles and got out on Mulholland Drive in the San Fernando Valley. It's dry and freaking hot. I'd train there, then go to Kona for a bit and tax the body a little in the humidity. Timothy Noakes, a South African sports physiologist, points out that your body will react to the stimuli you give it. So if you set out a training block, you can stimulate the body with the same conditions and it will tend to hold its form. You can do that by training at altitude and then later training in an altitude tent, for example.

I talked with Steve Moneghetti, an Australian marathoner. He told me an interesting story about the Barcelona Olympics. He was the favorite to win the marathon. Well, all the Australians and a lot of the teams were lying in this non-air-conditioned village, in the summer, sweating and stinking in the heat. They all thought they were getting acclimated.

Finally, the Germans couldn't take it anymore. They went and stayed in an air-conditioned hotel, and those Germans performed far beyond what was expected of them. I remember Steve telling me, "We were all weak and tired. We bought into the mind-set that living and training in the heat would be just what we needed." But the Germans would go out and train in the heat—stimulating the body's heat management system—then come back and rest in the cool.

Steve went back to Ballarat, Australia, and tried the same approach. He would train in the cool conditions, and then four times a week, he would throw three ringing wet towels in a dryer, close the door of his laundry room, lock all the windows and run on his treadmill. He told me it was like a sauna. Meanwhile, he would do his main, hard running in cool weather. He went to Athens and I recall him saying, "My problems with heat? Gone."

So now I train in the heat in Los Angeles. The great thing about LA is that if it's too hot, I can drop over the mountains onto the Pacific Coast Highway and it's twenty degrees cooler. Then I take training partners to Kona and work in the humidity, and then come back to LA and do it all over again.

It's unusual, of course. But I'm trying to get better at the bike, so don't tell me that I have a problem with heat. I already know that. Tell me how to solve it. That's why I find it interesting to talk to people like Steve, because he delves in like I do. I just asked, "You had a problem with heat—what did you do? How did you solve it?" Athletes are very open in telling you what they did to fix things if you just ask. It's like we're the sports scientists now. We have the theory and the application.

While I'm on the subject of training in Los Angeles, I should mention my training partner, Paul Ambrose, whom I've been training with for five years. We grew up in the same town near Sydney. From the beginning, I found him interesting because he was so abrupt and stern. He did things his way. He was tough. I met him when he was looking for the opportunity to race in Europe; he got my phone number from mutual friends and rang me up, just like that, to ask if I could help him get onto a team in Europe. I respected that this kid had the guts to call me.

I made some calls and got Paul posted to a small German team in the town of Hofstetten. The team had told me that he had to be in Europe in eight days, and I thought, *No chance*. But he booked a ticket and just flew to Germany. I knew the loneliness and disorientation he was flying into, and I respected this kid. I started training with him when he came back to Australia and brought him along with me to the United States. He has a pain tolerance like no one I have ever seen. He doesn't buy into the hype and is a real blue-collar worker in a white-collar sport. Paul races on pure heart. He won his first Ironman this year in Louisville and did it off the front, alone. I admire him tremendously.

Unconventional Wisdom

I don't know of any other professional triathletes who incorporate advice from other athletes—bodybuilders, sprinters, marathoners—into their training and racing strategy. I'm the only one to suggest a "fluffy" training regimen that listens to what the body needs. I came into the sport through the back door, going around the usual club system and the national federation—just showing up and winning while everyone looked at each other and said, "Who the hell is this bozo?" I've been unconventional my entire career. So I guess it's not surprising that during that career, other people have made a point of telling me what I couldn't do.

Supposedly, I couldn't win Kona. After I won it the first time, I couldn't possibly win it a second time. I turned against the sports scientists. When they told me, "Here's your perfect eating formula," I tried it and said, "This didn't work like you said it would. When I did what you told me *not* to do, I got better results." Everybody always wanted to talk about the problems I would have winning at Kona, but when I said, "Okay, what are we going to do about that?" they would call me a dreamer.

People always tell me that. I've been criticized for putting people around me who tell me what I want to hear. "He likes to get sunshine blown up his backside," they say. Well, yeah. I don't want people who kiss up and tell me everything's fine when it's not, but I do want people around me who dwell on the positive, not the negative. Don't talk to me about a problem unless you're also going to bring me a solution. I put people around me who are smart enough to see problems *before* they happen and confident enough to say, "Macca, here's how we're going to fix them."

The funny thing is, I have no entourage. As I said earlier, I've seen up-and-coming triathletes who haven't even won anything yet with fifteen people in their posse. Now, why would you need that many people around you? You might want your agent to handle business affairs, sure. You might want your publicist if you're going to do interviews. You might want your coach or a trainer if you're going to be working out or getting ready for a race. But beyond that, who do you need? Your personal chef? Your masseuse? Your valet? When you have that many hangers-on, most of them are there to leech off of you or to tell you how wonderful you are. And I surround *myself* with ass kissers? I don't think so.

Where's the New Information?

I don't need somebody else to make me feel good; I can take care of that on my own. My marriage and my daughters are all the reassurance I need. Professionally, what I need are problem solvers. If I tell someone, "Look, I sweat hugely, and if my heart rate gets over 152, I lose. What do you suggest?" I don't want to hear back, "Well, it's going to be hard." I know that. Give me information I can use to fix the situation.

I'm always resourcing new information. Tim Noakes, who wrote *Lore of Running*, has called bullshit on the lactate threshold model. The whole world, since the dawn of time, has said that lactate is the limiting factor in performance. If more lactate builds up in your muscles than your anaerobic system can eliminate, you reach your lactate threshold and stop being able to perform.

Noakes says that lactate is just one part of a more complex puzzle. He talks about a Central Governor System: Your body will protect itself at all times. In this model, the body never gets anywhere near the maximum effort that the muscles are capable of. The hormones and other variables within the body change as we put stress on it, in order to protect the heart and other vital organs. There's a predetermined governor on performance; the body won't let itself push to a level that will damage it. That can be slightly changed through training, but ultimately, it's a matter of genetics. I was genetically enabled to be a triathlete, while others were genetically programmed to be bodybuilders.

I believe this, because if lactate were the limiter, how would women lift cars off their trapped children, or people run superhumanly fast in life-or-death situations? Lactate doesn't stop people from doing those things. That's the kind of thinking I appreciate. You ask hard questions and accept nothing at face value. Then you look for answers.

Maybe because of my training as an accountant, I have an analytical, mathematical mind. If there's a problem, there's a solution, and positive thinking is the only way to find it. The trick is to think outside of the narrow, traditional wisdom of the sport and look for answers anywhere without prejudice. If you start thinking that football or track or climbing don't have anything to teach you because you're a tough triathlete, you're going to pass up a lot of wisdom.

MACCA'S (W)INSIGHTS

"You don't *play* triathlon. You play soccer; it's fun. You play baseball. Triathlon is work that can leave you crumpled in a heap, puking by the roadside. It's the physical brutality of climbing Mount Everest without the great view from the top of the world. What kind of person keeps coming back for more of that?"

Embrace the Suck

Ultimately, triathlon is about pain—enduring it, knowing when it will come, and persisting through it. Every triathlete has his or her own mechanism for dealing with pain, and many of them work. I am not the only athlete winning races; obviously, other athletes have systems that get it done under different conditions.

How you deal with pain has everything to do with whether you take a positive or negative mind-set into a race. I'm not much for affirmations, but the one thing I say to myself before every race is, "Embrace the suck." Because no matter how much you love being a triathlete, at some point a race is going to really, really suck.

Even when I was doing two-hour races, there was agony. You don't *play* triathlon. You play soccer; it's fun. You play baseball. Triathlon is work that can leave you crumpled in a heap, puking by the road-side. It's the physical brutality of climbing Mount Everest without the great view from the top of the world. What kind of person keeps coming back for more of that?

That's why your state of mind is so important. You have to be honest with yourself about suffering: It's going to come, it's part of the wholeness of being a triathlete, and it's totally real. It's you versus you. If you can be at peace in your mind and accept the pain, then you can see it as part of the whole amazing experience. But if you're dreading the suffering because you approach it from a negative frame of mind, when it finally comes you're going to check out.

The pain is a slow process. You feel it coming from a long way off. When the gun goes off, you think, *I feel good*. Then the fatigue starts to come, and then the body rebels. It's a raw reality: your will against the agony that's setting in. When that happens, your mind can go to some crazy places. But I've always found it blissful. I hate the pain, but I love it, too.

Ever talk to someone at the end of a marathon? They don't talk about how they cruised at mile twelve. They talk about how they hit the wall in agony at twenty-three miles but kept going to the finish. We're at our best when we're overcoming and striving, and in triathlon one of the biggest challenges is overcoming that part of your mind that says, *Knock this shit off, it hurts, stop, quit running!*

MACCA'S (W)INSIGHTS

"The pain is a slow process. You feel it coming from a long way off. When the gun goes off, you think, *I feel good.* Then the fatigue starts to come, and then the body rebels. It's a raw reality: your will against the agony that's setting in. When that happens, your mind can go to some crazy places. But I've always found it blissful. I hate the pain, but I love it, too."

That's why I laughed when people said I wasn't hungry enough to win Kona again. Not hungry? That race has challenged me more than any other in my career. The more you suffer for something, the more you value it. If I cruise through an event that didn't hurt, it doesn't mean as much to me. I've done some races where there wasn't much competition and I was there for the money, and it's not fulfilling. What you get is worth what you paid for it.

So pain is like an old friend to me. When it shows up I think, *There you are. I was wondering when you'd get here.* It's not that I'm looking forward to suffering, but I accept it as a sign that I'm pushing myself and overcoming something. I'm doing it right, because I hurt. I shake hands with the pain and keep going.

I tell other athletes to embrace the pain and start planning for it, instead of denying that it's going to come or thinking you can prevent it if you train hard enough. You should constantly be analyzing how you feel mentally and physically. If you do, you can feel the fatigue and pain coming, so you're not surprised by it and can make decisions based on it. You say, *What's happening around me at this point in the race? Do I go with this move, which means my friend pain is going to come a lot earlier than I'm prepared to face him, or do I hold back?*

But many athletes fear that analysis. They have doubts and fear about how they will handle their friend pain when he shows up. Are they going to stop? Are they going to quit? How are they going to deal? If they fear the pain, they make themselves powerless against it. If I gave into fear during a race, all my strategy and my mental game, which are my real strengths, would be useless.

I understand prerace nerves, because they are based on fear. I've often felt them myself and wondered, *Why am I nervous before a race I should dominate?* I've tried to say, "It's not nerves, it's excitement," but that's kidding myself. Nerves are outward manifestations of your fear that you don't have what it takes—that you'll lose it in the swim or not make a cutoff time. It's that worry that we all have: *I'm not good enough.*

That's why attitude is so critical. You have to love and embrace the pain. Start planning in your training how you will deal with the mental impact of suffering. That's not being negative; it's being realistic and empowering yourself. If you let fear blind you, then you're impotent against the pain.

My pain strategy starts with self-talk. I tell myself, "You've done this a thousand times. You know what's going to come, and you're better than it is." Then when the pain comes, you know what I do? *I smile.* People say, "Macca is always smiling." That's my way of honoring the pain. *All right. You're here. Let's buckle down now and get this job done.*

Then I focus on rhythm. I start with my breathing. Is that under control? Check. Second, my nutrition. How do I feel? Is there a nutrition issue? Is my blood sugar okay? Check. I focus on what I can control. If the pain comes when I'm on the bike, I might focus on pedal technique. If it's on the run, I might count my steps.

Your body is not that smart. It'll do anything you tell it to, but after a while it will rebel. So you treat the whole thing like a game. When the pain comes, stop for a second. The pain will go. Endorphins will kick in and then you're back in the game. The pain will be back again, but then you know you can beat it.

Mental Milkshakes

Sometimes I feel like I have beaten a lot of people that really I shouldn't have beaten. At the time, I might have thought, *Oh man, how did I get away with that one?* Oftentimes, the person I beat was what I call a "mental milkshake." That means their mind is whirling at a million miles an hour, like a blender making a milkshake. They can't source anything in their head. When they speak to you, it's clear they're an emotional wreck.

I have seen a lot of athletes come through this sport who are phenomenal on a physical level. I've trained with them, and many are still some of my closest friends.

I've got a really close friend who should have been the greatest ever. I watch him and think, *How the hell don't you beat me every day? You're a better swimmer than I am, a better bike rider than I am, and you're a far superior runner. How haven't you won everything?* I've never seen a better performing triathlete ever, on a physical level. In training, he's a world champion every day.

But in competition, he's a mental milkshake. On race morning, he's freaking out. I say, "Relax man, just do what you've been doing all week." I saw that in him when he was only nineteen and coaching didn't help. Most coaches understand only the physical. They watch trainees and think they've got the next great one. But often they completely neglect the mental.

For years, people have said, "When this guy gets it together, we're all dead." Well, he's thirty-seven now, and it's never happened, and it's never going to. It wasn't that he didn't train hard. He's just a disaster in the head. He'd stub his toe before the race and that would be an issue. He would let those little setbacks take him completely out of his game. That's a mental milkshake.

Turn Your People into Assets

One of the best ways to keep yourself positive and focused on solutions is to choose the right people to have around you and stick with them. I've had the same crew around me for years. They are people who know me and know the sport.

If you're a professional, it's important to have gatekeepers — people who influence who can come into your life. My wife is my main gatekeeper. Mick is a major gatekeeper. My agent, Scott, is another one. I've got my brother and his mates. They decide who gets access to me, which is important. I don't want someone with a problem-based mind-set infecting me with that sort of thinking. Be real, but be proactive. Attitude is the number one requirement for being around me.

In the end, it's this small core of people who sit down with me and do the nuts-and-bolts planning of my season, sponsorships, and everything else. When I need specialized information or a new way to solve a problem, that's when I might reach out to someone outside the inner circle.

It's also important to bring your family, if you have one, into your racing. Our sport has an incredibly high attrition rate; people quit because they can't balance the demands of triathlon with the demands of family. Or they get divorced. The divorce rate among triathletes seems to be extremely high.

That doesn't have to be the case. You can bring your family into the process—and you should. Your family can be your greatest source of strength and inspiration if you let them. You have to sit down with them and understand what they need. It's critical to balance the time you need to commit to the sport with family time. In my world, family life comes first. But it's a series of compromises. You set rules. You say, "On Saturdays you have the kids for soccer, darling, because that's my ride day. On Sundays, let's have a family day." You set the rules and boundaries and stick to them.

You should involve your family in planning your training and your season. I also believe it's important to explain to your kids what Mommy or Daddy does, even when they're young. That way, they can appreciate the hard work and sacrifice, and understand why Mommy or Daddy has to be away from home sometimes. Your spouse and children will become your biggest cheering section and source of strength. For me, the best moment of winning the 2010 Ironman at Kona was rushing into the embrace of my wife and girls, who have always believed in me.

My wife and family are part of my decision-making process. They have to be.

They're not outsiders. I see other athletes in all sports play it that way: They have the coaches and then they have their families, and the two have nothing to do with one another. I don't believe that can work. It's not just you as an athlete making sacrifices; your family makes them, too. So they deserve to be part of the planning process.

The decision of what races I'm running in 2011 was my wife's. That was my gift to her. She's spent years taking care of our daughters while I was traveling and away for weeks or months. She's earned the right to control how much I'm away at this stage of my career. My oldest daughter, Tahlia, is old enough now to understand that this is what Daddy does for a job.

Believe me, it's hard enough to make time for triathlon when you're a professional. I'm going to spend a minimum of twenty weeks per year in time-intensive preparation. If you're an amateur, it's even harder. Sure, the stakes aren't as high because you're not making your living racing, but you're still going to spend a lot of hours biking, running, and swimming—and you've got to make time for a real job. You'd better get the green light from the people who love you and involve them in every step of your process. Otherwise you're doomed.

I've seen it with many pro men. To them, their wives become nags because they're asking for more time, and to the wives, their husbands are abandoning them to race. Triathlon is a demanding mistress. She'll eat your marriage alive if you let her.

Let your spouse help plan your travel. Let your kids help choose the color of your racing gear. Help them understand why you race, whether it's because you want to be healthy and fit or because you are a professional and are trying to provide for them.

With family, it's also very important to acknowledge that this is an expensive sport. You're going to spend a hell of a lot on a good bike. It's a destination sport, so you have travel expenses. You have swim coaches and racing gear and gels and swim skins and all the rest. That can be a financial strain unless you plan for it as a couple. That's why a lot of the most successful triathlon families I see are the ones where both spouses do it together. It's their playtime. One athlete watches the kids while the other one trains or races. You can even do it with kids, though it's harder. It's all about working together.

There aren't many problems in this sport that can't be solved if you just look for answers. That's the advantage of age. I've made all the mistakes already; now I know where not to look for solutions. Let's face it, if you've done something for six or ten or fifteen years and not grown and learned, you're doing it wrong.

12

There Are No Short Cuts

I was living in Australia when I took up triathlon, so maybe I was naïve. I never heard about performance-enhancing drugs. I had never known an athlete who used them. I knew about steroids, but I thought only bodybuilders used them. It was with that innocent attitude that I started winning races in Europe.

It was back in 1997, and I was in phenomenal form. I was racing Olympic distance triathlons around Europe and living in Switzerland. At the time, I was training with Craig Walton, whom I've mentioned before, and Paul O'Brien, a friend from where I grew up. I was dominating the Credit Suisse triathlon series, winning French Grand Prix races, and was rated number one in the ITU World Cup. Since I was riding and running off the charts, I decided to do the ITU Duathlon World Championships. Duathlon is bike-run only, and the winner would get twenty thousand dollars. It was a big deal.

The race was in Guernica, in the Basque country of Spain, the town that inspired Picasso's famous painting. I went into it feeling great—I was running better than anyone in the field—but got absolutely torn up by Jonathan Hall, another Aussie and a brilliant rider. I thought I had second place wrapped up, but several other guys passed me and I ended up with one of my poorer showings. At the after party, I was a bit down on myself, thinking, *How did I just get smashed that badly? Maybe I'm not going as good as I think I am.*

After the party, I went out with some other athletes to this seedy, dirty little nightclub filled with smoke. I was in the back chatting with a Spanish athlete who had ridden with some guys who I knew. I remember him saying, "Chris, are you happy with your race? You had a good race, a solid race. What medicines are you using?"

I said, "What was that? What medicines?"

He said, "What medicines do you use? Come on, we're all big boys here."

I didn't get it. I said, "Oh, I take a bit of Vitamin C, and I'm on Coenzyme Q10 now. It's pretty good."

He gave me this smile, and it hit me. He thought I was on drugs. I said, "What? Drugs? You think I'm on drugs?" I think he realized that he had a real goody-two-shoes here. He shook his head and started to walk away, and I grabbed him. I said, "You think I take *drugs*, man? I don't take drugs. What makes you think that?" The Spaniard, looking disgusted, just left the club.

I was deeply offended by the idea that he thought I was taking drugs. The boys who were with me calmed me down, but I was furious. I'd also had my eyes opened: I realized for the first time that guys in our sport could be taking performance-enhancing drugs. I think that was the moment I went from being a naïve boy in my sport to being a real professional. Even though I had won all these races, I hadn't understood that this was the big time. There was a lot of money at stake, and that made the environment susceptible to cheating.

It's Not All About the Results

This realization nauseated me. I saw it as a weak cop-out, a coward's way to win, and I still do. You can't deal with the fact that you're not good enough, or you can't get past the fear that you're not good enough, so you cheat instead of finding a solution. To me, that is a direct outgrowth of our sport's obsession with results.

I've said that I love the entire process of being a triathlete and of breaking down races. That would be true even if I didn't win the races, because I enjoy the process of becoming the best triathlete I can be—the best *person* I can be. I love the process of finding the secret to winning a particular race as much as the win itself. Winning by cheating is taking an exam and getting my answers off the paper of the guy next to me. I might pass, but I wouldn't learn anything.

MACCA'S (W)INSIGHTS

"I think people like Julie Moss and many age groupers reflect the true spirit of our sport better than many professionals. They understand that the process of being a triathlete—training, surpassing limitations, developing strategy, finding the strength to endure the suffering—is transformative. You become a better person when you manage to do something as insane as swimming, biking, and running 140.6 miles in the same day."

Our sport should be about more than winning races. It should be about overcoming limitations, conquering fears, and inspiring other people. That's exactly what it is for the millions of amateurs who do triathlons every year. In a way, they're the stars of the sport, not us paid professionals! The age groupers train hard and endure the same kind of suffering in races that we do—usually for many hours longer—and at the end, all they get is a T-shirt and the pride of finishing. There's no big paycheck, no sponsorship money (some top amateurs have sponsors, but they are a small minority), no television interviews. Some amateurs race because finishing a triathlon is something they have dreamed of all their lives. Others do it to mark a life transition. There are physically challenged age groupers in wheelchairs or with prosthetics who do Ironman, and one guy who raced after having a heart transplant.

One of the most famous finishes in the history of Ironman reflects that kind of determination and will. Back in 1982, professional Julie Moss was leading the women's race when her legs buckled a half mile from the finish. She ended up losing a six-minute lead and crawling down Ali'i on her hands and knees to an agonizing second-place finish, all the while pushing away people trying to help her so that she wouldn't be disqualified. Since then, many people say that they began racing triathlons because they watched Julie crawling to the Ironman finish line that day. That's what this sport should be all about.

I think people like Julie and many age groupers reflect the true spirit of our sport better than many professionals. They understand that the process of being a triathlete—training, surpassing limitations, developing strategy, finding the strength to endure the suffering—is transformative. You become a better person when you manage to do something as insane as swimming, biking, and running 140.6 miles in the same day.

If all you want to do is win the race by any means necessary, you lose all that. If all that matters to you is the result, what kind of person does that make you? For years, pro cycling has been riddled with rumors of doping and positive drug test results. I personally know some great cycling champions who tested positive and wound up with what appear to be some severe psychological problems, including depression. I think that comes, in part, from getting to the end of your journey and realizing that you didn't earn it. You didn't learn anything about who you are, you don't know if you're any good, and it cost you your integrity.

A Shortcut to Destruction

If you define success in triathlon as becoming a better human being, not just a better athlete, then there are no shortcuts. You will get out of the sport exactly what you invest in it. Anything else is a shortcut to destruction. I came to understand just how badly endurance sports were riddled with cheating when I saw what came to be called the "Festina affair."

In 1998, Festina was dominating cycling, winning everything in sight. But according to many news stories—including pieces in the *New York Times* and *Sports Illustrated*, customs officers stopped their *soigneur* (caretaker) and found his car full of steroids, EPO, and other performance-enhancing drugs. The soigneur ended up convicted of drug trafficking, and the Festina team was tossed out of the Tour de France. The whole thing blew up into a massive scandal that nearly destroyed the Tour. Cheating destroyed those guys' careers.

That was the start of mainstream awareness of drugs in endurance sports. Cycling hasn't been the same since, and we've all been under suspicion. That was also when it finally hit me: Some of the guys I had competed against may have been dirty. When I saw them in later years, I called them cowards to their faces. I feel that way about anyone who cheats. I have no respect for them.

It takes courage to face the process in this sport. You're going to fail, and when you do, you need the guts to look at yourself, assess where things went wrong, fix them, and then come back and try again. That's an arduous process. But that's how you learn and become stronger—not just as a triathlete, but as a human being. Because even if you're a professional now, someday you won't be. Someday, you'll retire and become an age grouper and have the whole rest of your life ahead of you. What are you going to tell your kids about what Mommy or Daddy did? How are you going to look at yourself in the mirror and be proud of what you accomplished? The ones who cheat don't think about that.

Moments of Grace

Any juried sport can be done clean. I know that because I've never touched a performance-enhancing product in my life. I've had plenty of tests, but tests don't matter all that much. Plenty of athletes respond to accusations of doping by saying, "I've never tested positive." That's not the same thing as not having cheated, mate, and you know it. That probably just means you're good at not getting caught.

The hard part about competing clean is that you run the risk of being beaten by athletes who aren't as good as you are but who may be doping. Most of the time you either know it or suspect it, but unless they test positive, there's nothing you can do about it. Once the results are in, it's hard to get justice for a clean athlete who was cheated out of a place on the podium.

In the 2000 Sydney Olympics, my old friend and training partner Miles Stewart took sixth place in the triathlon. Triathlon Australia had refused to put me on the team, so I had taken off to Europe with Emma-Jane and I ended up watching the Olympic event in my hotel room. I saw guys I had been racing with for years, some of whom had muscles on their muscles, running with Miles. I thought, *They're having good days, but come on.*

Simon Whitfield, who's as clean an athlete as there is, won the gold. Miles is also clean as a whistle, and he's an incredibly talented guy who pays attention to detail, and does the sport right. I lived and trained with him, so I know what he's capable of.

Later on, one of the triathletes who finished ahead of Miles was suspended from the sport for two years for doping. So as far as I was concerned, Miles should have been the silver medalist at Sydney.

In 2008, Miles was retired from the sport. Plenty of athletes were now testing positive and programs were being racked by scandal. Miles was coming down to Sydney for work and I invited him to dinner. To surprise him, I made a silver medal out of aluminum foil and gave it to him. He couldn't believe it, and he was very grateful. I said, "This is my Olympic silver medal to you. In my eyes, you will always be the Olympic silver medalist. You got robbed, and I want to acknowledge it."

I will never forget what Miles said to me: "Macca, had someone told me ten years ago when we were training together that I would be sitting here, I would have said no way. I didn't know how to take you back then, and I didn't really like you. It's funny how as you get older you see people for what they are. The guys I thought I would be sitting with I haven't heard from or spoken to in years, but here I am having dinner at your place. I know what this medal means and respect that you do, too." It was a moving moment.

I was glad to do it; Miles was cheated by cowards who have done nothing since then. Miles and I had clashed when I left him and his father to train on my own; I think he found me abrasive because I always asked so many questions. But with him out of the sport now, we're not separated by that competitive drive. When I gave him the medal it brought us back together. I think he understands my character, and I understand him.

From time to time, this sport brings you moments of real grace. Another one came in 2002 at the San Jose International Triathlon. It was a big-money time-trial race, one of the most important races in California at the time. Only twenty-five professionals were invited. It was an interval race, so you couldn't rely on a group. We did the bike stage, then rested while the age groupers raced, and then did the swim and run off our bike time. I was first off the bike, so I went first.

Craig Walton caught me on the swim. In the run, we were going down a very steep hill together, and Craig suddenly did a face plant on the downhill. He went down hard and bloodied himself. I didn't think twice: I went back, picked him up, and helped him brush himself off. Craig, the big crowd, and the age-group racers all looked shocked; Craig Alexander and Greg Bennett were only about three minutes behind us and I had stopped! I let Craig compose himself, then we cruised down the hill, I told him to keep going, and I went on to win the race. It was just one of those things you do when you love the sport.

The Respect of My Peers

Moments like that one with Craig have earned me the respect of my peers, and I crave that even more than I crave winning. The Academy Awards have more prestige than anything else in Hollywood because the winners get the awards from their peers—actors vote for actors, directors for directors, and so on. There's nothing more satisfying than the respect of people who've gone to battle with you and know the sacrifices you've made.

After the 2010 Kona race, everybody started asking me about my legacy—how I wanted to be remembered. But while I truly appreciate the fans, I get more satisfaction out of how my peers view me. It's a thrill to have the Raelert brothers ask me for advice, or to have Mark Allen calling my 2010 Kona race the greatest Ironman he's ever seen. On a personal level, it means everything to be judged by the boys with whom you've raced and gone to war.

When you race alongside people, you get to know them. You learn their character, background, everything. Hopefully, you learn to respect them even if you don't like them personally. That respect is the heart of sportsmanship in any sport, including ours. And nothing—absolutely nothing—will destroy that respect among your peers faster than cheating. When you cheat, you're stealing from all the clean athletes who are working so hard to get better.

For example, Michellie Jones, who won at Kona in 2006 and who in my opinion is the greatest female triathlete to ever walk the planet, was outsprinted for the gold at the 2000 Sydney Olympics. Brigitte McMahon, who took the gold, tested positive for EPO in 2005 but insisted that she was not using any performance enhancers during the 2000 Games. She later retired rather than face a two-year ban.

The thing is, even if you pass every drug test and think you're getting away with something, other athletes always know. It's obvious. Someone on steroids or human growth hormone will lose all their body fat and become inhumanly lean but muscular, and they just won't fatigue. When you see someone with that kind of body who didn't look that way four months ago, you know. Then there's the corruption of character that comes with cheating. Your main concern stops being fair competition and becomes, "Will I pass the drug test?" Cheaters don't care what other athletes think of them, because if they did, it would ruin them. Nobody wants to be despised.

Spouses, coaches, and national federations can push athletes to start cheating. It makes sense — the administrators who work for the national federations have to justify their $150,000 salaries, and they get their budgets from success. If they produce winners or a gold medal, their sport gets a bigger budget and they have a job for another four years. There were well-supported, believable rumors a few years ago that one of the national federations actually had sanctioned a doping program. Other programs would supposedly give their athletes the old "You didn't hear it from us, but if you want to go see them, we'll look the other way" treatment.

Of course, everyone denies it now. It's all about damage control. The fact is, because things were so loose until recently, you can't point to any triathlete's performance and say unequivocally, "That was due to drugs." And I don't want to. I don't want to taint the sport I love in the way that pro cycling has been tainted.

Why Cheat?

If you think of sport, your career or anything in life as a journey, shortcuts rob you of everything that's sweet about that journey. In the end, cheaters might harm the sport temporarily, but they cheat themselves permanently. It doesn't matter if they don't get caught. They're tarnished. They're finished.

I suspect that the increasing money coming into triathlon is putting more pressure on some professionals to cheat. Some might do it even if the only rewards were accolades and pats on the back, because it's also about being the best. But money makes you take shortcuts. I don't think it's a coincidence that as tens of millions of dollars have flowed into the Tour de France, allegations of doping have run rampant in the sport. Money makes you do things you don't want to do. I doubt that Floyd Landis would have taken drugs if the reward for winning the Tour had been a medal and a pat on the back in Paris.

Don't get me wrong; money does matter. I race to feed my family and satisfy my sponsors. However, I think the biggest reason that some athletes use drugs is because of that dangerous emotion I've already touched on: *fear.*

What makes you stick that needle in your arm? Money? Maybe. Ego? Sure. But nobody wakes up one morning and says, "You know, I think I'm going to start using HGH or EPO today!" Fear drives them to it: fear of not being good enough, or of not having what it takes to meet other people's expectations. That's why when people say, "Macca's on the juice," I don't get offended anymore. I take it as a compliment, because they need an excuse for why they can't beat me. Their inner voice whispers, *I'm just not good enough to beat this bloke,* so they need a reason to dismiss me. That's all right. We all know the truth.

The people around me know me too well to even hint that I should try a performance enhancer. They know I would never consider it, not for a second. I have never even been tempted. After all, part of the reason I race is for my late mother and my daughters. How would I be honoring them if I was sticking a needle in my arm?

Most important, though, is that at the end of the day we all have to face that person in the mirror and ask ourselves if we're for real. I like knowing that I am who I say I am and that I've earned what I've gained.

Because I Love the Sport

Many of the people around triathlon—the journalists, the so-called experts, and the athletes—watch results. They don't watch races.

That's a problem if you're trying to walk the straight and narrow in this sport. The fact is, I might be prepared to win every race, but I'm also prepared for the fact that I might not win. After I lost to Stadler at Kona in 2006 despite running the best race I could have possibly run, I was still elated. I hadn't won, but I had performed beautifully. The athlete who beat me had a phenomenal day and deserved the win, but I took something precious away from that Ironman: the pride that I had excelled in my toughest race.

You can only have that mind-set if you're getting something out of the race besides the result. I got into the sport originally because it was play. I was traveling with my friends. We chased girls. We had fun. We pretended to run down Ali'i Drive. But part of that fun comes with knowing that there aren't any guarantees. You're going to lose sometimes, and accepting that gives you permission not to stress out if you do. You can treat the race as a puzzle to be solved. The challenge of getting better can be just as rewarding as finishing in the top of your age group.

It sounds hokey, but I think the guys who are clean and still at the top of the sport are there in part for a simple reason: They are passionate about it. That's why I still get so much out of it. I'm racing for the same reasons I did when I was a kid: the thrill of competition, the challenge of finding the solution to a particular race or a particular problem I'm having, and the knowledge that I'm getting better and smarter as a man. Okay, one thing has changed: I don't race for the chicks anymore.

Now I'm seeing other athletes admit to that same kind of passion for the sport. That's one of the reasons they're coming after me. I made it cool to be openly in love with triathlon. I don't treat it entirely like a business. Yes, it's serious, but it should also be a blast. Other athletes see and hear me and say, "See, Macca loves the sport," and they're not shy about telling everyone else how much they love it, too.

Of course, you don't have to love it to be successful. Simon Lessing, who with Craig Walton and me formed that great three-way rivalry I wrote about in an earlier chapter, was one of the greatest short-course triathletes who ever lived. But he absolutely despised the sport.

Simon won his first world title in 1992 and was near the end of his peak period when I came along and beat him in 1997. When I met him, he told me that he hated the sport. "You hate it?" I said. "You're the champ. How can you hate this? When I was a kid, I wanted to be you. Now you're telling me you hate it, and you're miserable?" I really wanted to hang around with Simon, because he had been such a role model for me. But when I got to know him and heard how negative he was, I couldn't stand being near him. I admired him, but he was such a downer.

You can succeed in this sport—or in any area of life—with pure talent and technical prowess, there's no doubt. But when you don't have the passion, and you hit the wall of age or injury, you're gone. Simon's first injury ended his career. Boom. He was looking for a reason to retire. He didn't have the love of the sport that would have made me or Simon Whitfield or the Raelerts fight to come back.

If you don't have the passion and love the process, if the results are all that matter to you, then there's no depth to your career. There's nothing to pull you out of the dark hole when you fall in. And if you do this sport long enough, you will fall in. I did it in 2004 after I cramped and took a dive into the sponsor car. I was done, ready to retire. Part of the reason I didn't is because I am madly in love with the journey of being a triathlete. I can't wait to see what's to come around the next turn.

If you don't love the sport, then when the opportunity to take a shortcut comes along, you're more likely to take it. That's a short, slippery slope. Your ego gets the best of you. I see guys who are second-tier athletes, which is nothing to be ashamed of, doping because they got desperate. They can't elevate their game, they can't leave the sport, and they can't accept being a few steps down from the podium. So they cheat. They see me and Simon Whitfield getting the accolades and the winner's checks, and they think it should be them.

What's sad and ironic at the same time is that some of the athletes who have juiced—the ones who've been caught and the others that haven't but who the triathlon community *knows* have done it—were great athletes before they started using drugs. Maybe if some of them had looked at their weaknesses honestly or learned from other sports, their careers might have lasted longer. Most had the talent. But something changed. The sport stopped being about passion and started being about something else. So they took the quick fix.

MACCA'S (W)INSIGHTS

"If you don't have the passion and love the process, if the results are all that matter to you, then there's no depth to your career. There's nothing to pull you out of the dark hole when you fall in. And if you do this sport long enough, you will fall in. I did it in 2004 after I cramped and took a dive into the sponsor car. I was done, ready to retire. Part of the reason I didn't is because I am madly in love with the journey of being a triathlete. I can't wait to see what's to come around the next turn."

A Two-Tone Life

When I read stories about the athletes who've been caught cheating, I wonder how they do it. To do what they do, you have to live a two-tone life in your head. On one level, you know you're a cheat. You're a coward. You're all about winning the game at all costs, and that must haunt you day and night.

On the other hand, you're still trying to convince yourself that you're an honorable person, maybe a good spouse and parent. Nobody ever sees themselves as the villain; everybody has a justification for cheating that makes sense to them at the time. Knowing you're a gutless thief who steals from clean athletes, while trying to convince yourself that you're actually not a bad guy, must be immense. It must haunt them for years.

The saddest part comes postcareer, when all you have is the ability to reflect on the things you did back in your glory days. The accolades are gone, and you're probably not in the sport as a coach (because no young triathlete wants to train with a known cheater), and the people are gone. It's just you, your wife, your kids, and maybe a few other retired athletes. What are you going to do? Tell that story about the time you had the really great dose of HGH that helped you finish third? Your kids don't want to hear your stories, anyway. They roll their eyes, then say, "Dad, we heard that one already. Can I borrow the car?"

Ultimately, the only audience you have is yourself. After your racing days are over, you could be sitting back on your porch with a beer, saying to yourself, *Yeah, that was a good day. That hill was hard, but I got through it.* Or you'll be thinking, *It was the drugs. Why did I do that? What did it get me?* You leave your career with a whole life ahead of you and nothing to look back on. That's a tragedy.

MACCA'S 1997 SEASON

- St. George Formula 1 Triathlon Series, Australia—FIFTH
- Australian Triathlon Championships—SECOND
- Australian Sprint Championships—FIRST
- Devonport Triathlon, Australia—SECOND
- Gold Coast Triathlon—FIRST
- Canberra Triathlon, Australia—FIRST
- ITU Triathlon World Cup Japan—FIRST
- ITU Triathlon World Cup Auckland—SECOND
- Toyota Alice Springs Time Trial Triathlon—THIRD
- ITU Triathlon World Cup Monaco—SECOND
- Triathlon St. Etienne, France—FIRST
- Triathlon Beauvais—FIRST
- Triathlon Codelet France—FIRST
- International Grand Prix Triathlon, Koblenz, Germany—THIRD
- ETU Hennezz Zurich Triathlon—FIRST
- Credit Suisse Triathlon, Nyon, Switzerland—FIRST
- Credit Suisse Triathlon, Neuchatel, Switzerland—FIRST
- Credit Suisse Triathlon, Lugano, Switzerland—FIRST
- ITU Triathlon World Cup Hungary—THIRD
- ITU Triathlon World Cup, Embrun, France—FIFTH
- ETU Triathlon Interlaken, Switzerland—FIRST
- ITU Duathlon World Championships, Guernica, Spain—FIFTH
- ITU Triathlon World Cup Bermuda—THIRD

- Nowra Triathlon, Australia—FIRST
- Lake Macquarie Triathlon, Australia—SECOND
- ITU Triathlon World Championships, Perth, Australia—FIRST (first world title)
- ITU Triathlon World Cup Series—FIRST

Season Statistics and Interesting Facts

- Flight miles accumulated for year: 70,379 miles
- Countries visited: 13
- Days away from home: 237

Training miles for the year

- Swim: 740 miles
- Bike: 11,790 miles
- Run: 2,311 miles

13

Everybody's Trying to Age Me

Muhammad Ali once said, "A man who looks at life the same way at fifty that he did when he was twenty has wasted thirty years." Amen. Age brings change. Whether it's positive or negative change depends on how you look at it. I added a family to my equation almost eight years ago when my first daughter was born. Now I have three; my latest was born just before the release of this book. That changes you. I've got other responsibilities now. That doesn't mean I'm less hungry. I'm just drawing inspiration from different things. But does it change what I will sacrifice for my sport? Of course it does. I used to do eight-week training camps away from my children, but I don't know if I have it in me to do that very much longer.

Age is the elephant in the room for every athlete in every sport, because there's no other area of life where you can be washed up when people in other professions are just hitting their stride. As a gymnast, you're done by twenty. If you're a swimmer, you're probably over the hill at thirty. And in most other sports, including triathlon, you're finished by age forty. There's a great deal of anxiety about that. You're slowing down, the work is harder, and it's easy to project your mind ahead in time and see a moment when you just won't be able to do it anymore. For some of us, that brings us face to face with our mortality. For others, I think it's about not being exceptional anymore. When you're a pro and your body is how you make your living, age can haunt you. Some guys stick their heads in the sand and say, "Nope, it's not going to happen to me," but that's just denial.

Also, athletes who are anxious about their own age-related decline start trying to undermine athletes who are still performing well at a relatively advanced age. Everyone has been trying to "age me" for years, especially after the 2009 Ironman Hawaii, when I had a bad swim. But even before that, peers and friends in the sport would start to point at how few thirty-seven-year-old or thirty-five-year-old champions there were. You'll have beers with your boys and they'll say things like, "Gimme a thirty-five-year-old guy who's winning races right now, in any sport," or, "So, mate, when are you gonna hang it up?" I'm sure glad I didn't hang it up before the 2010 race.

If you listen, it can become a self-fulfilling prophecy. When I say I'm not ready to retire yet, they roll their eyes, and you know they're thinking, *Macca's going to be like that beat-up old heavyweight fighter who just keeps going back into the ring to get pummeled.* Trust me, I will not be that guy. I just trust in what I can do at my age.

As I've said, my sport is very focused on the physical. We don't give enough credibility to experience and the effect it can have on a race. If you think of yourself as a complete being, then as your physical capabilities go down a bit, your experience goes up. You become smarter, more clever with your training, and wiser about how to read races and other athletes. Think of your career as a bank of experience and knowledge. I've been saving for sixteen years. Of course, you need to know how to spend it.

Experience Wins

Experience in any field is underrated. People tend to be overwhelmed by talent, especially new, young talent. But how many people in any profession are great from the moment they start? There are a few prodigies, sure, but most people need seasoning to reach their peak. Experience plus self-discipline plus talent equals success. You just can't dismiss experience and the knowledge that comes with years of watching how people perform under pressure.

Experience is a weapon. I won Kona in 2010 because of my experience, my knowledge of myself and my understanding of the minds of the other athletes. It's won me a lot of races in the last few years against guys who, based on physical gifts alone, should have beaten me. But I also lost races in my early years through fear. I lost the Australian national title in 1996 to Brad "the Croc" Bevan, who was my idol, and I should have belted him. But he was a cagey bastard. He sat on me and talked to me, saying stuff like, "You know, you race well," and he played me. Before I knew what happened, he'd buried me.

If I have to choose between the guy with awesome physical gifts who's a mental milkshake and the above-average talent who's disciplined, experienced, and smart, I'll take the smart guy every time. When you cross the line and the guy who shouldn't have beaten you is standing above you on the podium, you know you've had your pocket picked. That should teach you a few lessons. I was schooled a few times by more experienced athletes early in my career and I picked up their lessons. If you don't pick up experience from your losses and turn it into an advantage, then you've got nothing. When you hit thirty-five, you're gone.

The Old Bull and the Young Bull

There's an old joke that goes like this: An old bull and a young bull are standing at the top of a hill, looking down at a pasture full of cows. The young bull says, "Hey, why don't we run down there and screw some of those cows?" The old bull looks at him and says, "Why don't we *walk* down there and screw them all?"

That's how I think about experience in triathlon: It's the old bull versus the young bulls. The old bull conserves his energy to spend it at the right time, when it matters. The young bull is all about ego, showing off and thinking he's invincible. But winning a triathlon is about more than winning the race in water, on the bike, or in the marathon. It's about intelligence and will. Those things don't diminish with age. They increase. As you get older, you learn more about what you can take on. You learn what your real limits are. I'm a much better athlete now than I was at twenty-three. Am I faster and more resilient? No. But as an overall athlete, it's no contest. I was a boy, and now I'm a man.

Experience brings with it a whole life history of the training, tactics, and mental tricks that bring out the best in you as an athlete. You have a better perspective on what makes you better. I have a bigger catalog of knowledge because I've raced hundreds of races and know how to make small adjustments that yield big benefits. For me, it's no longer about humbling the other guy. That takes too much energy. All I want is to find that one key that will let me beat him.

But the greatest compensation of age is that your ability to endure suffering increases. As I've said, triathlon is at its core about who can continue to fight through the agony when others give in to it. When you're old, you can draw from a much greater reserve of will than you had when you were young. When you're young you're full of energy. You think that you can breeze through a race at full speed and it shouldn't hurt. But it does and I've seen young athletes quit because they didn't expect it to be as bad as it is.

When you're young, everything is a crisis. When my daughters are sixteen, everything for them is going to be the end of the world. That's youth. Age teaches you to chill out. Whatever you're feeling, you've been there before. It's not a big deal. You know what your body can take. You have more points of reference. You know to save something in reserve for the time when your good friend pain comes calling. The most I've ever suffered in a race was at Kona in 2006, when I was thirty-three—well past the age when a lot of triathletes have retired. I was able to do that because I knew my body so well. I knew precisely how hard I could push myself without blowing up. I knew that while what I was experiencing was excruciating, it wouldn't kill me.

That's why the old bull can beat the young bull. Your ability to have a slugfest with another athlete definitely comes with age. You know when to counterpunch, when to lay back and let the other guy beat himself, when to be patient, and when to attack. The deciding factor in my showdown with Raelert in 2010 wasn't my physical ability. It was my experience and self-knowledge. You can't see experience on a TV monitor, which is why everybody thought he'd caught me and was going to run me into the ground. Now everyone knows better. I was the old bull that day.

Age Is Just a Number

You should be wiser at thirty-five or thirty-seven. If you're not, then you haven't grown, and that's a waste. When I was winning races at twenty-three, I had no idea why I was good. I was an idiot. I didn't have a clue why I was a world champion. If you don't know your strengths and weaknesses, you don't know what to change when you run up against someone who knows how to beat you—and that happens to all of us. Today, I know why I'm successful. I know what to tweak when a race doesn't go the way I want it to.

When you get older, you also have to plan everything much farther in advance. When I was in my twenties, I could jump out of bed after a few hours of sleep, throw some junk down my throat and run, bike, and swim a ten-hour training day. If I tried to do that today, I wouldn't last six hours. You have to prepare when you're older. You have to plan for more rest and a longer training period so you can avoid injury. You can't just flip the switch anymore, so preparation becomes critical. That's why my team and I carefully plan out every part of my season long before it starts.

MACCA'S (W)INSIGHTS

Train smarter with age

- Give yourself more recovery time. Build more days into your training program dedicated to either light work or total rest.

- Add more strength work to your plan. With age, you will lose speed and flexibility, but you can compensate by becoming more powerful.

- Invest more time in warming up to loosen your muscles, and consider working dedicated flexibility exercise such as yoga into your routine.

- Take advantage of your experience. Analyze your past performances in races and adjust your training to attack them. With age, your mind becomes even more important than your body.

Doing that means accepting what's happening, but it also means refusing to listen to those idiots who are so eager to tell you that you're too old to compete. Age is just the number after your name that tells people when you were born. It doesn't have anything to do with what you can or can't do.

In the wake of my win at Kona in 2010, I would love to see some older guys start trying to compete at a high level instead of accepting a premature decline. I hope they say, "If Macca can do it, I've got the same physical skills he does, so maybe I can do it, too." There are a lot of "old" guys who are actually younger than me but considering retirement. You know you're getting old when that happens.

Groupies, Not Experts

The reporters are the ones who were really trying to age me before Kona in 2010. They hyped the fact that I was thirty-seven, like it was shocking that I could still get out of bed. In every profession, people love to label you. They want to get a handle on who and what you are. So with me, it was, "Macca is thirty-seven; therefore he's too old to win at Kona again." Now they have dismissed me and can move on to the next person. That's a very human impulse.

My response is, maybe we should retire all the young guns in the sport, because they got taken to school by a grandfather. I'm the oldest athlete ever to win Kona—four months older than Mark Allen was when he won his last world championship. Heck, Chris Lieto is older than I am, and I don't hear anyone talking about how he's too old to be taken seriously! Craig Alexander is only four months younger than me, so where are the "Crowie is too old to win at Kona again" columns?

One of the problems with the sport is that we don't really have experts writing the magazines and doing the interviews. We have groupies. They look at results, not races. They don't have any interest in analysis of how an athlete performs. It's all about times, ages, and finish positions. Rather than look at my evolution as an athlete—or dig into the race data and find out that the only reason I wasn't racing for first in 2009 was because I'd had a terrible swim—the press decided I was too old. I was too big. I'd fought too many wars. I didn't want it enough. I was too wrapped up in my family. Anything to drop a neat label on me, relegate me to the Former Champions Hall of Fame, and move on to the Raelerts or some other young stars.

Let me tell you, being aged before my time and dismissed as a threat added a lot of satisfaction to my 2010 win. Because of that, more people are starting to realize that they just can't take some of the triathlon press seriously. For instance, the media have been gushing over a Czech triathlete, Filip Ospaly, as the next big star. He's a great athlete; he beat me by a minute to win the 2010 Ironman 70.3 Austria. But they were saying that he was a nobody who beat Macca, so they had another excuse to declare my career over. But this guy was a two-time Olympian—hardly a nobody! The press looked like fools. Now the fans are starting to question the hype and saying,

"Who's writing this stuff? They don't know what they're talking about."

There was a time when I felt like I had to justify what I did to the press, but not anymore. When they made me a ten-to-one shot at Kona in 2010, I remember thinking, *After knowing me for fifteen years in the sport, you never really knew me.* But they know me now.

No Matter How Old You Are, There's Somebody Older

I think the other factor that's helped me defy all those predictions about my early demise is the mentoring of my friend and trainer, Mick. Having the vainest man in the world in my corner all these years, preaching to me about the realities of aging, has been a real benefit.

Mick is in phenomenal shape, especially for a guy in his fifties, but what really made our relationship work was that from the beginning, I was interested in how age changed the body and how to compensate for those changes. Mick liked me because I would listen to what happens to this muscle when it contracts, how age affects its recovery from injury, and so on. But I was truly fascinated, even if it was for selfish reasons: I wanted to get some insight into how my own body would age and how it would affect my performance as a professional.

So I was always asking questions, and Mick was always answering them. He'd say, "You'll see, mate. When you get to thirty-five, you will be able to do this and this, but this will happen, too." I would ask him, "So at thirty-two, could you do so-and-so?" and he would tell me. I learned a lot.

Mick is almost fifteen years older than I am, and the difference in our ages has been a blessing. When he went with me to Europe at the beginning of my career, he was the age I am now, so it was really interesting to watch how his physicality has changed. I've been lucky enough to piggyback my whole career on a guy who is athletic but also able to talk honestly about the changes that have occurred as he's aged. It's helped me be realistic, but also to look at growing older with anticipation instead of the sense of doom that I think most athletes have about it. Age becomes just one more challenge for me.

I think any athlete who's serious about this sport should spend time with athletes, mentors, or trainers who are older but aging really well, because it's a great way to get perspective on what age really means. It doesn't have to mean the end of your career. It just means that change is coming. Heck, Tim DeBoom ran an 8:49:26 and finished thirty-third at Kona in 2010 at age forty. If you approach aging with a positive attitude and a plan, there's no reason you can't be just as strong and competitive at forty as you were at thirty.

14

A Goal Is a Dream
with a Plan

When Sean Maroney and I were dreaming about all the triathlons we were going to conquer, we would always talk about leading Ironman Hawaii at the turnaround point, in the town of Hawi. We'd argue about who would go around first if we both got there at the same time. I'd say, "I'll go around first, but then let you come up close because the TV camera would be following us both and we'd punch the air at the same time." It didn't matter what happened after that. Hawi was our defining moment. Leading at the turn became rounding Cape Horn to us.

Then Sean died in 2002, and a few months later I was in my first Ironman at Kona, leading in the bike stage. Two miles from the turn, I rode up next to Thomas Hellriegel (who would save my ass three years later by telling me to drink Coke when I was near collapse) and said, "Do you mind if I take the lead here, mate?" He looked at me like I was out of my mind, because of course he was thinking about the race. But he backed off and let me lead around the turn, and I was in heaven. All I could think about was Sean and how we were going to punch the air after this moment. For ten years, this was all we'd talked about. I spoke to him in my mind: *How cool is this, mate, we did it*. The emotion was overwhelming. Earlier in the year, I'd equaled Mike Pigg's record by winning my fourth Escape from Alcatraz, and now I'd led my first Kona at the turn. Wow.

Too bad that was the high point of the day. As you know, the day went downhill from there and I didn't finish. But looking back, I think one of the reasons I was so quick to step off the course in 2002 was that I'd really been there to fulfill that dream—Sean's and my dream. I probably could have fought and muscled and stayed in the race. I had such a big lead off the bike that I only had to run a 3:10 marathon and I would have finished third. My cramps were brutal, but they weren't what stopped me. After Hawi, I'd checked out. It was easy for me to say to myself, *I've had a good year. I'll be back next year and kick their asses.*

Leading at Hawi was our dream, but we also had a plan to make it a reality. We could have settled for sitting back in Australia and imagining what it would be like, but that wasn't enough. Our list of races wasn't just a fantasy. Our goal became conquering each one of those races. There's a saying that goes, "A goal is a dream with a plan." Well, in wrapping up this book, I thought I would talk about how someone who aspires to do a specific triathlon—or any other endurance race, for that matter—can take it from a distant dream to an achievable goal.

Break the Big Thing Down

When you're an athlete of any kind and you look at a big race or event, it can seem impossible and remote. If you're a triathlete who wants to do Kona, you might think, *I'm years away from being able to do that. How do I get there?*

With something that big, you can't take it all at once. When I started my pro career, I didn't set out to become world number one or Ironman champion; I just wanted to make some money, learn from the older guys, and make the Olympic team. You have to break the big dream down into smaller steps that don't intimidate you. Then you can set each one up, reach it, and move on to the next.

I find it also helps to write things down. Declare your intentions to the universe. Put yourself out there and tell the people around you what you're going to do. Say, "I'm going to do an Ironman race in the summer of 2013 and Kona by 2014." Now it's no longer a dream or vision. It's a goal. Then you build your process, the strategy you'll employ to reach that goal.

I've given you some of the building blocks for that plan in this book:

- Work with a coach and create a training program that works for your body and your schedule.
- Develop a nutritional strategy.
- Watch races on video and live and learn about tactics.
- Talk to triathletes and learn from them.
- Join a triathlon club near you and train with a group.
- Learn about gear and get the best you can afford.
- Get out your calendar and start setting goals for the future: *This race, this weekend.*
- Go to your first race.
- Accept that you're going to be a nervous wreck, because we all were.

That first triathlon is terrifying and exhilarating, but you get through it. When you do, you feel incredible. The word *hope* becomes obsolete. You go from thinking *I hope I can do this* to *I can do this.* Damn, you're a triathlete. You're one step closer to your goal.

That's the whole story of my career: a dream of two twelve-year-old boys inspired by the champions in the sport, a goal for turning that dream into a career, and a plan to make that happen. And even though I've won just about every major triathlon on the planet, I still have that dream. I've never wavered from that initial passion that brought me to the sport. That's really the secret of my longevity. Even when I'm no longer a pro, I will still do triathlon. I like what it makes me learn about myself. I like what it makes me have to do. That's why I haven't retired. There are more mountains to climb.

Believe, But Be Tough

Unfortunately, too many people—would-be triathletes and others—deny their dreams. They talk about what they plan to do someday, but that's as far as they take it. They're afraid to fail, so they don't even take a risk. They don't honor that passion they feel or believe it's worth sacrificing for, so they aren't prepared to pay the price of reaching their goal—and that price can be steep.

If your goal is to compete in a triathlon, or to step up your game and compete at Kona or another major race, you're definitely going to make sacrifices. You're going to spend money. You're going to spend time away from your family. You're going to hurt. You might blow up in a race and feel like a loser. It's no different if your goal is to be an actor, a writer, a doctor, or anything else. When you chase your dream, there's a good chance you're going to trip and fall. That can paralyze you.

I was just as fearful as any normal kid would have been about leaving behind everything I knew and running off to compete on the European circuit in 1996. I made it a little easier by quitting my job and selling all my possessions, leaving me with no choice. I pushed all my chips into the middle of the table. There was no turning back. Even if I had failed miserably as a professional triathlete, I would be able to say that I had given it everything. It's the things we *don't* do that we regret.

I think the reason I was able to walk away and take that risk was that I honored my burning desire to race and to see the world. I believed that my passion was worth pursuing, and that gave me what I needed to break out of my "comfortable prison." And that's what I wish more triathletes would do: honor their passion for getting better, doing bigger races, and setting loftier goals. Your dreams are no less important than mine. So what if you're younger or older than I was when I started, or have a career and can't commit as much time to training, or are an average athlete who won't ever finish an Ironman in less than fifteen hours? Your dreams matter.

I wouldn't have been able to do all that if I hadn't believed that what I was doing was right, not only for me but for my sport as well. You will always have people telling you what you can't do. *Always.* But in the end, the only opinion that matters is yours. It's true that Emma, my daughters, Mick, and my agent, Scott, have always believed in me, and their faith has given me strength as surely as any electrolyte drink. But if I hadn't believed in myself, all their belief couldn't have made me endure suffering or work to solve the puzzle of Kona.

MACCA'S (W)INSIGHTS

"I wish more triathletes would honor their passion for getting better, doing bigger races, and setting loftier goals. Your dreams are no less important than mine. So what if you're younger or older than I was when I started, or have a career and can't commit as much time to training, or are an average athlete who won't ever finish an Ironman in less than fifteen hours? Your dreams matter."

Of course, believing in your passion is only part of the formula. You have to follow through, and that means being tough and relentless. Plenty of aspiring triathletes never make it to their goals because they get fired up with the vision and the plan—and then quit at the first injury or other setback. There will always be bumps in the road. Triathlon will demand everything you have and more. If you think, *I've made the decision and now everything should just fall into place,* you'll never make it. Remember, when I went to Kona in 2002, I assumed the race would fall before the greatness that was Chris McCormack. It took me six years to finally capture the race I had been so certain I would own.

It's hard to turn a dream into a plan. If the results aren't what you want the first time around, retreat and regroup. If you can't retreat, then attack in a different way. Keep moving forward. The reason I was able to finally win at Kona was because I didn't accept the failures of previous years. I kept looking for new ways to attack the race and finally found one that worked. When the race changed again in 2008 and 2009, I regrouped and came back to capture another title.

It's About Respect, Not Being Liked

That persistence, drive, and passion have earned me as much respect in this sport as my race results. Respect matters to me more than being liked. I've said a lot of things in my career that have rubbed people the wrong way, and some of those people have said, "Macca, you're dead wrong, mate," as well as some things that were less polite. That's okay with me. I'd like to be liked by the people in my sport, but when I started winning races, I quickly learned that there are plenty of people who only like you when you're going well. When I was a kid in the sport, older athletes treated me like just another young punk—until I was world champ. Then they were my friends. Sean would get in their faces and defend me. "Do you like us now, mate? Do you?" he'd demand.

Worrying about being liked is like chasing phantoms. That's why I don't have an entourage. If your fortunes turn and the money and acclaim disappear, guess what? You'll look over your shoulder and the only things left of your posse will be their bar tabs. I also think a big entourage tells other people that you lack confidence in your ability. A great example of this was a 2001 boxing match I saw between the Russian Kostya Tszyu and the American Zab Judah. Zab was the IBF junior welterweight champ and a flashy, skilled fighter. Kostya was a hard, disciplined boxer with only one loss in his career, one of the greatest welterweights of all time.

Well, Zab Judah started calling out Kostya and talking a lot of trash. I noticed that Zab was beating the daylights out of some really great fighters who were a lot younger than the Russian, who was nearing the end of his career. They scheduled a fight and met in Las

Vegas. Watching it on television, I saw Kostya walk into the ring. Now, I've become good at noticing if guys look scared before a big event, whether it's a triathlon or a fight. You can see it in their eyes. Kostya looked like he'd been there a million times before. His entourage was his coach, Johnny Lewis, and his son.

Zab Judah came down to the ring with about sixty guys, including a cadre of rappers and Mike Tyson. He was chewing gum. I was floored. *What are all these guys for, Zab? What are you hiding behind?* He looked scared; it looked like he had pulled all his people together hoping to intimidate his opponent. But in walking out with just two people, Kostya had made it clear that he didn't need anyone to tell him how good he was.

The result was predictable: Kostya knocked Zab out in the second round.

I don't need the entourage. I care about the opinions of the people I'm close to—my wife, my children, friends like Mick, Scott, Susanne, Paul Ambrose, and some others. But beyond that, I want my peers to respect me—and fear me a little. I'd also like to be recognized as someone who took the sport to a new level in the sense that I made it about more than swim, bike, run. I made it about swim, bike, run, *think.* I want people to look back and ask, "What was Macca's strength?" and have them say that I was an incredible tactician and a hard-ass warrior, that I could suffer with the best of them, and that I was the smartest guy in the sport.

There are a lot of guys who have much more finesse than I do. Andreas Raelert looks like a gazelle; I'm a brute. But I have the ability to plan and execute that plan. I'd like the people who really know the sport to respect me for those reasons.

My Legacy

Now that I've won Kona for the second time, everybody's asking me what's next. My obvious answer is, "More time with my family." But don't think I'm going to be leaving the sport. I will be involved with triathlon as long as I'm breathing. I'm just not sure in what capacity. I can't deny that my professional career is slowly winding down. Even if I can still compete at an elite level with the young bucks, I'm not sure that I want to for much longer. This is an endurance sport in more ways than one; I've endured many months half a world away from my wife and my girls. That's going to end.

What about my legacy? First of all, just the word makes me feel ancient, like I should already be in a rocking chair. But I guess if you ask me how I'd like to be remembered, it would be like Ali is remembered. He was outspoken and disliked in his time, but now he's regarded as the greatest ever. I'd like people to come to see me like that.

But not yet. I still have dreams. For one, I would love to make the Olympics. I contacted the Australian Triathlon Federation and said, "I am here to help, not hinder, Australian progress in triathlon." They presented me with a scenario for completing my career with an Olympic berth. If I can meet the criteria and earn the points necessary to qualify for the Games, they'll put me on their radar. Now everyone thinks I'm a dreamer again. These kids are almost half my age and faster than I ever was. The odds are against me, but that's the way I love it. It is going to be awesome fun.

I could also see myself coaching on a small scale. I would love to run a school or camp. It's a natural for someone like me who's in love with tactics and breaking down races and other athletes. Or maybe I could run my own school of coaching philosophy and principles, training other coaches to be better coaches. I might also be interested in running a national program, because it would give me access to the young athletes. I could train them the right way from the beginning—mental toughness, strategy, self-awareness, skeleton training, and more.

Most important, I would teach athletes to always ask questions and be aware of weaknesses, both their own and those of others. You identify the weaknesses in yourself and strengthen them, and you find the weaknesses in others and work out ways to exploit them.

Everybody you're going to be racing has weaknesses. It might be as simple as finding someone who's fearful or overly sensitive, then teasing them in a press conference and watching them explode. There are a lot of ways to win a race.

One More Kona?

But I know what you're wondering. Everybody has been wondering it: Will I defend at Kona in 2011? Here's the official word: Due to family needs and the immense time commitment, Kona 2011 is a no-go for me. A lot of people I respect immensely, like Bob Babbitt, a six-time Ironman finisher and cofounder of *Competitor* magazine, have said things to me like "What an incredible career, Macca. You should be proud of yourself, very, very proud of yourself. There's no need for you to go back to Kona again. Walk away on top, be that guy. Your career deserves that."

As for racing in Kona…never say never. I love the race. It's where I perfected my process-driven approach to winning. I think anybody who has this event in his blood is always drawn back to it. I will stay involved with Kona for the rest of my life. Will I pin a number back on my chest again? I suspect that one day, someone will appear who I would enjoy competing against, and I will throw my hat in the ring again. I have bled too much on those lava fields to simply walk away.

My team and I have tossed around a couple of other options for the 2011 season. In one, I would try to break the world record for an Ironman, 7:50:27, which Luc Van Lierde set at Ironman Europe in 1996. The first person to break the 7:50 barrier would become the Roger Bannister of the sport, an immortal. Even if I didn't get it, no one would smack me around for giving it the old college try.

The other possibility is that I go on another rampage of races that I haven't done yet, or try to win ten of the toughest 70.3-mile half-Ironman races in the world in a single season, which no one has ever done or even approached. All the sports physiologists have said that it's impossible and puts too much strain on the body, and you know how much I love confounding the guys in the lab coats.

I might do VineMan in the Napa Valley, San Juan, Puerto Rico, Ironman China, maybe Austria and Singapore. Who knows? I'd like to target events I haven't done or haven't won. But even if I *only* won six of those races, it would still be one of the greatest seasons of all time. As I said, by the time you're reading this, my final season will probably have been decided. I might decide to try something that I haven't even thought of yet.

Nothing Left to Prove

I always said that I want to walk away on my terms, on top. My 2010 Kona race will be talked about forever. It's part of my legacy. I've got nothing left to prove to anybody. I don't want to hang around for the accolades; that's the wrong reason. If I go back to Kona or do anything else in the sport, it will be for passion. That's the right reason. The other great reason is to raise money for my foundation and to bring attention to the sport that has given me everything.

Emma will also have a lot to say about what I do next. It's as much her decision as mine. If wanting to break the world record or win ten races in a season is my ego bubbling up, she'll let me know. From this point on, I belong to those ladies back in Australia who have kept the fires burning and always welcomed me home.

I'm a lucky, lucky man, mate. I've turned my dreams into goals and then achieved every one of them. Whether you're a novice triathlete trying to get off on the right foot, a professional trying to move up in the ranks, or an athlete in a totally unrelated sport, I hope I've given you some things you can use to do the same.

Acknowledgments

Emma-Jane...you brought balance into my life and a peace to my being that is bliss. You are my best friend, my wife, and my life, and this entire journey would have been nothing without you. I love you more than you can ever imagine.

Tahlia, my daughter...I blinked and you were seven. I hope you enjoy this book. You grew up around the world, and you were present as a baby for many of these stories. You will always be everything to me. I love you, darling.

Sienna, my darling little baby...you're Daddy's little girl. You light up my life and your smile owns me. I love you so much it hurts.

My unborn child...As I write this, Emma is pregnant with you. By the time this book is published you will be a part of this world. Welcome! My journey has brought me here, and the rest of my life will be about you and your sisters. I cannot wait to hold you. I cannot wait to have you in my life. We are so blessed and excited to have you in our family.

Dad...I am here because of everything you did for me as a boy. You kept me levelheaded, called it straight, and gave me the tools to be my own man. All the days you took me surfing as a boy, all the runs we did together, every athletics carnival I ever did, you were there, and to be the best athlete in the world in my chosen sport was a product of your guidance and your time. Dad, I love you and I thank you. You are the best father a person could ever have, and I hope to guide my girls with the same love and energy you gave me.

Mum...I miss you, love you—I wish we'd had more time. Cancer took you so fast. One minute you were my mother, and the next minute you were gone. I would trade everything I have accomplished for one more day with you. I will never forget you. You will always be remembered, and I thank you for my life and your love.

Greg, my older brother...thanks for letting me win that running race when we were boys. As the oldest brother, you could have crushed my spirits, but you allowed me to believe for all those years that I was a winner. You're my big brother and I don't say it enough, so thanks for being you. Thanks for keeping it real, and thanks for the love. Being older, I finally appreciate your love and support. You are an awesome big brother. The Easter show was the best!

Sean Maroney...what can I say, mate? I did it! I would give anything to have you see what's transpired in my life. You were the one who always believed in me, even when I didn't. *Always.* We laughed, we won, and we believed, and I will never forget our bond. I miss the beers and the talks and the laughs. I miss the old days of dreaming about doing this sport while we trained and partied. I miss the days when I was winning and the laughs we had when nobody realized what huge triathlon geeks we were. They were the best days ever. I miss you, brother, and I will never forget you.

Scott Fairchild, my sports agent...mate, it's been eleven years, and we have come a long way. You are one of my best friends and I don't say it enough, but thanks for your unselfish drive and belief in me. We took on this sport together and we nailed it. You have been at every victory and shared every defeat of the past decade, so this journey is yours, too. I could not have had a better wingman.

Warren and Lindy...thanks for giving me Emma-Jane and for welcoming me to the family. It's been an eventful journey, and we have shared many highs and some big lows. That's what makes any journey special. Thanks for your love and commitment and everything you do. I love you both dearly.

Kerry...thanks for your support and belief. It means a lot. I know how hard Stephen and Dad can be, so you're an Ironman for putting up with them. I really appreciate it.

Michael "Mick" Gilliam (MG)...you're a brother from another mother, mate. You know how much I love our friendship. When all the lights die down, it will still be us, kicking back on the balcony drinking beers and breaking down problems. Those are some of my favorite talks ever. Your knowledge is simple and exceptional, and I hope you share it with more people. Thanks for being there for so long, mate. We've come a long way since that day at Brighton Bike Chain, haven't we? Just so you know, I am only calling you Michael here for your mum. You will always be Mick. I know you hate it, but get used to it, because now it's immortalized in print.

Susann, my brilliant mental game coach...am I your thesis study? I am waiting for this sport to be over and for you to finally diagnose me as mentally unstable. I cannot tell you how much I enjoy our friendship and our talks. You're a huge part of my life and my team. You burrow so deep into my thoughts sometimes it's uncanny. I absolutely love it. It's been a great ten years knowing you and Arne. You are special people in my life.

Jillian Manus, my literary agent...you are also my friend. Without you, this would never have been possible. Thank you for the insight and the belief that we could pull it all together. I had a story to tell and you believed it was worth telling. This is only the beginning! Thanks for coming into my life. You are amazing and an inspiration.

Tim Vandehey, my cowriter and partner in this story...mate, you are a wordsmith of grand proportions and a genius with the English language. To turn this rough Australian accent of mine into a gripping story is impressive. More than anything, you're a friend, and I thank you for the tireless work and commitment you've shown in getting my story down. Getting a book published is a serious endurance challenge, but you never faltered or complained. For this I am forever grateful, mate.

Rolf Zettersten, my publisher, and Kate Hartson, my editor... from the moment I crossed the finish at Kona in 2010 you wanted this book, because you shared my vision of creating something that would be more than a "here's how I won" book. Thank you for your faith, dedication, passion, and talent in making this all happen in such a short time. You and your team at Hachette are incredible.

Guy Hemmerlin, my French club coach from back in 1993... you're still around the sport, and there are not many of us left, mate. Thanks for your support and friendship. You have been at so many of my victories in Europe and Hawaii, and I seriously appreciate that. Who would have ever thought all of this in 1993? *Vous remercier mon bon ami.*

Dave "Turtle" Cavaco... mate, you have magic hands. Thanks for the work on my muscles and the tireless commitment to helping me hold everything together after all the work we do. You're the body technician, keeping me fine-tuned and ready. I cannot thank you enough. You're a legend.

My sponsors... there are so many, but I have to call out a few:

Clif Bar, for your belief and long-term support of my dream. Dylan, you are the man and an absolute pleasure to work with. Thanks for helping me achieve my goals.

Under Armour, you epitomize everything I have aspired to be: driven, focused, real, and better. Kevin Plank, you are my idol. I model my pursuit of being better on the same mind-set you built this company with. Thank you for believing in me a long time ago. Where many people thought I was full of hype, you thought I was full of potential. Thanks for building the best gear in the world, and know I will protect this house forever.

Specialized, thanks for understanding our sport and putting your faith in an athlete like me. Three years and two world titles—not a bad synergy! Guys, you make my job so much easier. You never say no, always pushing for me to be better and faster. I cannot say thanks enough to you all.

Zipp, Sram, Profile Design, Yankz, Triathlon Lab, Orca, Biest-milch, Yurbuds, Speedplay, FuelBelt, Compex—each of you is spe-cial in my journey. You have all been with me for a long time, and you all took a chance on a guy who was a little different. Thanks for your unrivalled support. To Karen at Profile, Alex at Sram, Lloyd at TriLab, Jacquie at Compex, Scott at Orca, Arne at Biestmilch, Rich-ard and Sharon at Speedplay, Vinu at FuelBelt, Greg at Zipp, Rich at Yurbuds, and Pierce at Yankz...THANK YOU.

Paul Ambrose...you have been a warrior for me, mate. We have done some outlandish training and punished our bodies many times, but you keep getting up. It's been a lot of fun, and I thank you for the endless days on the road, riding or running beside me. You have your own career, but know that you were a big part in mine over these past five years. Keep being real; that's your best quality!

Bob Babbitt...you took me under your wing when I arrived in the USA as a young guy. Many people were happy to dismiss me, but I thank you for taking me at face value. You have become a good friend and a special person in my life.

Kim and Simon...thank you for all those years you came out to support me in Kona. I will never forget it and appreciate it so much. You're special friends. I look forward to returning the love when you step up to race the big dance one day soon.

Chuck...what can I say? It's been a long time and we've come full circle. Thanks for all those years, mate: our talks, our long days train-ing, and our funny times over the past decade. It's been great fun and filled my life with laughs. With the stresses of parenting two girls, it's going to be a fun journey to come, too.

Julie and Lloyd...thank you for your driving support of me and for your friendship and love. You're family. Jules, "You know you love it." I had to say it.

Rob and Irene...I love you both. Thank you for all you do in my life and for being such grounded friends. It means more than you can imagine.

Derek King...you have become one of my best mates. Thanks for just being you and putting up with my babble. We always have great laughs and good times eating chicken parmigiano at Rostis in Santa Monica. It's one of my favorite things to do in the US.

Terenzo Bozzone...I believe in you. You're an awesome training partner, an absolute gentleman, and a super talent. I wish you only success and prosperity in this sport and hope you achieve all you are capable of achieving. If you ever need anything, I am only a phone call away.

Michellie Jones, Miles Stewart, Helen McGuckin, Col Stewart, Dick Caine, Clinton Barter, Peter Coulson, and Mark Allen...your guidance at particular times in my career gave me the foundation and knowledge to grow. I respect you all for that, and thank you for being so giving and helpful. They say you are a product of the people you learn from, and I could not have had better mentors.

To my training partners over the years who have endured my singing on the bike and long hours together...it's a tough gig, and you are all warriors. It's the guys you suffer with that give you the fight to win. Kerry Classen, you were a stalwart and a great mate. Paul Amey and Benny Harley, we did some solid days and some big months together. Thanks for your diligence and time. Stanto, your crash is still the best I have ever seen, and our talks in Boulder are always a laugh. Cainey, it was always fun out there in those trails around the Shire. Great times and great laughs, and I look forward to many more. Randy, thanks. You are a solid friend, and I appreciate all those long training days in France and Spain more than you can imagine. JTo, you're a legend. Thanks for the LA time. Those long rides would not be the same without you. BP in Boulder, Tyler Butterfield, James Bowstead, Tim Marr, and Browny—cheers, boys, for the time. Know that it was and is much appreciated. To all of you who suffered with me, thanks very much.

To my friends who supported me and never stopped believing... Struggler, you're a rough diamond, but I love your support. Battler, you're one in a million, and after fourteen years knowing you, it gets better every year. Marijo and Danny Murphy, we love you. Pat, Mac, and Cal in Santa Monica, thanks for taking me in way back when and giving me the Batcave to sleep in. I loved it and miss it. Mac, chase your dreams, mate. I look forward to watching you rock the stage with your band.

Finally, I would like to acknowledge some of the phenomenal triathletes I have raced and suffered with over the years. We have had our wars on the racecourse and for some of us, wars off it as well. But through it all, I have always had the utmost respect for all of you. Thank you for inspiring me and pushing me to find my limitations and go beyond them. Thank you for teaching me by example. Thank you for showing me what it means to be a professional. Thank you for making me better.

Andreas Raelert
Brad Bevan
Craig Alexander
Craig Walton
Eneko Llanos
Greg Bennett
Greg Welch
Hamish Carter
Miles Stewart
Normann Stadler
Simon Whitfield
Timo Bracht

VISIT CHRIS MCCORMACK ONLINE

Twitter: Follow Macca and his racing around the World on Twitter: www.twitter.com/MaccaNow

Facebook: Stay up to date with Macca on Facebook at www.facebook.com/MaccaLive

MaccaNow
www.MaccaNow.org
The Chris McCormack Foundation

The MaccaNow Foundation was set up in honor of my mother, Theresa McCormack, who lost her battle with breast cancer in 1999, at the age of 53. It has become my mission to raise and donate $2,735,373 over the duration of my career and to give this money to the cold face of the disease by directly donating to hospitals that help patients and families who have been struck with this disease. I came up with this figure simply because my mother, at 53 years of age, had lived 19,455 days on this earth. Racing Ironman events around the world requires me to push my body for 140.6 miles. I decided I would raise 140.6 dollars for every day my mother was alive, and this is how we came up with our figure. The money we donate is given on a no-questions-asked basis to be used by the families and the hospitals in any way they desire and to help the women who are fighting this disease to focus entirely on their health and not worry about anything else.

Visit the MaccaNow Foundation to be inspired and to help us in the fight against breast cancer.

MaccaLive
www.MaccaLive.com

Check out this website for up-to-date travel, race video, race reports, video blogs, photos, and all the latest news on Ironman World Champion Chris McCormack as he races around the world. Register here for free newsletters, sponsor giveaways, and prizes. This site is active and alive and offers people a solid insight into life on the road as a professional endurance athlete.

MaccaX
www.MaccaX.com
Dream, Believe, Succeed

The MaccaX site will give athletes of all abilities the opportunity to learn his special methods of training and adapt them for individual use. We offer free video blogs, information, and recommendations for training for all types of endurance events. We have programs for athletes to download, coaches to work with, and direct access to Macca and his team. We have a semi-restricted online coaching system, personalized and generic programs for all athletes, and a competitive racing team to join. Our online members' club has huge sponsor discounts, giveaways, and access to Macca and his coaching staff. Register here for newsletters, up-to-date training videos, and live chats with some of the most influential athletes and coaches in triathlon on the planet.

Chris McCormack Career Summary

IRONMAN RACES

- 2010 Ironman Hawaii—FIRST
- 2009 Ironman Hawaii—FOURTH
- 2007 Ironman Hawaii—FIRST
- 2006 Ironman Hawaii—SECOND
- 2005 Ironman Hawaii—SIXTH
- 2002 Ironman Australia—FIRST
- 2003 Ironman Australia—FIRST
- 2004 Ironman Australia—FIRST
- 2005 Ironman Australia—FIRST
- 2006 Ironman Australia—FIRST (course record)
- 2003 Challenge Roth Germany—SECOND
- 2004 Challenge Roth Germany—FIRST
- 2005 Challenge Roth Germany—FIRST
- 2006 Challenge Roth Germany—FIRST
- 2007 Challenge Roth Germany—FIRST
- 2008 Ironman European Championships—FIRST (course record)

- 2009 Ironman European Championships—THIRD
- 2010 Ironman European Championships—THIRD

HALF-IRONMAN TITLES

- Ironman 70.3 Hawaii—2006–2008 (course record in 2007)
- Wildflower Half-Ironman—2001, 2002, 2004, 2008 (course record in 2001)
- Ironman 70.3 Mexico—2007
- Ironman 70.3 Austria—2009
- Ironman 70.3 China—2009 (course record)
- Ironman 70.3 UK—2006
- Soma Half-Ironman, Arizona—2003 (course record), 2006
- Silverman Half-Ironman, Las Vegas—2007, 2008, 2010
- Challenge Germany—2009 (course record)
- Challenge France—2008, 2009 (course record)
- Desaru Half-Ironman, Malaysia—2005
- Half-Ironman Australia Gold Coast—2006, 2007
- Cairns Half-Ironman—2003

MAJOR CHAMPIONSHIPS

- ITU Triathlon World Champion
- ITU World Cup series Champion
- Runner Up, ITU World Cup series
- Four-time ITU World Cup Japan Champion
- ITU World Cup Canada Champion
- ITU World Cup Switzerland Champion
- ITU World Ranked #1
- Goodwill Games Triathlon Champion
- Two-time USA Professional Triathlon Champion

- Australian Triathlon Champion
- Oceania Triathlon Champion
- Fourteen National Championships, including France, Switzerland, Australia, and the USA
- Australian Sprint Triathlon Champion
- Four-time Escape from Alcatraz Champion
- Two-time Mrs. T's Chicago Triathlon Champion
- Three-time San Diego International Triathlon Champion
- Two-time San Jose International Triathlon Champion
- Two-time Los Angeles Triathlon Champion
- Seven French Grand Prix titles
- Eleven Credit Suisse Switzerland Professional Triathlon Series Victories
- European Ironman Champion

INTERESTING STATISTICS

- Won 76% of career events
- Finished on the podium 88% of the time
- Won 200+ races around the world since 1993
- Twelve Ironman victories, more than any other male
- Broken eight hours in Ironman distance races four times—only man to break eight more than twice
- Only man to break eight hours for the Ironman at two different courses
- Five-time International Triathlete of the Year
- Four-time Competitor of the Year
- ESPN World's Fittest Man

Photo Credits

SWIM COURSE
2.4 miles - 3.86 km

PALANI RD.

FINISH & TRANSITION

START

ALI'I DR.

KAILUA BAY

IRONMAN
WORLD CHAMPIONSHIP
®

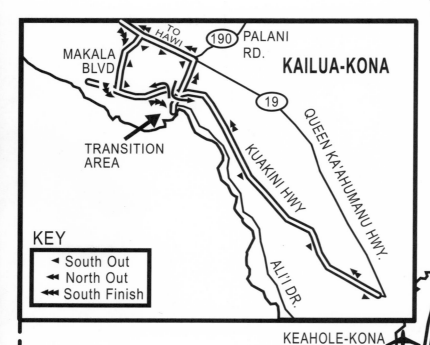

TO HAWI

190 PALANI RD.

MAKALA BLVD

KAILUA-KONA

19

TRANSITION AREA

QUEEN KA'AHUMANU HWY.

KUAKINI HWY

ALI'I DR.

KEY
- ◄ South Out
- ◄◄ North Out
- ◄◄◄ South Finish

KEAHOLE-KONA AIRPORT

190

BIKE COURSE
112 miles - 180.2 km

HONOKOHAU HARBOR

KAILUA-KONA

map by matkindesign.com